Praise for *Sex Lives of Superheroes*

"Super-sex?? Super-duper awesome! Dangerous and daring! Pushes the envelope and all the buttons! I was riveted throughout!"

—Rob Liefeld, creator of *Deadpool*

"An exhaustive, meticulously-researched treatise on a truly ridiculous subject. You'll learn something new and interesting on every page, regardless of whether or not you want to know it."

—Jason Pargin, *New York Times* bestselling author of *John Dies at the End*

"It has been 55 years since the great Larry Niven let us all know that not only were we not the only people who were wondering about superhero sex lives, but that you could discuss it in a (somewhat) serious fashion. Now, 55 years later, Diana McCallum is proving Niven's point for him by giving us serious answers to all of our superhero sex questions (even the ones we didn't know we had), while also embracing some of the bizarre attempts that comics have made over the years to incorporate sex into superhero stories. As an expert in radioactive sperm and time-traveling Founding Father sexcapades, I can attest that she hit all the right notes in this book."

—Brian Cronin, senior writer at *Comic Book Resources*

"*Sex Lives of Superheroes* is both funny and impressively scientific, diving into questions that would make even Superman blush. As McCallum writes in her intro, it's a little weird how few deep dives there are when it comes to the erotic escapades of Marvel and DC's finest, but *Sex Lives of Superheroes* more than makes up for it. Far from being a one-off joke, McCallum has written the definitive look at what happens to comic book icons when they're between the sheets. I will never look at Reed Richards the same way again."

—Daniel Dockery, author of *Monster Kids: How Pokémon Taught a Generation to Catch Them All*

"Finally, a book written for every nerd who wants to know everything there is to know about their favorite superheroes—including what they do between the sheets. What makes *Sex Lives of Superheroes* fascinating and sets it apart is that Diana McCallum does not just conjecture about how having superpowers might affect our heroes' sex lives. She also incorporates science to back up her hypotheses and come to some conclusions, with input from experts, from biologists to uranium scientists to fertility experts. Just for fun, the book also delves into the weirdest sex stories in superhero and comics history—which is really saying something considering there are plenty of weird things happening in every superhero iteration. If you've ever wondered why the Hulk gets lucky way more than Bruce Banner, how the Thing gets it on without a 'thing' or whether Reed Richards should take advantage of his penis-stretching abilities, this is the book for you. Or maybe you need to know what kind of horrifying penises the Mutant Ninja Turtles probably have, or how the Deep gets it on with Ambrosius the octopus, or why Mystique might have the best orgasms EVER. I confess that some of these questions have never crossed my mind, yet I was drawn into the creative conjectures and then thoroughly satisfied by the meticulous research that went into finding some actual answers. And what's better than a book that leaves you . . . satisfied?"

—Lynn Zubernis, professor at West Chester University, clinical psychologist, and editor of *Supes Ain't Always Heroes: Inside the Complex Characters and Twisted Psychology of The Boys*

SEX LIVES OF SUPERHEROES

Wolverine's Immortal Sperm,
Superman's Porn Career, the Thing's Thing,
and Other Super-Sexual Matters Explained

DIANA McCALLUM

Smart Pop Books
An Imprint of BenBella Books, Inc.
Dallas, TX

Smart Pop is an imprint of BenBella Books, Inc.
10440 N. Central Expressway
Suite 800
Dallas, TX 75231
smartpopbooks.com | benbellabooks.com
Send feedback to feedback@benbellabooks.com

BenBella and *Smart Pop* are federally registered trademarks.

Printed in the United States of America
10 9 8 7 6 5 4 3 2 1

Library of Congress Control Number: 2024025748
ISBN 9781637745496 (trade paperback)
ISBN 9781637745502 (electronic)

Editing by Rachel Phares
Copyediting by Elizabeth Degenhard
Proofreading by Denise Pangia and Lisa Story
Text design and composition by Aaron Edmiston
Cover design by Brigid Pearson
Cover image © Shutterstock / KennyK.com Custom Mascots (buildings);
© Shutterstock / Yurlick (halftone); © Shutterstock / Alhovik (font)
Printed by Lake Book Manufacturing

Special discounts for bulk sales are available. Please contact
bulkorders@benbellabooks.com.

To Andrew,
for always committing to the bit

CONTENTS

Part 3—Mind Over Mattress: Psychological Issues That Affect Heroes in the Bedroom

Part 4—Secret Origins: Pregnancy and Childbirth Among the Superpowered

Part 5—Do It Like an Animal: Insect and Animal Powers in the Bedroom

INTRODUCTION

I was probably too young when I saw *Mallrats* for the first time. I remember being drawn in by the movie's comic book–inspired poster that promised a fun romp through the mall with a couple of nerds joined by Stan Lee himself. And what I got was indeed a fun romp through the mall with a couple of nerds and Stan Lee, but also a movie that was shockingly R-rated, with more sexual content than my ten-year-old self was prepared to see at the time. Among the raunchiest of characters in *Mallrats* is Brodie Bruce, a comic book nerd who is described by Stan Lee as "really hung up on superheroes' sex organs." A fair description. Brodie is so enthralled by super genitalia that he uses the few minutes he has with the great Stan Lee to ask if Reed Richards can stretch his penis like the rest of his body or if the Thing's "dork" is made out of orange rock like the rest of his skin. In the movie, Stan doesn't answer any of these burning questions.

But this book does.

I never really wanted to be like Brodie in *Mallrats*. He wasn't exactly a shining model of success or happiness, and he was kind of mean, but my lifelong love of superheroes eventually led me to launch my webcomic, *Texts From Superheroes*, in 2012 with my partner Andrew to surprising success. For over a decade we wrote three comics a week that delved into the minutiae of superhero life, and let me tell you, it doesn't take long before you stop wondering about innocent things like how Batman got that giant dinosaur into the Batcave and start pondering the intimate details of a superhero's life, like how Amazons reproduce and whether Daredevil's enhanced senses would make sex good or bad. Every week questions started to form in my mind and my Word documents, questions that were too big to be explored in a text message–sized comic strip. *Is the Flash actually fast in bed?* I would ask myself. *Could Bruce Banner ever have sex without Hulking out? Is the Thing's penis* actually *made of rock?*

These were all questions that haunted me, both for their comedic potential and my need to just *know the answer*—because in the world of comic books, there's virtually no superhero fact, figure, or backstory that can't be tracked down. If I want to know just how strong Superman is compared to Wonder Woman I can check DC's official strength listings for both characters. If I want to know how Alfred joined the Wayne family, well, there's a ridiculous 1943 origin story for that. If I want to know more about Peter Parker's parents, I just need to watch 2012's *The Amazing Spider-Man* (unfortunately). Every question has an answer in comics, sometimes more than one depending on continuity and the retcons involved, but usually at least one—except for questions about sex.

And there are a lot of questions to be answered, especially when you consider that the things we're taught in sex ed don't apply to our superpowered friends because most heroes aren't even human—they're aliens, or gods, or mutants. It stands to reason that their bedroom exploits are cosmically different from the human sexual experience, yet most superhero books and movies remain family-friendly affairs that refuse to divulge any specific sexual information about these characters. We can know everything about a hero's superpowers, their jobs, their battles, even their pets and coworkers, but we have almost no canonical accounting of how those nifty superpowers affect their sex lives, whether it be for good, bad, or weird. Which is frankly unacceptable. True nerds want to know *everything* about superheroes; we pride ourselves on our wealth of fandom knowledge and cataloguing every minute detail about a fictional world, and that includes what goes on in the bedroom (or space or another dimension or wherever else heroes want to bang). Since official sources have been as tight-lipped with this information as Stan Lee was in *Mallrats*, I became determined to fill this gap in our collective knowledge. Thus, this book came to life.

I wrote *Sex Lives of Superheroes* for myself, for Brodie, and for every other nerd out there who loves to dive too deep into the details of a super-hero's life. I wanted to offer up a comprehensive look at just how superpow-ers would affect the sex lives of the heroes who have them, in a lighthearted discussion based on superhero facts from comics and movies combined with science to back up my conclusions. In addition to digging deep into comic and film canon for supporting evidence, we're going to look at things like real scientific studies on uranium levels in soldiers' semen to deter-mine whether Spider-Man could accidentally give his wife cancer just from having sex. We'll talk to fertility experts about whether Wolverine's sperm would retain his healing ability and be functionally immortal and discuss the history of sex education in the 1930s to figure out just how much Cap-tain America actually knows about sex. Then we'll find out why Mystique has the best orgasms of any hero out there, and discuss the horrifying impli-cations to a hero's sex life if they have animal-based superpowers. Along the way, we'll stop for a few Sexual Interludes where we'll break down the weirdest sex stories in comic book history, including the time Superman tried to marry his cousin. And yes, we'll figure out exactly how long Reed Richards can stretch his dick. For Brodie.

So prepare to laugh (hopefully), not cry (probably), and have a few holy-shit moments as science takes us to weirder places than comics ever could (except for a few *really* weird ones).

And most importantly, get ready to learn the answer to every question that Stan Lee was too scared to tell you and find out more than you ever thought you would know about the sex lives of superheroes.

Just to say:

In this book, and most of the scientific studies relied upon to write it, male and female are being discussed predominantly in terms of sex assigned at birth and not gender identity. When we explore the sexual differences between men and women (such as who has better orgasms, and so on), the pronouns and language used are largely in reference to sexual biology, with the acknowledgment that sex does not equal gender.

This book respects the gender identity of every reader who picks it up (and also those who don't, but they're not reading this).

Part 1

A HERO'S SACRIFICE

Superpowers That Wreck Your Sex Life

Part 1

A HERO'S SACRIFICE

Superpowers That Wreck Your Sex Life

IS SEX WITH THE HULK AN AUTOMATIC THREESOME?

"Hulk SMASH!"
—The Hulk, all the time

Poor Bruce Banner. Thanks to a dousing of gamma radiation, he's cursed to transform into the green-skinned rage-monster known as "The Incredible Hulk" whenever he's angry, scared, or stressed out, which in this day and age is pretty much all the time. Imagine the embarrassment of changing from a brilliant scientist into a shirtless, dim-witted body-builder who can barely string a sentence together and has the self-control of a frat boy at a kegger. Then imagine that dumb bodybuilder has a way better love life than you! What a kick in the purple pants that must be.

It's true, the Hulk is like the James Bond of incoherent rage-monsters. He has had not one, but two relationships with beautiful alien princesses (named Jarella and Caiera), and not only did they love him for the furious beast he was, but he also became emperor of both their worlds. Caiera's world was even renamed Planet Hulk after him, which is wild. It's normal to take someone's name in marriage, but the rest of the planet doesn't usually do it, too.

But while the Hulk is off bedding beautiful princesses, Bruce Banner spends most of his time alone—on the run from the military, or in a lab making discoveries he can name after himself and quietly mumbling that it's just as cool as naming a whole planet.

So why is brilliant scientist Bruce Banner alone while the vocabulary-challenged Hulk has a Tinder account full of royalty begging for a slice of green? Here's one theory: it's because Bruce Banner can't seal the deal, physically. Or rather, he's unwilling to try out of fear that if he gets too excited the Hulk will show up to finish what he started. And three's a crowd in the bedroom, especially when one of the three is a murderous, steroidal version of yourself.

Conversely, we know the Hulk has no trouble performing in the bedroom. In the Marvel Cinematic Universe he has a giant green son named Skaar, which is impressive considering that exposure to mutating levels of radiation isn't usually a boost to fertility. If Bruce really can't pull off a two-person tango without transforming into a raging murder machine, it explains why women might consider him an Incredible Sulk in comparison to his alter ego.

But is this a legit concern? Can Bruce get busy without Jekylling his Hyde, or must there be an inevitable Hulk in the bedroom? The question seems like a no-brainer that even the dim-witted Hulk could answer. If Bruce only transforms when he's angry or stressed, then of course he can have some nice, relaxing sex and stay on the Bruce side of the equation while doing it. He and a lady friend can just light a few candles, put on some Enya, and hope that for God's sake nobody barges in on them and makes Bruce mad. But the situation's not that simple.

The Science of Hulking Out

In 2008's *The Incredible Hulk* movie, we see Bruce and his love interest Betty Ross lying in bed about to get to the film's next "action" sequence when Bruce's heart rate monitor goes off in warning. He begrudgingly tells Betty he "can't get too excited" or he might accidentally Hulk out. Not willing to risk a pounding of a different nature than they had intended, the lovers decide that's the end of that and separate for the night (cue sad Hulk music here).

What we can learn from this exchange is that Bruce is worried he *might* transform into an unfortunate bedfellow if they keep going, but he doesn't know if it will happen for sure (unless there are some pulverized ex-lovers in Bruce's past that he neglected to mention).

So it's an open question: Is Bruce capable of having sex without transforming into his monstrous alter ego? To answer that we are going to turn to our good friend, science (the Marvel Universe kind), which is appropriate because Bruce loves science (even though it's literally the cause of all of his problems). First, we need to identify exactly what triggers Bruce's transformation into the Hulk. If we adhere to comic-book canon, we know the change is based on Bruce's adrenaline levels, adrenaline being the fight-flight-or-freeze hormone that speeds up our heart rate and breathing and preps us to throw down, book it, or otherwise exert ourselves in times of trouble. As the people at Marvel Comics put it in *World War Hulk: Gamma Files* (2007):

> *Banner's adrenal medulla secretes large amounts of adrenaline in times of fear, rage, or stress, which hormonally stimulates the heart rate . . . in Banner's case it triggers the complex chemical-extra-physical process that transforms him into the Hulk.*[1]

This makes Bruce Banner quite literally the world's biggest adrenaline junkie and also coincides with what we see in *The Incredible Hulk* movie. One of the signs that someone's adrenaline is spiking is a rapid heartbeat, and we see Bruce constantly monitoring his heart rate in the film to gauge if he's about to Hulk out. And while the scientific advisors to *World War Hulk* are correct that fear and stress trigger an adrenaline rush, the hormone is also released during exercise, general exertion, and, most importantly, sex. So it's smart of Bruce to worry, but for his own personal fulfilment it would be even smarter for him to figure out just *how much* adrenaline needs to be pumping before the Hulk turns up . . . and how busy in the bedroom he can get before reaching that threshold.

To answer these literal life-or-death questions, let's turn back to science, this time of the real-world variety: specifically, a 1984 study by Southern Illinois University School of Medicine on the body's chemical response to stress.[2] This study found that the average adrenaline levels in the blood of someone at rest are approximately 34 picograms per milliliter (pg/ml), so we'll use this as our base level for regular non-Hulky humans going about their day. The researchers conducting this particular study, however, were analyzing the most stressed-out people they could find, and though none of them were mutated rage-monsters on the run from the military, the subjects *were* suffering from chronic stress severe enough to put them in intensive care. On average, the adrenaline concentration in these folks was 140 pg/ml, about four times higher than the base level. Since the comics show us that Bruce's transformation into the Hulk requires a hefty emotional stressor, we'll say that Bruce is at a risk of transforming when his adrenaline reaches that quadruple level of 140 pg/ml.

Okay! So we have a good idea of how much adrenaline it takes for Bruce to transform into the Hulk—all that's left is to compare this amount to how much adrenaline the body produces during sex. To figure that out, though, we'd have to measure the exact adrenaline levels in a person's bloodstream during orgasm, and surely no one would . . . holy shit, someone did a scientific study on exactly that.

Adrenaline-Fueled Science

In this 2003 study[3] done in Germany (oh, Germany; that makes sense), ten male subjects were asked to masturbate while an IV automatically took a sample of their blood at one-minute intervals (imagine writing the grant application for that one). Once the researchers were done hosing down the equipment, their data revealed that the average level of adrenaline in a person's blood during orgasm was 125 pg/ml . . . which is definitively below the minimum Hulk-out threshold we established of 140 pg/ml. This sounds great for Bruce's sex life, but keep your ripped purple pants on, Dr. Banner: that 125 pg/ml was only the *average* of the ten participants. The highest level of adrenaline produced during orgasm was 165 pg/ml, well above our established Hulk safety levels. Uh-oh.

So Bruce *may* be able to have sex without transforming . . . as long as his peak adrenaline levels are on the low side of normal. But he can't know that they are for sure (unless he wants to sign up for the next scientific study in Germany), so any attempt at sexual intercourse would be at the risk of inviting an Incredible Bulk into the bedroom, and not the kind most potential lovers would be excited about.

Also, since the study involved men masturbating alone in a lab it only quantified the adrenaline produced by orgasming and didn't factor in the adrenaline produced from the physical exertion of sex with someone else, or from emotions one might experience during partnered sex, such as nervousness or fear. Like, say, the fear of turning into the Hulk halfway through sex and breaking a whole lot more than a condom. And the emotional component should be a pretty big part of this calculation since we know that Bruce isn't winning any awards for emotional control at this point in his life.

The Heart(beat) of It All

Let's return to the previously mentioned bedroom scene from *The Incredible Hulk*. In it, we find that before he ends his brief sexual meeting with Betty, Bruce's heart rate is a whopping 154 beats per minute (bpm) just from lying in a bed and kissing her while fully clothed. To give you some perspective on how high that is, the average heart rate for a middle-aged man during intercourse is only 112 bpm, which means Bruce's heart is hammering so hard we might as well call it Mjölnir. What would it even take for a healthy human to get their heart rate to 154 bpm? It turns out, a lot. Researchers at Stobhill General Hospital in Glasgow[4] did an experiment where they gave volunteers the same amount of adrenaline found in patients who just suffered a heart attack, and found it increased the heart rate of the subjects by just 7 to 9 bpm. So an average man would have to be mid-intercourse and receive a dose of adrenaline that's six times as powerful as a heart attack to get his heart rate anywhere close to 154 bpm. Since Bruce is not yet exerting himself physically in the abovementioned scene, we have to assume his heart rate is skyrocketing from mental stress and anxiety alone, which is understandable, since he knows if his adrenaline spikes too high it will kill the mood *and* his girlfriend. It seems safe to say at this point that the combination of physical exertion, stress, and orgasm-induced adrenaline would easily push Bruce past his Hulk-out threshold if he tried to have sex. The odds are great enough, at least, that the safest thing Bruce can do for everyone is keep it in his pants (which shouldn't be too difficult since his pants somehow stay on even when he transforms into a monster that weighs a literal ton).

However, all may not be lost for Bruce Banner's sexual exploits. Sex with a human partner is off the table, but he may be able to find a super-powered lover somewhere out there in the Marvel Universe who can handle a potentially risky sexual encounter with his dual personality. And if he can't find any takers on superhero Tinder, he may still be able to safely participate in some singular entertainment. Masturbation shouldn't bring about the same fear of injuring someone as sex with a partner would, especially if he was alone in a secluded place (or in a German science lab with multiple onlookers; I can send him their number). With some cautious experimentation, Bruce might even find out exactly what his adrenaline levels are like during orgasm. And if they stay in that sweet Hulk-free range, he can then proceed past third base with a partner without fear of waking up the next morning in a pile of rubble.

Until then, though, Bruce will have to do the responsible thing and choose not to partake in any potentially orgasmic encounters with another person for fear of Hulking out. Which means letting the Hulk continue to get all the action while Bruce lives the life of a monk. I guess that explains why he's so angry all the time.

LISTEN BUD, HE'S GOT RADIOACTIVE BLOOD (AND SEMEN)

Spider-Man, Spider-Man, Radioactive Spider-Man.
Spider blood, spider blood, radioactive spider blood (repeat three times).
—From "Spider-Man: The Animated Series Theme Song" by Joe Perry

Spider-Man might just be the most popular superhero of all time, and with great popularity comes great moments in superhero (and cinematic) history. Moments like the upside-down kiss with Mary Jane in the rain, the multiple Spider-Man team-up in *Spider-Man: No Way Home*, and Miles Morales's leap of faith from *Into the Spider-Verse*. But a hero's life can't be all highs, and no hero has experienced more lows than Peter Parker, a man whose origin story involves the death of his uncle, whose first love interest was killed by the recoil from his own webbing, and who had to make everyone he ever met forget he existed in order to save the world. Eep. When you think about everything Peter's been through, it's incredible that this guy is still so upbeat and full of puns—and we haven't even touched on what might be Spidey's most infamous moment, that time Peter Parker killed his wife with his radioactive semen.

What's that, you want to learn more about that last part? That's genuinely shocking, but sure, let's talk about Spider-Man's deadly splooge.

The Infamous Semen Comic

If you somehow aren't familiar with this absolutely wild sequence of events, the previously mentioned spermicide (a homicide caused by sperm, obviously) occurred in the 2006 miniseries *Spider-Man: Reign*, an officially sanctioned Marvel comic. In this story we are introduced to a geriatric Peter Parker living alone in New York, having retired from being the friendly neighborhood Spider-Man after the death of his wife Mary Jane Watson-Parker years earlier. How did she die? Well, this is how Peter explained it (while clutching her decaying, unearthed corpse, if you're curious):

> The doctors didn't understand how it happened! How you had been **poisoned** with **radioactivity**! How your body slowly became riddled with **cancer**! I did. I was . . . I am filled with **radioactive blood**. And not just blood. Every fluid. Touching me . . . loving me . . . **loving me killed you**! Like a spider crawling up inside your body and laying a thousand eggs of cancer . . . I killed you.[5]

So there you have it, straight from the spider's mouth. According to Peter (who, I'll remind you, is a goddamn scientist), Mary Jane died from cancer caused by radioactive fluids exchanged when a couple touches and loves each other. So . . . semen. He's saying he killed Mary Jane by infecting her with radioactive semen whenever they made love. Which feels like a wild claim to jump to without proof. For a man who constantly brings up his "radioactive spider blood" in conversation, he seems pretty certain that his semen, and not his blood or some other bodily fluid, was what caused the multiple cancers that claimed Mary Jane's body. And while it's well known that exposure to radiation can cause cancer,[6] so can a lot of other things, like smoking, sun exposure, or just a poor diet.[7] Heck, maybe Mary Jane lived near some power lines or something. Knowing Peter's self-deprecating nature, though, it makes sense for him to automatically blame his radioactive bodily fluids for his wife's demise, and maybe he just assumes it was his semen because that's the only bodily fluid he knows for sure made contact with her body via unprotected sex. Or maybe he knows something we don't.

This leads us to a few questions that need answering. One, why would Marvel publish any of that? And two, is it actually possible that Peter killed his wife with his radioactive spider-semen?

We'll never know the answer to question one, but we can answer question two with shocking accuracy.

With Great Power Comes Great Radioactivity

The first thing we have to talk about when it comes to solving this spermicide is good old terrifying radiation itself. We know that Spider-Man is radioactive, not just because it's brought up in all his theme songs, but because it's the backbone of his origin story. While going about his business one day, Peter Parker was bitten by a spider that gave him spider-like superpowers (and thankfully for his social life, not a spider-like appearance). For most people a spider bite just gives you an annoying bump on your skin, but the spider that bit Peter had been exposed to high levels of radiation and caused what's known as internal radiation contamination (and also caused him to develop superpowers that kept that radiation from killing him, unlike poor Mary Jane). According to the Centers for Disease Control and Prevention (CDC), internal contamination occurs "when radioactive materials enter the body through an open wound or are absorbed through the skin" and a spider bite definitely qualifies as an open wound (as opposed to "external contamination," which is when radioactive material comes into brief topical contact with a person's skin, hair, or clothing). But the CDC also backs up Peter's claim that his bodily fluids would be radioactive enough to contaminate others.

People who are internally contaminated can expose people near them to radiation from the radioactive material inside their bodies. The body fluids (blood, sweat, urine) of an internally contaminated person can contain radioactive materials. Coming in contact with these body fluids can result in contamination and/or exposure.[8]

Now, you might notice the researchers at the CDC did not specifically mention semen as one of the bodily fluids that can expose someone to radiation, but don't worry, braver scientists than them assure us later in this chapter that semen is also brimming with radiation in a person who has been internally contaminated.

So, we've established that Peter's semen is in fact radioactive, but so are all the other fluids in his body. To prove it was indeed his semen that killed Mary Jane, we need to know how much radiation semen holds compared to other bodily fluids. And to do that we're going to have to explore some weird places with our good friend science or you won't even believe the answer when we get there.

To prove Peter's radioactive Semen-Man theory, we need to know what type of radiation he was infected with back when he was a skinny little nerd. Unfortunately, no comic or movie has ever provided us with the exact type of radiation the spider that bit Peter was irradiated with; we're just told it was generally radioactive. We have places to be and semen to discuss, so we can't run through every radioactive element in existence right now, but there are a few deadly and well-documented suspects we can consider. For example, in 2006 a former Russian spy named Alexander Litvinenko died several weeks after his tea was poisoned with the radioactive element polonium-210. After he was diagnosed with radiation poisoning, the British government shut down several restaurants and nightclubs Litvinenko had recently visited[9] in case he had excreted significant amounts of polonium as he went about his day. This means scientists and governments agree that radiation exposure through bodily fluids is something to be concerned about with this element. However, polonium is not likely to be what Peter was infected with, as this stuff is so potent that it kills in about a week and is not commonly associated with cancer, which is what killed Mary Jane.

It's much more likely that the spider that bit Peter was exposed to something like uranium, which is what we'll assume from this point on. Uranium is a radioactive element that can exist in the body for long periods of time without killing the infected person (as we're about to learn) but is also known to cause lethal instances of cancer[10] over long periods of exposure. In fact, a 2015 study found that uranium miners had a 32 percent chance of dying from cancer,[11] which is double the global cancer mortality rate of 16 percent. So uranium exposure could definitely explain MJ contracting multiple cancers that formed over several years in *Spider-Man: Reign*. As a bonus for our purposes, scientists have been studying the effects of uranium on bodily fluids for some time now, so strap in for what is hopefully the only roller-coaster ride you will ever go on that includes radioactive blood, urine, and semen.

Which Bodily Fluid Killed Mary Jane?

For the information we're about to explore, we must thank the US Department of Veterans Affairs (USDVA) and their study titled *Semen Uranium Concentrations in Depleted Uranium Exposed Gulf War Veterans: Correlations with Other Body Fluid Matrices*.[12] What this long title boils down to is that in 2009 a group of scientists worked with thirty-five veterans of the Gulf War to study the effects of long-term exposure to uranium, which specifically included checking the uranium levels in their blood, urine, and semen. And for that, we salute them.

The participants in this study were all exposed to uranium during the Gulf War in 1991, but their bodily fluid samples were taken in 2009, eighteen years after exposure—and wouldn't you know it, after all that time, *all of their bodily fluids* still contained radioactive uranium elements. This is relevant because Peter was with Mary Jane for at least a decade in the comic before she started getting sick from radiation poisoning, so we can safely assume Peter was still excreting significant amounts of radiation from all of his bodily fluids ten years into their relationship. This also means he was unknowingly being the menace J. Jonah Jameson claimed he was for all those years.

So Peter was right that "every fluid" in his body was likely still radioactive years after his famous spider bite. Now, let's get to the main event and talk about splooge. The researchers of the aforementioned study created a scale of what they expected the uranium levels in the semen of their subjects to be, which ranged from low (5 picograms/gram) to medium (50 pg/g) to high (1,000 pg/g). What they ended up finding was that half the participants had uranium levels that were considered high and above. One participant even had a uranium count in their semen of 3,350 pg/g, which is more than three times the "high" mark they expected. So not only were their subjects still excreting uranium eighteen years after exposure, they were releasing significantly more than predicted.

That makes semen a prime suspect in the killing of Mary Jane. But to determine once and for all that Peter's semen was indeed responsible for this deadly spermicide (so we can, I don't know, send him to sperm jail or something), we need to know for certain which bodily fluid holds the most radiation. So next we'll look at exactly how much uranium was found in equivalent amounts of *each* bodily fluid, including blood, urine, sweat, and semen. (The USDVA study didn't actually include an analysis of the uranium levels found in sweat. Fortunately, they aren't the only bodily fluid game in town. A different study from the University of Alberta[13] tells us that, on average, sweat will contain ten times as much uranium as urine, so we'll use that estimate in our calculations for sweat.) With that in mind, here are the average amounts of uranium found in the participants of the USDVA study, sorted by bodily fluid:

Blood: 0.16 pg/g
Urine: 5.39 pg/g
Sweat: 53.9 pg/g (estimated)
Semen: 306.91 pg/g

Holy web shooters, semen is *bursting* with radiation compared to other bodily fluids. These numbers tell us that semen has about six times more radiation than sweat, fifty-seven times more radiation than urine, and almost *two thousand* times more radiation than blood! At that rate it's a wonder that Peter's testicles aren't emitting a soft radioactive glow to warn women away from his deadly little swimmers or setting off his own spider sense every time he goes near his genitals. All the evidence so far is certainly pointing to spider-semen as the killer, but the final question is whether Mary Jane was exposed to enough uranium from Peter's web fluids to make her sick. According to the CDC, "in order for uranium inside the body to cause cancer, the levels of uranium have to be so large that they are easily detected by laboratory analysis."[14] Since scientists detected these radioactive bad boys pretty easily and found that the levels were literally higher than high, we can safely slap the handcuffs on semen as being the bodily fluid that struck Mary Jane down. Talk about a neogenic nightmare, and a twist on the accepted lore.

The Spider-Man mythos is consistently hung up on Peter's "radioactive spider blood," but looking at these numbers, the amount of radiation in his blood is frankly negligible compared to his semen and other bodily fluids. We're going to have to do some controversial rewrites of a few Spider-Man theme songs for accuracy is all I'm saying. But before that, we might owe *Spider-Man: Reign* an apology for dismissing their autopsy results, as Peter turned out to be right—his radioactive semen definitely killed his wife. And it's safe to say no one saw that coming. Considering how dangerous it is to be married to Spider-Man, deadly sperm was a pretty low contender on the list of things that might kill MJ. Personally, I had money on the Kingpin.

While killing your wife is one potential side effect of having radioactive spider-semen, unfortunately it's not the only one. We also have to consider what effect this deadly load may have on the couple's ability to conceive a child and how it may impact said child. But let me just say before we dive into the results, it's not nearly as bad as killing your wife (though not many things are).

The Itsy-Bitsy Spider Baby

Most people know that high doses of radiation exposure to the testes or ovaries can lead to temporary or permanent sterility, but it turns out that radiation has shockingly little effect on the sperm or eggs when it comes to things like birth defects, miscarriage, or mutation. While it's possible that Peter's radioactive fluids would make it difficult for him and MJ to conceive at all, if they do manage to get pregnant, the risk of their child having birth defects or mutations is shockingly low. Everything you've ever seen or read about exposure to radiation may tell you that this can't possibly be right, as you may be picturing the radioactive three-eyed fish from *The Simpsons* right now or pointing out that Peter Parker himself mutated into a spider man from a radioactive spider bite, but in real life it turns out that eggs and sperm are not as easily mutated as comic books would lead us to believe.

An extensive study[15] on the effects of radiation exposure from the Chernobyl nuclear power plant disaster in 1986 looked at the genetics of the children of two hundred survivors of the incident and found there were no mutations in the survivors' children. None! Scientists concluded that radiation could absolutely cause DNA damage and increase the risk of cancer to those directly exposed to it, but found that the number of germline mutations (a mutation passed on from parents to offspring) was no greater in the children of highly exposed parents than those of children born to parents who were not exposed at all. So basically, radiation can change your own DNA, but not the DNA you pass on to your children. What does this mean for a potential friendly neighborhood spider-baby? Well, if Peter and Mary Jane did have children, they would likely have no radiation-related mutations, which means Baby Parker-Watson wouldn't inherit any of Peter's spider-powers and would just be a regular baby. That baby would still be a menace in the way that all babies are, but less of a menace than one with super strength and the ability to shoot webs out of its wrists.

Using Protection in the Bedroom

We know now that it was indeed Peter's semen that killed Mary Jane, but let's explore a little further and figure out if there was any way he could have protected her from his little radioactive relatives. After all, he wouldn't be the first superhero who had to figure out how to safely have sex with their partner because their powers were on the murderous side. Rogue and Gambit of the X-Men have been an on-again, off-again couple for decades, partly because of their genuine relationship issues and partly because if Rogue's skin comes into contact with Gambit it would literally suck the life out of his body, which is both a mood killer and a killer-killer. The couple have only managed to be intimate a handful of times when Rogue's powers have been dampened by one plot device or another, but most of the time they must simply keep a physical distance for safety's sake and refrain from touching each other. So, an abstinence-based approach with no sexual-thwipping of any kind is one option to protect Mary Jane, but Peter might be happier emulating DC power couple Harley Quinn and Poison Ivy, who managed to overcome a similar sexual conundrum as our friendly neighborhood Spider-Man. As her name suggests, Poison Ivy is, well, poisonous. She's capable of secreting toxic substances from her body, including the ability to kill with a poison kiss, which is useful when you're trying to murder horny billionaires but annoying when you're trying to make out with your girlfriend. A death kiss would definitely be a safety concern in the bedroom, but Poison Ivy is also a scientist and used her most beautiful body part (her brain!) to create a vaccine to inoculate Harley against Ivy's more poisonous traits. This antitoxin allows the couple to safely be intimate and includes the fun side effect of giving Harley increased strength and stamina, which is something that will never go astray in the bedroom. Heck, maybe Ivy just threw those powers in there because she thought it'd be fun. Respect, if so. Either way, her workaround shows that it's possible for a potentially toxic couple to use creative forms of protection to practice safe sex, and Peter had several very good options to choose from to protect Mary Jane if he had known his downstairs web fluid was dangerously irradiated.

As discussed, Peter was contaminated with radiation internally, which means he is not emitting waves of radiation outside his body, and the only way he can contaminate another individual is through physical contact with his bodily fluids. Since Mary Jane died from direct semen exposure, we can deduce that the couple regularly had either oral or penetrative sex without using a condom, which has to be the weirdest way to ever verify a superhero is rawdogging it with his wife. A great way for Peter and Mary Jane to stop this exposure from happening is to just use condoms during sex—this would have kept her from coming into contact with his semen, which we now know was the leading cause of her cancer. Using condoms wouldn't have stopped her from coming into contact with Peter's sweat during sex, but this would be far less of a concern considering that sweat contains five times less radiation than semen and also that very minimal amounts would go inside MJ's body. Considering his spider-strength and stamina, it seems doubtful sex is even an intense enough activity to make Peter start sweating in the first place. And even if he was sweating up a storm, condoms definitely wouldn't have hurt as an added precaution.

But condoms aren't the only protection Peter could have used; there are also a few radiation treatments that can be administered after exposure. As mentioned earlier, we can only guess at the exact type of radiation that Peter was exposed to by his spider bite, but if he happened to be infected with, say, radioactive iodine instead of uranium, Mary Jane could have taken potassium iodide pills after sex to counteract the effects, kind of like a morning-after pill but for radiation exposure. The CDC warns[16] that to be effective "a person must take [potassium iodide] before or shortly after exposure to radioactive iodine," though, so she'd have to be quick.

Similarly, if Peter's body excretes cesium or thallium then Mary Jane could be treated with a pill called Prussian blue, which prevents the body from absorbing the radioactive material. This pill can save your life but will also turn your mouth, teeth, and stool blue, so Mary Jane would be alive but would look like the girl who turned into a blueberry at Willy Wonka's chocolate factory. Finally, if Peter was radiated with plutonium, americium, or curium, a more extreme treatment called DTPA (diethylenetriamine pentaacetate) could help treat any resulting infection MJ incurs. This treatment must be taken either through an IV or as a mist that is breathed into the lungs, and it would have to be administered each time they had sex, which would certainly bring a whole new meaning to "playing doctor" in the bedroom. So, Mary Jane definitely has some treatment options for radiation exposure, but when all is said and done, the easiest and safest method is for Peter to just wear a condom, which you wouldn't think would be difficult for a guy who wears a full-body spandex suit as part of his day job.

Much like Peter Parker, we need to wrap things up, but let's close out this chapter by exploring how the radioactive revelations we've uncovered might affect the rest of the superhero world.

Other Radioactive Heroes Waiting to Kill

Unfortunately for all the potential human sexual partners in the Marvel universe, Peter Parker is not the only superhero out there who may be waiting to kill via repeated radioactive orgasms (or even just one).

Other famously radioactive heroes include the Fantastic Four, who obtained their powers by being bombarded with cosmic radiation. Luckily for team members Reed Richards and Sue Storm, the risk of infecting a lover with radiation during sex is of little concern as they are happily married to each other and have no other sexual partners. Plus, since they got their powers from the same source of radiation, it seems pretty unlikely their bodily fluids could hurt each other. Ben Grimm similarly doesn't have much concern in this department, as we will discuss in a later chapter how he likely has no penis with which to ejaculate, therefore eliminating the risk of this particular contaminant. That just leaves Johnny Storm, aka the Human Torch, a known playboy who has dated dozens of women over the years, which could be good or bad in this scenario. It's definitely bad that he's possibly poisoned dozens of women with radioactive semen when he "flames on" during intercourse, but the fact that he doesn't date women for a particularly long time also makes it less likely that he's exposed any one partner to a particularly dangerous amount of radiation. After all, we're told that Peter's deadly semen slowly killed Mary Jane over many years, so Johnny's fear of commitment may have saved the lives of many of the women he's dated. What a hero. Also, judging by the lack of little Johnnys running around the Marvel universe, it seems likely that Johnny wears a condom when he has sex, which might be the only example we have of Johnny Storm displaying a sense of responsibility.

Of course, we can't discuss radioactive superheroes without mentioning the gamma-radiated green rage-monster, the Hulk, aka Bruce Banner. In the previous chapter we discussed the danger of Bruce potentially hulking out whenever he orgasms, but an even better reason for him to abstain from carnal pleasures is the fact that his semen is likely powerful enough to kill on contact. Remember, Peter got his powers from a small spider bite, and that was enough radiation to kill his wife after a few years of exposure, but Bruce got his powers from standing directly in the blast radius of a gamma bomb. We already know that Bruce's blood contains enough radiation to kill someone—in *The Incredible Hulk* movie a man accidentally ingests a small drop of Bruce's blood mixed into a soda and immediately falls unconscious from "gamma sickness." If Bruce's semen is like Peter's and contains two thousand times more radiation than his blood, well, I'm not even going to bother with any fun math in this instance, I'm just going to say that's too much radioactive semen for any human to handle. We're talking about a substance so toxic it would melt a person in half immediately upon exposure. So, for everyone's safety, don't make Bruce horny; you wouldn't like him when he's horny.

As for Peter Parker, well, it seems he has another tragedy to spur on his superhero exploits as he is now indirectly responsible for the death of both his uncle and his wife. But maybe a lesson can be learned here, which is that being a hero means protecting people. And protecting people can be as simple as putting on a spandex supersuit—or putting on a condom.

IS THAT A STAKE IN YOUR POCKET OR ARE YOU JUST HAPPY TO SEE ME?

"Vampire sex is like pizza, in that even when it's bad it's good."

—Nandor, *What We Do in the Shadows*, season 1, episode 9

Vampires are sexy. This is the general consensus the world has come to. Sure, they're walking undead corpses that lurk in the shadows and try to kill you, but damn, do they look good doing it. Some vampires invoke a sexual response in the audience through the seduction of their victims, while some are sexy due to an air of mystery or their brooding nature, and some are just traditionally attractive, which on rare occasions involves skin that sparkles in sunlight. Though there has been an influx of sexy-vampire media representation in recent years, from *Buffy the Vampire Slayer* to *Twilight* and *Interview with the Vampire*, the sexualization of the blood-sucking undead is not a new trend. Vampires have been romanticized since their inception in 1897's *Dracula* by Bram Stoker, wherein the title character was intimate with his female victims in a way that was as yet unseen in the Victorian age. In today's media it's hard to find a vampire that isn't oozing sexuality and the promise of carnal pleasures, but that brings up an important question that humans should be asking: Are vampires even capable of having sex? After all, these undead beauties have no heartbeat, no blood flow, and a serious sun allergy, making them quite literally a different species than humans—all facts that must be considered when discussing their sexual behavior. So how does the undead status of the children of the night affect their desire for sex and their ability to participate in it?

From a biological standpoint, it doesn't seem possible for vampires to partake in traditional human sex acts. Their lack of a heartbeat means they have no blood flow to cause arousal or get an erection, so their sex life should be as cold and dead as they are. And yet a large range of vampiric media tells us that vampires do indeed have sex like us lowly humans. In *Buffy the Vampire Slayer* it is a load-bearing plot point that Buffy and her vampire boyfriend Angel had sex at least once (this culminated in a true "moment of happiness" for Angel, which is TV show speak for orgasming so hard he lost his soul). More lighthearted vampire fare such as *What We Do in the Shadows* shows us that vampire intercourse is happening almost constantly, while in *Twilight* the vampires not only have sex, but Edward Cullen is even able to get his human wife, Bella, pregnant. But how?

Logic tells us that a vampire's lack of blood flow would be more of a bedroom killer than they are, and yet it seems vampires across multiple universes are sinking their teeth into humans in a variety of different sexual ways. Let's figure out how these interspecies relations might be possible, starting with vampire erections, or the lack thereof.

Erections and Undead Anatomy

Before we dive into whether the abovementioned bitey boys could get erections or not, let's break down exactly what an erection is. An erection begins when impulses from the brain tell local nerves to stimulate the penis, which causes the muscles to relax and allows blood to flow in. This blood flow creates pressure, making the penis expand and harden, thus creating an erection. Then the membrane surrounding these newly filled spaces (specifically the tunica albuginea, if you *must* know the scientific term) helps to trap the blood, sustaining the erection. This all boils down to three basic ingredients needed to bake an erection cake: nerve stimulation, muscle response, and blood flow. But do our sexy undead fulfill all of these criteria?

This is a hard question to definitively answer, as the lore about a vampire's physical traits changes slightly or drastically depending on the fictional property being discussed. In the most general terms, it's fairly universal to say that vampires are undead creatures that feed on blood to live, have no heartbeat, don't need to breathe, and can be killed by sunlight. Mileage may vary for other myths like being burned by crosses, hating garlic, and dying from a stake to the heart, but the above criteria are a good starting place in terms of bodily functions.

So back to our erection cake—let's look at our first ingredient, nerve stimulation. Nerves transmit electrical impulses throughout our body, including the central nervous system (which includes the brain and spinal cord) and the peripheral nervous system (which is basically everything else), telling our body to do pretty much everything it does, from basic muscle movement to digestion. We would be pretty hard-pressed to argue that any vampire doesn't have a functioning nervous system when they are all constantly doing nervous system–reliant things like walking around, talking, putting on dark red clothing, and licking blood off their lips like it's the most delicious thing in the world. So, clearly, when someone becomes vampirically undead, their nervous system remains intact. That's one requirement down.

The second requirement for an erection is muscle response, meaning the body responds physically to the signals being sent out by the nerves. We could list all the times this has happened in media, but as with the nervous system, it would be literally every vampiric appearance ever, as it's difficult to recall ever seeing a vampire incapable of movement. In fact, it's just the opposite: most vampires have increased strength and speed compared to humans, which would imply that their nervous system and muscle response are not only functioning, but work better than they do for us living folks.

This is great news for vampires so far. Break out your dental dams, because we're two-thirds of the way to achieving a vampire erection. The last hurdle the undead must face before being able to bone is . . . blood flow. Uh-oh.

As discussed, the beautifully undead creatures of the night have no heartbeat. To become a vampire, a person usually has to die, and then come back to life as a member of the undead, but their heart doesn't tend to join them on this ride of resurrection. But if a vampire's heart doesn't beat, that means there is no force to power their circulatory system and carry blood throughout their body, and, importantly for this discussion, to their penis.

Logic tells us that since these vampires have no blood flow they should be incapable of achieving an erection to partake in any traditional sexual acts, an idea backed up by the abundance of vampire lore wherein vampires do not engage in sex at all. Take Dracula, for example. For all his history of being a seducer, he never actually engages in sexual activities with his victims, nor do the vampires in the Marvel Universe. There are a few vampire-adjacent characters in Marvel, like Morbius the Living Vampire and Blade, that are capable of achieving erections and having sex the way we humans are familiar with, but Morbius and Blade both have functioning circulatory systems, as they are living men who simply have the supernatural abilities of vampires. Blade in particular "possesses all of a vampire's strengths without their weaknesses,"[17] which would explain why the Marvel vampires all hate him so much—they're probably jealous that he can go out in the sun and out on a date. This is in stark contrast to the vampires he hunts, who are generally quite sexual in nature and enjoy a good make-out session, but don't partake in full sexual acts.

Probably the most interesting vampires out there not having sex are the characters in Anne Rice's Vampire Chronicles, best known for the first book in the series, *Interview with the Vampire*. In this universe, the vampire characters are hypersexualized beings but their allure is just a tool to entice their human prey to let their guard down so they can feed off of them. In the insect world this is called aggressive mimicry and can be seen in creatures such as the crab spider,[18] which makes itself look like an ant to lure its prey in closer. Much like the vampire in the Anne Rice universe, the spider has no interest in having sex with the creature it is drawing in, but feigns the possibility in order to eat. For all the sexual tension between the characters in the Vampire Chronicles series, the vampires never actually have sex (in the books). Interestingly enough, they are capable of getting erections in extreme circumstances, but it seems like more of a hindrance for them than anything else. For example, the main character, Lestat, once had his body briefly transformed after drinking the blood of an ancient vampire and described himself as follows in *The Queen of the Damned*:

I studied my reflection—my chest was like a marble torso in a museum, that white. And the organ, the organ we don't need, poised as if ready for what it would never again know how to do or want to do, marble, a Priapus at a gate.[19]

Priapus, if you're wondering, is an ancient Greek god of fertility notable for being portrayed with an oversized, permanent erection. His name is the basis of the medical term "priapism," which is when the penis remains uncomfortably erect for hours. Literary references aside, it's a shocking and rare thing to hear a man describe his erect penis as an organ he doesn't need, want, or know what to do with. It feels impossible for any penis-endowed being, alive or undead, to not intrinsically cherish the lowest hanging member of their family, but Lestat's reaction to this marble erection as more of an inconvenience than anything else makes it pretty clear that he hasn't had, or desired, sex for as long as he's been a vampire, which is more than two hundred years when this incident occurs. This means that Rice's vampires, at least, do not consider their penis to be a vital part of their anatomy, which makes sense when you remember that vampires aren't actually human. As much as they look like us, vampires are a parasitic form of life that survive in the husks of dead human bodies (a helpfully unsexy thing to keep in mind if one ever tries to seduce you). These walking corpses are destroyed by the sun, eat blood to survive, and also turn into bats, which is just a tad different from how human biology works, so it makes sense that vampire sex would be different than what we humans do as well. Some vampires may partake in human penetrative sex acts from time to time, but they also have their own kind of sex, in a way. It doesn't involve anything with a penis or a vagina, but it does involve a kind of penetration.

The Bite as a Sex Act

Think about why humans have sex—from a biological standpoint it's mostly about reproduction. Sure, sex is fun, but that's Mother Nature's way of tricking you into doing it. We have sex because it feels good, we orgasm because it feels even better, and for some couples this involves a vagina being penetrated, semen being released, an egg being fertilized, and our species continuing to procreate. That's how it works for humans, collectively: sex feels good, we do it, we perpetuate the species.

But vampires are not human; from an evolutionary standpoint they are something else entirely, more like a virus or separate entity that takes over the body of a human. In general, vampires cannot reproduce through human sexual means (though there are rare exceptions that we'll discuss later). For a vampire to procreate they have to bite a human, drink their blood, and also feed that human some vampire blood as they're dying. The human will technically die from blood loss and then resurrect a short time later as a vampire. In most lore, this newly turned vampire will be considered a "childe"[20] and the vampire who bit and turned them is their parent or sire. That means for most vampires the bite functions as the penetrative act to begin procreation and the drinking of blood is the fluid exchange that perpetuates their species. It makes sense, then, that vampires would no longer be driven to have sex like they did when they were human, as it serves no biological function for them anymore. For a vampire, the bite is both a reproductive and sexual act, further emphasized by the fact that a vampire bite is often portrayed as an orgasmic experience for those involved. Sure, not every feeding results in a new vampire being born, but humans also don't get pregnant every time they have sex. Vampires *could* reproduce every time they bite someone if they were to feed their blood to their victims and resurrect them, and some humans *could* get pregnant every time they have sex if they didn't use birth control, but reproduction isn't necessary for the act itself to be fun. Honestly, vampires likely view the option of not feeding blood to their victims as a form of abstinence. And as birth control options go, it's a pretty damn reliable one.

But even if vampires don't need to have sex to procreate, we can't ignore the fact that many vampires are capable of achieving erections, having sex, and even ejaculating, as Edward Cullen in *Twilight* and Angel in *Buffy the Vampire Slayer* both fathered children in their respective franchises. So how are these guys getting their little coffins to rise?

The Blood Must Flow

In terms of empirical data, we have only a small amount of information from source materials about exactly how vampires are capable of human-style sexual exploits.

In *Buffy the Vampire Slayer*, the show's most prominent and sex-crazed vampire, Spike, explicitly states that drinking blood is both an aphrodisiac for vampires and what makes them "hard."

> *Blood is life, lackbrain. Why do you think we eat it? It's what keeps you going. Makes you warm. Makes you hard.*[21]

This line tells us that Spike likes to overshare during group conversations and, more importantly, that ingesting blood is what makes a vampire capable of achieving an erection and participating in sex. Which makes sense. As discussed earlier, the thing holding bloodsuckers back from achieving an erection is essentially blood flow. They don't have the flow part, but it's not as though vampires are in short supply of the main ingredient. Blood is literally a vampire's only food source; they need it to survive just as much as an erection does, and this may be why none of our sexually active bloodsuckers are suffering from erectile dysfunction. In a living human, our digestive system breaks down the food we eat and then the nutrients from that food are absorbed into our bloodstream to be carried to each cell in the body. It's possible that when a vampire drinks blood their digestive system allows the fresh blood to be absorbed directly into the bloodstream and from there it could move on to the genitals.

Now, it might seem unlikely that ingested blood could make its way to the penis without a functioning circulatory system, but we must also consider gravity, the sweet mistress that holds us all down. If a vampire ingests a large amount of blood, and then that blood travels directly into their nonflowing circulatory system, gravity would likely pull the blood down into the lower half of the body, specifically the legs and genital region. Even living human bodies depend on gravity for this. Because our bodies know that gravity will naturally send our blood downward, we spend very few bodily resources pumping blood to the lower regions of our body. In fact, astronauts in space with zero gravity have issues with blood pooling in their heads and chests because their bodies aren't accustomed to having to pump blood down to the legs and genitals—that's gravity's job as far as the body is concerned. So we know that ingested blood would naturally flow down to where it's needed if a vampire did want to have a coffin party for two.

We established earlier that nerve stimulation and muscle response are still functional in vampires, so if ingestion and gravity are able to bring blood into their genital region, it stands to reason that their penis may be able to function normally, with their nerves telling their muscles to relax and allow the fresh blood to flow into the penis and cause engorgement. And just like that, you've got a vampire erection.

This sexual achievement doesn't just apply to the penis-laden members of the undead—the vagina also needs to be engorged with blood to allow for arousal and sexual enjoyment. The same basic principles of nerve stimulation, muscle response, and blood flow apply to both sex organs, which means that all the undead creatures of the night are able to go be a freak in the streets *and* the sheets, as long as they're having sex on a full stomach. If they haven't ingested blood recently, though, there would be no fluids to engorge the genital regions, which means any vampire that skips supper has to go lurk in the shadows and find someone to eat before they find someone to eat out.

This theory about blood ingestion and gravity aligns well with most vampire sexual lore, but to do a thorough analysis we have to consider all available information regarding a vampire's ability to have sex. What makes that job incredibly easy is when a creator explicitly states how a fictional process is possible, and in this regard no one has done a greater service, or provided a crazier answer to the vampire-sex question, than Stephanie Meyer, the author of the Twilight books.

When asked how the vampires in her series were capable of not only having sex but impregnating a human, Ms. Meyer took to her blog and supplied an entire essay outlining the process in detail. As she explains it:

> A fluid similar to the venom in their mouths works as a lubricant between the cells, which makes movement possible (note: this fluid is very flammable) . . .
>
> Throughout the vampire's body are many versions of venom-based fluids that retain a marked resemblance to the fluid that was replaced, and function in much the same way and toward the same purpose. Though there is no venom replacement that works precisely like blood, many of the functions of blood are carried on in some form . . .
>
> The normal reactions of arousal are still present in vampires, made possible by venom-related fluids that cause tissues to react similarly as they do to an influx of blood. Like with vampire skin—which looks similar to human skin and has the same basic function—fluids closely related to seminal fluids still exist in male vampires, which carry genetic information and are capable of bonding with a human ovum.[22]

There's a lot to unpack there, not the least of which is why Meyer felt the need to point out that all the liquid in a vampire's body is hella flammable, a fact that is hopefully irrelevant to somebody's sex life. What is relevant here is that we're told the vampires in Twilight have very venom-reliant bodily functions, which accounts for their super strength, paralytic bites, erections, and seminal fluids (venom is truly a must-have in any vampire's body—it does it all). Unfortunately, venom is not a common component in most vampire lore, so while we have an explanation for the sexual exploits of the vampires in Twilight, we can't in good scientific conscience apply this answer to other franchises or vampires in general to explain their ability to have sex.

But maybe the definitive answer to the question of how a vampire can achieve an erection doesn't lie in fictional vampire venom, or gravity, or the possibility that vampires digest their food differently than us. Perhaps the answer is as simple as the fact that dead people can just get erections.

Raising the Dead in Real Life

A death erection (or *rigor erectus* if you're nasty and know Latin) is an erection that some corpses in the real world have been found sporting well after death. This pointed condition is most commonly found in those who died by hanging, but it can also occur after a death related to a spinal cord injury, gunshot wound, or poisoning. And a death erection doesn't just stick around for a minute or two; if an erection forms at death the penile membrane will hold the blood in place for longer than anyone involved would like, honestly, and makes for some uncomfortable trips to the morgue for emergency personnel. This isn't one of those flukes of nature that only happens once in a while—the possibility of getting a death erection is about one in three for a person who died by hanging. Basically, if you die a violent death, there's a good chance your body is going to head to the funeral home looking like a "Priapus at a gate," as Lestat would say.

What's important to note here, though, is that regular human bodies are capable of significant blood flow and even achieving an erection after death, so it's not much of a stretch to believe that the bloodsucking children of the night, who were formerly human, would be able to achieve erections as well and have a full and unsafe sex life, despite their undead status. So go forth and have a good time, our vampire brethren, but maybe keep those sexual exploits away from any lit candles, just in case Stephanie Meyer's right about those flammable bodily fluids.

THE NEVER-LOVIN' BLUE-EYED THING?

"The Thing! Is his dork made out of orange rock like the rest of his body?"
—Brodie to Stan Lee, *Mallrats* (1995)

When we first meet Ben Grimm of the Fantastic Four, he's a handsome young astronaut working with his friends on the noble quest of getting to space before the Russians. But while up in space he and the team are bombarded with cosmic rays and return to Earth with amazing superpowers (and hopefully an even more amazing sign that said, "Suck it, Russia!").

For most of the team these new powers were just swell. Reed Richards could stretch to incredible lengths and became Mr. Fantastic; Sue Storm was able to become transparent and called herself the Invisible Woman; Johnny Storm could light on fire and was deemed the Human Torch . . . and Ben Grimm was changed into a monstrous orange rock man called "The Thing." (By, like, his friends. Nice guys.)

After being one of the first people in space, Ben should have been welcomed home with a stampede of women knocking on his door. Instead he got the worst makeover of all time and found himself with no ladies interested in his literally rock-hard bod. In the 2004 *Fantastic Four* movie his fiancée even breaks off their engagement after she sees his new and unimproved face (but Ben's probably better off; he doesn't want to be with someone prejudiced against the orange and rocky). After that kind of treatment, it's no surprise that one of the features of Ben's new body was a heap of emotional baggage.

When discussing his notably orange form, Ben frequently mentions that he feels like a "monster" and on at least one occasion said he can never "be a man"[23] again. The monster part makes a kind of sense; he's made entirely out of rock (and not in the cool Dwayne Johnson kind of way). But why would he think he was no longer a man? Well, that's the worst part—you see, the Thing's got no . . . thing. No thing at all. His underwear is as empty as the seats to 2015's *Fant4stic* movie. Little Ben has left the building. His one-eyed monster has resigned. Which is all a roundabout way of saying, Ben Grimm has no penis.

To be clear, I'm not saying that Ben has a penis that is now an orange rock like the rest of his body. No, I'm saying that when he was transformed by those pesky cosmic rays he lost the appendage entirely. And the proof (or lack thereof) is constantly staring us in the face. I've never seen a photo of Ben Grimm where there was a rock penis visible under those tights of his (and surely the outline of a granite-encrusted member would be fairly noticeable). But the real evidence can be found in the previously mentioned *Fant4stic* movie when we see Ben Grimm lose his humanity, his penis, *and* all his clothes. Yes, Ben spends half of a children's movie romping around completely naked. But that's kind of okay because there's really nothing for the kiddies to see (and not just because the movie tanked and no one bought a ticket). Ben is shown multiple times in the film in all his full-frontal glory, and it's shockingly clear that he now has the pelvic endowment of a Ken doll (which is terrible news for Ben, but at least means his action figures are anatomically correct).

If Ben woke up from his rocket ship crash and realized he was made of orange rock *and* had no penis, well, it would be quite a blow to his self-esteem and explains why he constantly wonders if he is a monster or a man. It also explains why he chose such a demeaning code name for himself as the Thing (but still doesn't explain why his supposed friends agreed to call him that). Ben, of course, shouldn't wonder what he is, though, even if his penis has gone incognito. If he was born as a man and identifies as a man, he's a man, and also a hero, and also a rock. He's everything. So we know that Ben has no penis and is definitely still a man, but we have a lot of other burning questions, like what exactly happened to Ben's penis, what effect would this have on his bodily functions, and, most importantly, what does this mean for Ben's sex life?

What Happened to the Thing's Thing?

Let's start our fantastic journey by figuring out where and why Ben's penis went MIA. The where is easy enough. When Ben transforms into the Thing we can see that his head gets bigger (and rockier) but his eyes sink far into his head, his nose gets smaller, and he completely loses his ears, making his face more jack-o-lantern than human. Basically, any appendages not made of bone become sunken in or lose their defining features when they become rock. Boner jokes aside, the penis also lacks bone structure; it's made up entirely of skin, muscle, and other soft tissue. So it's probable that, like his ears and nose, "little Ben" was just absorbed away when Ben's body was transformed.

Having your new superpowers completely destroy the most beloved part of your body is a pretty good reason to feel less than human. But even though Ben resembles a walking Mount Rushmore as the Thing, his transformed body still functions a lot like a human's—it just works a little differently now.

For example, we just discussed how the Thing has no ears, or even holes where his ears used to be, but we know that Ben is not deaf; he hears just fine (though he tunes out when Reed launches into one of his long-winded science monologues). According to *Marvel Anatomy: A Scientific Study of the Superhuman*, an official Marvel resource book, even though Ben's ears aren't visible, his ear canal is still working below the rocky surface and sound is entering through the cracks in his rock skin.

The Thing lacks any external ear structure, and his auditory sensors are housed beneath his thick dermis. His perception of sound may thus be contingent on the presence of a tympanic membrane on each side of his head, below the layer of visible rock. Instead of sound entering through an auditory canal, this tympanum would interpret the vibrations passing through the Thing's rocky hide, transmitting those signals to the tympanic cavity in the middle ear.[24]

Since his ears still function despite being visibly missing, it makes sense that Ben's other appendages that seemingly disappeared might also be hiding out and doing their jobs elsewhere. This means Ben's missing member may not be missing at all; it may just be playing the worst game of hide and seek ever.

For example, in *Ultimate Fantastic Four #8,* Reed questions Ben about his transformed body, to which Ben reports that he can "still go to the bathroom" but "you don't wanna know the details."[25] And he's totally right, keep that info to yourself, Ben, because the fact that you have a functioning digestive system is all we need to know. If Ben still digests food, it stands to reason that his urethra (the tube that carries urine from the bladder to the outside of the body) must have remained intact when his pelvis turned into a rock quarry, much in the same way that Ben's ear canals still exist without his ears. We know that Ben hears through the cracks in his skin, so if he still goes to the bathroom he's likely emptying his bladder via the cracks in the rocks that cover the area where his penis used to be, which could be messy, but means that at least some function of the penis remains intact.

A functioning digestive system also means Ben still has to eat, which means he's alive and not just a talking hunk of rock, or a monster, as he sometimes calls himself. Since we know what happened to his penis and that he's still alive and human, despite his concerns, let's move on and ask what we're really here to figure out: Can the Thing have sex?

To which the answer is yeah, but probably not how you'd think.

The Thing's Sex Life—Not So Grimm After All

The fact that Ben has no external penis means he can't have traditional penetrative sex with a woman (unless we're talking about him penetrating her heart of course, but we're not). Thanks to his rocky transformation, he's got literally nothing to work with, but that doesn't mean he isn't capable of having an active and interesting sex life.

A penis entering a vagina may be considered the traditional way of having heterosexual sex, but there are many sex paths worth exploring in this wonderful world we live in. And don't forget, Ben Grimm is an astronaut; exploring is what he does. This may sound crazier than the time Ben went to heaven and found out Stan Kirby was God (don't ask), but a penis is in no way necessary to have a fun and fulfilling sex life, no matter your gender or sexual orientation. Oral sex, sex toys, and manual stimulation are all perfectly acceptable and fun forms of sex that leave both partners satisfied whether a vagina is being penetrated by a penis or not.

Which is good news for Ben's longstanding girlfriend, Alicia Masters. Even if Ben no longer has a penis, or is now sporting a barely visible micropenis (which is any penis that is smaller than about seven centimeters in length), he's still fully capable of pleasing his partner in the aforementioned ways. Heck, with the size of his fingers he wouldn't even have to splurge on sex toys as he's basically rocking the equivalent of five of them on each hand. Even better news for Alicia is that nonpenetrative sex doesn't end when a man climaxes; it's like the Energizer Bunny—it just keeps going and going. That means Ben can please her for as long as she wants, which would certainly explain his nickname as the Ever-Lovin' Blue-Eyed Thing.

So Alicia's covered in the sex department, but we haven't touched on perhaps the most amazing part, which is that Ben may still be able to orgasm, *even without a penis*.

Whoa. Let me explain. Now, rock isn't exactly known for its abundance of nerve endings, but we know that Ben's body still experiences sensations. During battles he clearly feels pain, he enjoys the taste of food, and he can feel when someone touches him—all his senses seem to be intact. If Ben still experiences sensations, it's possible that the rocky area of his pelvis that was once his penis is still sexually sensitive and that he could achieve orgasm through stimulation of that area.

In terms of finding this release, however, Ben would have to explore new "clobbering time" methods than those he used before his penis made its disappearing act. He can no longer partake in penetrative sex like he used to or masturbate in the traditional manner, but he may be able to quite literally "rub one off." To illustrate this point, let's look at a *New York Magazine* article from 2014 that interviewed a man with a two-inch (non-erect) micropenis who had incredible difficulty participating in vaginal sex but still enjoyed masturbating. Like, so much. "I do what some people call humping the bed,"[26] he explained. This involved lying face down on a towel and rubbing against it for friction until he reached climax.

As a rock man who weighs a few tons, Ben would need a pretty strong bed to lie on and a towel probably wouldn't get the job done, but a partner like Alicia helping out (or a literal grinding stone to rub against) could provide enough stimulation for Ben to reach orgasm in this way, even without a penis.

If you think that sounds unbelievable, well, it wouldn't even be close to the craziest form of orgasm that the human body is capable of.

Medical journals are filled with reports of men and women with spinal cord injuries who have lost all sensation to their genitals, and thus their ability to experience orgasm, who later found that another part of their body—such as their breasts, ears, neck, or even thumb—had become so sensitized that they could climax through stimulation of these areas instead. This wonderful phenomenon is known as a transfer orgasm.[27] It usually occurs after serious injury that has removed sensation in the genitals, and involves the brain rewiring itself to create new erogenous zones. Basically, the body's need for an orgasm is like life in Jurassic Park: it will find a way.

All of that is to say that if the bodies of people with spinal cord injuries can reroute their nervous systems to orgasm via places like their neck and thumb, it's completely conceivable that Ben Grimm's rock-transformed body would find a way to reorient itself in a similar fashion. His transformation into the Thing cost him his penis, but it didn't necessarily cost him his sex life. With a little experimentation he should be able to figure out how to get his rocks off (quite literally).

Now if you're thinking that Ben Grimm losing his penis in a space-related rock transformation is the weirdest sex story that has happened to the Fantastic Four, you'd be wrong, because there was also . . .

Sexual Interlude #1: The Time Johnny Storm Had Sex Dreams About His Sister

There are few mainstream comics as wholesome as the Fantastic Four. The first family of Marvel is known for their wacky hijinks, bright blue costumes, and G-rated adventures, which is what made it so surprising when they managed to sneak a plotline about sex dreams into the background of a regular story.

This sneaky sex tale begins in *Fantastic Four #525* with the team gathered in the family kitchen looking exhausted and complaining about having weird dreams. When Johnny Storm enters, looking particularly tired and on edge, his six-year-old nephew Franklin asks him if he had any "cool dreams last night," to which Johnny yells, "WHY CAN'T YOU PEOPLE JUST LEAVE ME ALONE?!?" even though it is literally the first thing that's been said to him. So, a normal reaction to a child, we can all agree.

Johnny's sister, Sue, tries to take him aside to find out what's wrong, but Johnny just gets more upset as she approaches and flies away rather than spend a single moment with her. If the person reading this has siblings, I'm sure you can relate.

After a second night of the family having weird dreams, Reed calls a team meeting and asks everyone what they have been dreaming about lately. Johnny is noticeably silent throughout the questioning process until Reed lets them know that "I believe we're all having each other's dreams," to which Johnny enthusiastically screams, "Oh thank GOD!" without elaborating why this is such a huge relief. *What* was this man dreaming about?

It's eventually revealed that the Fantastic Four caught a "dream fever" the last time they were in the Microverse that is causing them to see each other's dreams at night. The "dream fever" is eventually cured by some hand-wavey science using a weapon they stole from a villain named Diablo, but they all still remember the things they saw in their sleep, good and bad.

After they're cured, Sue tries to talk to Johnny yet again because she thinks she knows what's wrong with him (spoiler: she doesn't).

Sue: Think I haven't noticed that you've been on edge and avoiding me lately Johnny? Think I don't know why?

Johnny (wildly nervous): Um . . . do you?

Sue reveals that she saw Johnny's dreams during the "dream fever" and knows that he dreams about his flame powers accidentally hurting the people he loves and thinks that's why he's been acting so weird. To which Johnny literally just says, "Um . . . sure. Whatever" in response and leaves again, happy to let Sue think that's why he's been acting weird, because he definitely doesn't want to talk about the real reason, at least not with anyone who isn't a licensed therapist.

The story ends with Reed telling Sue that he isn't sure who was having his dreams, but if you're a reader with a little more information than our resident genius was given, it's easy to figure out by process of elimination that Johnny was the only one who could have been seeing Reed's dreams. Boring old Reed? What could that guy dream about?

Well, Sue asks him that exact question:

Reed: I do not dream about blackboards and equations . . . dreams aren't only about stresses and worries, they're also about wants and desires.

Sue: Do tell. And what do you want, Mr. Richards?

Reed: At the end of each and every day . . . only you!

Aw, so Mr. Fantastic mostly has dreams about how much he desires his wife. That's kind of sweet except . . . if Johnny was having Reed's dreams, then he was having sex dreams about Reed's wife, who happens to be Johnny's sister! Oh dear God.

But it gets even worse. When Sue describes seeing Johnny's dream she says that she experienced them "with me in your place" so the shared dreams weren't like watching a movie or something, the dreamer was fully immersed in a first-person experience of whatever was happening. So Johnny was having dreams where he actively had sex with his sister . . . with no idea that they weren't his dreams for like two days. That poor guy, of course he was freaking out and not telling anybody what was happening. It's usually not a good idea to keep secrets from your super-family, but in this case it's probably best that Johnny kept this piece of information to himself—it definitely helps with being able to make eye contact with his team in the immediate future. Oof. Flame off!

Part 2

PARTNERS IN CRIME FIGHTING

The Pros and Cons of Superhero Relationships

THE FASTEST MAN ALIVE . . . IN BED

Hawkgirl: That's fast.
The Flash: Fastest man alive.
Hawkgirl: Which might explain why you can't get a date.
—Hawkgirl and the Flash, *Justice League*, season 1, episode 8

The Flash can do a lot of things. After being struck by a combination of lightning and chemicals, he gained access to the Speed Force and a whole host of wonderful abilities. Hailed as the Fastest Man Alive, the Flash can move faster than a speeding bullet, can vibrate his molecules to phase through objects, can create little tornados with his arms, and frequently runs faster than the speed of light to travel through time. He has a truly incredible set of powers that he's used to save the world countless times, and yet after all these amazing feats, people still say with a snicker, "I bet the Flash is also fast . . . in bed." Which is to say, because of the Flash's super speed, it's widely assumed that during sex he ejaculates very quickly, resulting in an unsatisfying sexual experience for his partner. Which is a much funnier thing to imply than explain.

There is no denying that the Flash is an all-around fast guy, but let's discuss just how those speedy powers of his would affect his relationship, his ability to orgasm, his potential career as a sperm donor, and his vibrational capacity. And most importantly, we'll find out whether we should send sympathies to his wife.

Now, many characters have worn the Flash symbol over the years, but for this chapter let's focus on the most famous Flash of them all, the star of both *The Flash* TV shows and *The Flash* movie, Barry Allen, and his regular human wife, Iris West.

A Speed Force to Be Reckoned with

To know how Barry's powers would affect his sex life, we first need to break down exactly how the Flash's powers work, starting with his basic super speed. Yes, Barry Allen is capable of running at the speed of light, but he is equally capable of moving at the speed of a regular human, and he spends more time casually walking around than he does breaking the sound barrier. This is because Barry draws energy from an entity called the Speed Force to use his powers. And that's the thing about Barry's powers: he has to choose to use them. He's not like, say, Superman, who can't turn off his super strength so has to be careful not to crush the world (or his girlfriend) at any given moment. Instead, Barry can easily live his life at normal speed, then tap into the Speed Force to activate his powers when he needs them.

This would heavily imply that Barry could simply have sex with his wife at a normal human rate and never tap into the Speed Force that would cause his potential fast finish. But of course, accidents do happen. After all, it's not uncommon for a woman to request her partner go "faster" when nearing orgasm, and there's no one who could go faster than the Flash. It's also a fact that as men reach orgasm some motions, such as pelvic thrusting, can become involuntary and increase in speed.[28] So a blissed-out Barry Allen could try to have normal sex with his wife but end up accidentally tapping into the Speed Force as he climaxes, the results of which would be absolutely catastrophic. If the Flash was thrusting his body against his wife at the speed of sound, the impact would decimate Iris in every way imaginable, except sexual satisfaction.

To figure out just how destroyed she would be, we'll look to the good scientists at McMaster University who did some lengthy and impressive calculations for us based on *The Flash* TV show and concluded that Barry Allen's acceleration at his maximum speed was 100,013.60 m/s^2 and his mass was 84 kg.[29] As you might remember from high school physics, Force = Mass × Acceleration, so we can deduce that that if Barry was tapped into the Speed Force during sex he would be thrusting his hips against his wife at a force of 8,401,142 kilograms m/s^2 or 1,888,651 pounds. Oh God, don't use the force, Barry! To put that into perspective, that's like getting hit with 6,400 wrecking balls *at once*. At least if Barry had sex with his wife at super speed there would be no point in asking if it was good for her when he's done, as she'd be dead a thousand times over.

Or would she?

While it's true that in the real world the Flash would kill his human wife if he had sex with her at super speed, in the fictional world of the DC universe it's been established that the Flash creates a friction cushion or "aura" around anyone he is in contact with when tapping into the Speed Force. According to the *DC Comics Encyclopedia*, the Flash "can lend his speed to moving objects or people by touch,"[30] which explains how Barry can carry regular humans around at supersonic speed without them being killed by friction, heat, or g-forces like they should be. It's safe to assume that this aura would also extend to his wife during intercourse, which means if Barry did accidentally start thrusting at super speed, Iris would simply enter the Speed Force with him and they would both start having the fastest sex of all time and, more importantly, they would also both survive. Which, most people would agree, is the ideal way of having sex.

The Flash's Finishing Speed

Now that we've addressed the question of Iris's survival during sex with her husband at super speed, we can move on to the next obvious question—just how fast *does* the Fastest Man Alive have sex?

Well, to answer that we need to know how fast a regular human male has sex, and guess what, it's already pretty fast.

According to *The Journal of Sexual Medicine*, it takes just six minutes for an average heterosexual male to reach orgasm during intercourse, in comparison to the average heterosexual woman who takes 13.5 minutes.[31] Anyone with a basic understanding of time can figure out that that's a problem for opposite-sex couples. Digging into the data from a different study shows us just how much of a problem it is, as 87 percent of husbands reported consistently experiencing orgasm during sex, while only 49 percent of their wives reported the same thing. So, a large percentage of men reach orgasm faster than their wives and literally aren't willing to put the extra time in to get their partners past the orgasmic finish line.[32] Maybe we should all leave the Flash alone with those "finishing fast" in bed jokes, as plenty of men without super speed are also disappointing their wives with a high level of frequency. But I digress. Let's get back to the matter at hand: how fast the Flash cums.

The next thing we need to know is how fast the Flash actually is in relation to a regular human. Obviously, the Flash is really, *really* fast, but let's figure out exactly how much faster he is than the rest of us. According to data aggregated from running apps, the average running speed for a male is 10.6 km/hour or 2.94 m/s.[33] The Flash can move pretty much as fast as he likes, up to and including the speed of light, but that's when he's really booking it. So for the sake of comparison, we'll use a slightly slower benchmark and estimate that the Flash is generally moving at the speed of sound, which is 343 m/s. Compare that to the average running speed of a human and some quick math tells us that the Flash is zipping around about 116.66 times faster than a regular human male. If we divide the speed at which an average Joe orgasms (360 seconds) by 116.66, we find that when moving at the speed of sound, the Flash likely orgasms during intercourse in about 3.08 seconds. So . . . pretty fast. That makes sex with the Flash the very definition of a "quickie." Now, some may be tempted to yet again joke about premature ejaculation at this juncture, which is comedically understandable but doesn't actually apply here. Except it kind of technically does. A little.

Scientifically speaking, premature ejaculation is not defined by simply orgasming quickly every now and then, as many people seem to believe.

This misconception has led to the claim that 20 to 30 percent of all men have gone through premature ejaculation, but there are actually four criteria that must be met to diagnose the Flash, or anyone else for that matter, with this condition, and most people simply don't meet it. When the actual criteria are taken into account, it turns out only about 4 percent of people experience true premature ejaculation, and everyone else is just getting a little excited too quickly (which also sounds like a description of Barry Allen in general, to be honest). The actual criteria for premature ejaculation include:

1. the ejaculation almost always occurs unintentionally within one minute of penetration,
2. this has been occurring for more than six months,
3. the premature ejaculations are very distressing, and
4. no other medical problem is identified as a cause.[34]

Despite the fact that we just worked out that the Flash climaxes in well under one minute as the first condition outlines, he doesn't actually meet any of the other criteria for premature ejaculation and would therefore not be diagnosed medically with this condition.

So, we know that the Flash doesn't technically suffer from premature ejaculation and climaxes in about three seconds, but what about the Flash's wife, Iris? How does having sex at the speed of sound affect her experience?

Well, let's figure out just how long it would take Iris to orgasm if she entered the Speed Force with Barry while boning. According to the same studies we just used, the average running speed for women is 9.6 km/hour or 2.66 m/s.[35] If Iris does indeed slip into the Speed Force during intercourse and matches Barry's speed of 343 m/s, then she is going 128.95 times faster than a regular woman, and she would therefore orgasm in approximately 6.28 seconds . . . which is pretty fast, but still twice as long as it takes Barry to orgasm.

On first glance, this would indicate that even if both of them are banging it out at super speed, the Flash would probably leave his wife unsatisfied at the end of intercourse, unless of course the Flash can keep going and going and going, which generally speaking is something he's very good at. But can he keep going *in the bedroom*? Yes, he probably can, thanks to a little thing called a refractory period, and his lack thereof.

How the Flash Keeps Going and Going

Scientifically speaking, a refractory period is the span of time after having an orgasm during which a person is no longer sexually responsive. During this period a person might lose interest in sex and not be able to get an erection, ejaculate, or orgasm, so basically it's the sleepy time after an orgasm when you don't feel like having sex again. Depending on age, the refractory period can be anywhere from fifteen minutes to about twenty hours, but the average for all men is approximately half an hour. So what are the chances that the Flash has a very, very short refractory period and can go about pleasing his wife again almost immediately after orgasm? They're actually very good. Things are looking up for Iris West.

Scientists aren't exactly sure what causes the refractory period in men, but a prevailing theory is that after ejaculation the seminal vesicles (a pair of glands that produce semen) lose muscular wall tension and send a feedback loop that won't allow the penis to become erect again until wall tension has been restored. Basically, the muscles get tired and need a rest. As men age, the time it takes to restore tension in the seminal vesicles increases and their refractory period becomes longer. This increase closely correlates with the change in a person's overall ability to heal and recover from injuries. For example, a teenager may completely recover from a cut on their leg in a few days, while an elderly person can take a month or more to heal from the same injury. More specifically, since we're talking about muscle recovery and people who run a lot, we can turn to a study in the *European Journal of Applied Physiology* from 2010 that showed that after running a marathon, the muscles of young runners in their twenties and thirties were 100 percent recovered after twenty-four hours while older "master" runners in their forties and fifties only recovered 86.4 percent of their muscle strength in the same amount of time.[36] This indicates that the faster a person heals, the shorter their refractory period will be, and as we've mentioned several times already, nobody's faster than the Flash (except maybe one of the other Flashes, but that's a whole thing).

It's fairly well known that the Flash heals from injuries almost as fast as he runs, but DC has never specifically quantified just how fast he heals compared to a regular human. We can work this out on our own, though, by looking at one of those other Flashes I just mentioned, specifically Barry Allen's grandson, Bart Allen, also known as Kid Flash, who, for all intents and purposes, has the same powers as his grandfather (but is also a teenager, so we're only going to talk about him briefly in this book about sex). In *Teen Titans #3* (2003),[37] Kid Flash gets injured in a quantifiable way when he's shot in the knee by the villain Deathstroke. This is extremely bad news for Kid Flash but good for us, as we see Bart get taken to the hospital, where he undergoes surgery to replace his shattered kneecap, a surgery he completely recovers from after just fifteen minutes. In regular humans this surgery has a recovery period ranging from three months to a year, depending on age and severity. We'll average the time to six months as getting shot in the knee is pretty severe, but as mentioned above, young people tend to bounce back from injury fairly quickly. So, if Kid Flash's knee heals in fifteen minutes, and a human heals in six months (or 262,800 minutes), and we assume this healing ability "runs" in the family, so to speak, we can estimate that the Flash heals at a rate 17,520 times faster than a human. Holy shit, if you thought he orgasmed fast, you won't believe how fast he can orgasm *again*.

So what does this mega healing mean for the Flash's refractory period? We know that an average male's refractory period is approximately 30 minutes (or 1,800 seconds). If we divide 1,800 by 17,520 that means that after orgasming, the Flash is capable of being sexually active again in approximately *0.102 seconds*. And just like that, we're no longer worried about his wife not being satisfied in bed because the Flash can indeed just keep going and going. Look out Energizer Bunny, because the Flash is coming for your job. And this isn't even the only evidence that supports Barry's sexual super speed.

Is It Possible to Learn This Power?

If it sounds a little crazy that the Flash would be able to achieve an erection again almost immediately after orgasming, it shouldn't, as scientists have studied several men in real life who were able to orgasm multiple times in a row with no refractory period in between, despite having no connection to the Speed Force (that we know about). In fact, one of the subjects studied was able to orgasm an astonishing six times in thirty-six minutes[38] and maintained his erection the entire time, which would be an impressive feat to do alone at home, let alone in a lab being observed by a bunch of scientists (unless you're into that kind of thing). A separate study looked at thirteen different men who were all capable of multiple orgasms with no refractory period in between. The goal of the research was to study the lack of refractory period in men, but the scientists definitely also asked them "How?! For the love of God, how are you doing this? Teach me!" Several men reported that their secret could not be taught as they were always able to achieve multiple orgasms. Some reported that they taught themselves to become multiorgasmic, and a few outliers explained that they did it accidentally, such as one subject who became multiorgasmic after occasionally performing pubococcygeal (PC) muscle exercises and another who orgasmed during sex with his wife, kept thrusting for her benefit, and found he could simply orgasm again and again.[39] Now that's a man who deserves the power of orgasming multiple times as he will clearly use that power for good.

By studying these men of multiple orgasms, researchers found several notable similarities among those with little to no refractory period. Most commonly these men were achieving erection and orgasming several times in a row, but they would not ejaculate until the final orgasm (which they all described as the best and most intense one). It was only after ejaculation that a refractory period kicked in and these men found themselves unable to achieve an erection any longer or orgasm again. This has led to a theory that the refractory period isn't just related to the seminal vesicles as discussed earlier but is likely also connected to a hormone called prolactin, which is released by the body during orgasm and may prevent a person from becoming aroused again until the hormone dissipates. This theory became more prevalent after a 2002 study of a multiorgasmic man who ejaculated each time he orgasmed but still had no refractory period in between. Blood tests showed one potential explanation for this—his body wasn't releasing prolactin after each orgasm, likely explaining his lack of refractory period.[40]

Following this alternate theory, let's assume for the moment that a man's refractory period is actually related to the release of prolactin, and not the wall tension in his testicles—what does this mean for the Flash's potential refractory period? Well, if he has to wait for the prolactin in his body to deteriorate before he can become aroused again, his refractory period may just be a normal human length of time. But it's also possible that the Flash could *choose* to be able to orgasm again quickly by burning the prolactin out of his system. One of the side effects of the Flash's abilities is his increased metabolism, which forces him to eat about 10,000 calories per day to have enough energy to run around like he does. This high metabolism alone would burn off calories and chemicals in his body pretty quickly, but Barry can also ramp it up even higher than usual if he needs to by tapping into the Speed Force, such as when he was poisoned by Poison Ivy and managed to run the toxins out of his body before they could reach his heart and kill him.[41] If he's able to increase his metabolism to burn away toxins, he can likely also burn away prolactin after orgasm and sexually hit the ground running, as the Flash likes to do.

But just because the Flash may be able to burn the prolactin out of his body doesn't mean he necessarily should. After all, the human body has built a refractory period in for a reason. No one is 100 percent sure what the reason is, but the prevailing theory is that it gives the body a chance to replenish seminal fluid and sperm post-ejaculation. But that might not be something Barry has to worry about.

A Wealth of Sperm

In regular humans, the testicles make several million sperm a day, or about 1,500 new sperm every second.[42] That sounds like a lot, but the body also loses anywhere from 20 to 300 million sperm in a single milliliter of semen, so if there is no refractory period to stop someone from orgasming again for a while, a person's sperm well could run dry pretty quickly. But what would sperm production look like for the fastest man alive?

Well, we know the Flash heals 17,520 times faster than a human. If his other bodily processes, like sperm generation, are equally fast, then that means the Flash's testicles make 26,280,000 sperm *per second*. Since there are 86,400 seconds in a day, that means his body would make 2,270,592,000,000 sperm every 24 hours. At that rate the Flash would have to ejaculate 7,568 times a day before he ran out of sperm, and since we've established he has little to no refractory period, that's something he could totally do. If it takes the Flash 3.08 seconds to orgasm and his refractory period is 0.102 seconds, that means he would only need 24,081 seconds, or 6.7 hours, to ejaculate enough times to run through his daily supply of sperm. For most people, ejaculating around 7,500 times in a day would result in a lower-body friction burn so bad Captain Cold wouldn't even be able to cool it down, but the Speed Force actually protects the Flash from the forces of friction, so there's really no reason why he can't just take a day (or 6.7 hours) and enjoy life to its literal fullest (or emptiest, as the case may be).

As of this book's publication, DC has not asked me to write a special edition Flash comic about the time he orgasmed 7,500 times in a day, but my inbox remains open if they change their mind. For a sneak peek at this potential book, though, we must also consider the bodily fluid loss involved in ejaculating 7,500 times, which is . . . a lot. The average semen ejaculate is 3.7 ml; multiply that by 7,500 and the Flash would be losing 27.75 liters of fluid in a day during this orgasmic outing. For some perspective, the average male's body is made up of about 42 liters of fluid altogether, so the Flash would be losing more than half of his bodily fluids, which is very bad considering that death from dehydration occurs when you lose just 15 to 25 percent. But that doesn't mean it's not possible for the fastest man alive to achieve complete testicular depletion. With a constantly running IV into his body and maybe a few dozen bottles of Gatorade, it would indeed be possible for the Flash to replenish his bodily fluids and expel all of his semen supply in a day. But if the Flash is truly generating trillions of sperm a day, it seems obvious his calling is not to be the world's fastest man, but the world's greatest sperm donor. In general, sperm donors earn about $100 per sperm donation. At 7,500 potential donations per day, the Flash would be earning $75,000 daily. This goes up to $2.5 million in sperm earnings if he donated every day for a single month. Forget Bruce Wayne paying for everything; the Flash has the Justice League's finances covered. Just don't ask him where the money came from.

All of this is presuming that we are correct about the Flash having almost no refractory period and that he can indeed keep going and going, but as mentioned earlier, scientists aren't exactly sure what causes the refractory period or what determines how long it lasts, so it's also possible that the Flash may simply orgasm in three seconds and then not be able to cum again for twenty minutes or more. Where would this leave his wife then, sexually speaking? Well, she likely won't have orgasmed during intercourse in that short amount of time, but there are plenty of other ways to satisfy a woman, and the Flash has some wonderful built-in features in that regard.

Those Good Vibrations

One of the Flash's potentially titillating superpowers is that he can vibrate his molecules so fast that he can phase through objects, which means he essentially has the potential to be the world's fastest vibrator (and best husband). Of course, Barry would have to slow things down for this to work, as a vibrator that literally phases through your body isn't what most people are looking for in their sex life. In fact, his powers would have to be toned down pretty drastically to be anywhere near something his wife could handle. Researchers at Idaho State University tested seven of the most popular personal vibrators on the market to study the "range of stimulation" they provided and found that the most powerful vibrator performed at an acceleration of 311 m/s^2.[43] That's pretty powerful, but you may recall that we found out earlier that the Flash has an acceleration of 100,013.60 m/s^2, which is a worrying 321 times faster than the fastest known vibrator on the planet, and once again causes concern that the Flash might accidentally make his wife explode during sex, in a decidedly messy and unsexy way. As it is, 16.5 percent of women who use vibrators not powered by the Speed Force already report that they can experience genital desensitization from using them, which is the opposite of the desired effect.[44] This condition is usually mild and temporary, but even so, it says that the Flash would have to drastically lower his vibratory abilities to provide an enjoyable and safe sexual experience for his wife, especially as vibrator use is not without its risks, even in real life.

Generally speaking, using a vibrator is a low-risk activity, but accidents have been reported to happen, including multiple incidents that involved trips to the emergency room to have devices removed and at least one real-life death caused by a vibrator perforating the rectal wall of a user who had inserted the device beyond reach.[45] So the Flash could most definitely use his vibrating abilities on his wife in a sexual manner with great success, but it's probably for the best if the Fastest Man Alive takes things slow just this once.

All this is to say that the folks who like to joke that the Flash is "fast in bed" probably aren't wrong, but that's not necessarily a bad thing. As we've discussed, his powers allow him to cut his refractory period down to practically nothing, let him be a personal vibrator to his wife, and provide him with a secondary source of income as a potentially limitless sperm donor. If the cost of being "fast" in bed is a lot of orgasms, a fully satisfied partner, and a couple million dollars in extra cash a month, it's a price a lot of people would be willing to pay.

BUILDING THE BEST ORGASM WITH MYSTIQUE

"What's the matter, baby? Don't you think I look pretty like this?"
—Mystique, *X-Men: Days of Future Past* (2014)

When it comes to the X-Men character Mystique, you never quite know what you're going to get. Is she a villain or a hero? A savior or an assassin? A freedom fighter or a terrorist? A human color, or blue? In many ways she is all of the above, changing her role in mutant society as easily as she changes her physical skin. With her mutant shape-shifting abilities she is able to physically become anyone she desires, man or woman, in any shape or size, which is useful as she is also a wildly ambitious woman who uses her powers to help her accomplish her goals, whether they be wealth, power, or mutant liberation. But what if her goals were different? What if her ambitions weren't political but geared more toward personal satisfaction? And what could be more satisfying than figuring out the physical form that would give her the best orgasms during sex? Literally nothing, that's what.

Here's the thing about orgasms: they're not the same for everyone. Some people's orgasms are more intense, some people can only orgasm in certain positions or from certain stimulation, and some people, I'm sorry to say, can't orgasm at all no matter how hard they try. Some orgasm potential is decided by a person's choice of partner, setting, and sexual skills, but there are also physical characteristics that can influence a person's success in the wonderful world of O-facing, and when we know what those characteristics are we can put them all together to help Mystique create a body capable of having the absolute best orgasms in mutant- or humankind. And who would be opposed to that? A fool. And Mystique's no fool—she's a woman who's been known to use sex as a tool from time to time to get what she wants. So why not help her build the absolute best tool out there?

Or at least we can try, because achieving the "best" orgasm might look different for different people, including men and women. (A quick note to say that the following statistics predominantly refer to men and women in terms of sex assigned at birth and not on the spectrum of gender identity.)

The Battle of the Sexes

The first question Mystique has to ask herself before choosing a sex shape is how frequently she wants to orgasm, and for how long, as it varies wildly among the sexes, with women coming out the absolute winners of this particular battle. Whereas men experience orgasms for about five to twenty-two seconds, women can orgasm for nearly a minute,[46] going into a state of ecstasy for double, triple, and even quadruple as long as men do. And not only do they orgasm longer, they can also do it again and again and again. Because most women have a much shorter refractory period than men, they are able to orgasm again in as little as a few seconds, whereas the average man needs a few minutes to twenty hours until he can go back to sex-town.

But these statistics are all averages, and Mystique isn't building an average body, she is building herself the perfect body for her own sexual pleasure, so we must consider the exceptions to the refractory period rule. As discussed in the previous chapter about the Flash and how fast he performs (in bed), scientists have discovered that a small number of men have almost no refractory period, including one overachieving participant who was studied orgasming six times in just thirty-six minutes *in a lab!*[47] Imagine what he could do at home with some mood lighting and Vaseline. Scientists have speculated that the reason men have a longer refractory period is because of a hormone released during orgasm called prolactin, which men with no refractory period don't seem to create. So if Mystique can shapeshift into a male body that doesn't produce prolactin after orgasm, she could make herself capable of having just as many orgasms in a row as the average woman, but they would likely still be shorter in length. The question then becomes, can Mystique affect her hormone levels the same way she can change her skin? According to *Marvel Anatomy*, Mystique's abilities allow her to "manipulate her form on a molecular level to mimic virtually any humanoid being."[48] The only thing she can't do with her shape-shifting abilities is copy the powers of other mutants, so if she can mimic any humanoid being at the cellular level, it's very likely she can mimic the short refractory period of the men found in these studies, unless that turns out to be a mutant power that some guys just have, and considering how few men are capable of multiple orgasms, it might be.

It's also worth noting that according to *Marvel Anatomy* (an official Marvel publication I'll remind you), "Mystique's control over her anatomical structure allows her to shift the placement of her internal organs to avoid fatal injury." If you're thinking this means she can move her kidney a little to the left or something before Wolverine tries to stab her, think bigger, because this statement is accompanied by an illustration that shows Mystique can move her entire heart all the way down into her thigh and can shift her whole brain to be in her upper arm, like some kind of messed-up surgery performed by Dr. Nick Riviera on *The Simpsons*. If Mystique is officially walking around with a leg-heart and an arm-brain, I'm gonna say that, yeah, she can choose whether her body makes prolactin or not after orgasming. So, in conclusion, Mystique can likely choose to have no refractory period, no matter what sexual organs she chooses to shift into. Enjoy your multiple orgasms.

Other factors to consider when choosing the best body to orgasm in are just how likely that body is to have an orgasm at all and who her sexual partner is. Thankfully for Mystique, she's bisexual, having dated several men and in recent years marrying her long-time girlfriend Irene Adler (aka Destiny) in the comics. This provides a wide range of sexual partners who could appeal to her, so let's work out which partners would statistically provide her the most pleasure.

If Mystique is looking to orgasm while having partnered sex, as opposed to masturbating, she's definitely going to want to choose a male body, because a woman's chances of orgasming during intercourse are comparatively low. A 2014 study found that men experience an orgasm during sex 85 percent of the time, and that percentage was the same whether the men identified as straight or gay.[49] For women, however, the numbers were not so great, but some have it worse than others. Lesbian women said that they orgasm during sex 75 percent of the time, but heterosexual women only climax 62 percent of the time. So basically, guys will almost always cum, women will look after women, but ladies who date men should maybe look into some nice vibrator options. If Mystique is determined to stay in a female form to have sex, she should look to hook up with a female partner to increase her orgasmic odds, but if she chooses to shapeshift into a dude she can sleep with whomever she wants and have an 85 percent chance of orgasming. Even though Mystique has literally every option in front of her, this somehow feels wildly unfair.

The Ideal Woman

At this point we've basically boiled down the better orgasm argument to the fact that women cum longer during sex and men are more likely to cum. But if she chooses the female body route, there are other ways that Mystique can increase her chance of orgasming. For example, women who are shorter than average and have small breasts often find it easier to reach orgasm,[50] so Mystique will want to keep herself short and sweet—and that doesn't just mean body length. A woman's orgasmic capacity can also be affected by the distance between the clitoris and vaginal opening. Scientists have found that the shorter the distance between the two, the easier and more likely it is to reach a vaginal orgasm. If she wants to orgasm via clitoral stimulation instead of penetration, then she will also want to make sure her clitoral hood is not too thick or large. The clitoral hood looks like a fold of skin connected at the inner lips near the front of the vulva. If it's too large it can make it harder to reach orgasm, though the hood can be pulled back and more pressure applied to compensate.[51]

Putting all these physical factors together, it seems obvious that some people are naturally more inclined to be able to orgasm, and scientists agree that genetics play a huge part in whether a woman will climax. According to a study from St. Thomas's Hospital in London that interviewed identical and fraternal twins (i.e., twins that have the same DNA and twins that do not), "after taking into account other factors that could influence orgasm, the scientists estimated that 34 percent of the difficulty women face in reaching orgasm during intercourse is due to genes."[52] This means for all the physical reasons listed above, and many others we don't know about, some women are more naturally inclined to orgasm, which is actually great news for Mystique. After all, she is able to "copy detailed physical attributes of other individuals, including retinal blood vessels, fingerprints, and voice patterns," and if that includes the ability to copy a person's genes, she just needs to find a woman who naturally has great orgasms, copy her DNA, take on her physical form, and be on her way to ultimate sexual satisfaction.

Yet another physical feature to consider on the road to orgasm is the effect pregnancy can have on the body. Orgasms can be less intense for someone who has gone through childbirth, as their pelvic floor may be weakened by all the pushing, shoving, and stretching the vagina goes through.[53] In the comic books, Mystique is the mother of Kurt Wagner, better known as Nightcrawler, so she has indeed given birth, but it seems unlikely that the pregnancy would have been physically taxing on her pliant physiology. Mystique is able to shapeshift into a body twice her natural size and even grow extra appendages with her powers, so it's not a stretch to think she probably played with expanding the dimensions of her vaginal opening during childbirth to make things a hell of a lot easier on herself. Heck, Kurt could have just crawled out. (Maybe that's how he got his nickname.) In either case, Mystique's pregnancy probably wouldn't affect her ability to orgasm, but if she is looking to orgasm in a female body, she needs to remember to put in a strong pelvic floor to make her orgasms more intense.

The last physical factor to consider when orgasming in the female body is age. A survey of 2,600 women found that age thirty-six and older is "the prime time for the perfect climax,"[54] though it was heavily indicated that this orgasm sweet spot was influenced more by women feeling more confident and comfortable in their sex lives at this age than by any physical changes in their bodies. This is great news for us, though, as in the most recent *X-Men* movie, 2019's *Dark Phoenix*, Mystique is fifty-eight years old, so it's likely that at this point, no matter what age she physically makes her body, she's going to have the confidence and experience to get herself to a "perfect climax," which is helpful when you're trying to build the best orgasm that's ever happened.

It's a Man's World

We've covered all the known physical factors that affect a woman's ability to orgasm, but let's not forget, Mystique can shapeshift into a man as well. After reading this lengthy list of physical requirements necessary for a woman to orgasm easily, you may be eager to find out what the men of this world need to overcome in order to achieve a peak orgasm. Well, you will either be excited or disappointed to find out that, generally speaking, men are just naturally great at orgasming and there isn't really much a man needs to do to reach peak orgasmic performance. As was already mentioned, men orgasm during sex 85 percent of the time, every time, regardless of sexual partner. As they are generally not having trouble getting their rocks off, very few studies have been done to determine exactly what makes a man orgasm more easily. There are some very basic physical attributes that don't hurt—being physically fit and maintaining healthy blood pressure are key components, especially as erections are reliant on blood flow, but this is true just as much for women as it for men. Much like the penis, the vulva and clitoris also get engorged with blood when aroused, which helps lead to orgasm, so these physical factors aren't even male-specific. A male body that has naturally relaxed blood vessels in the penis would also get easier erections, and thus be able to orgasm more frequently, but that's really all it would take to make a peak climaxing male body. So, when it comes to orgasming, like many other things in life, women have to work extra hard and men just get one handed to them.

Let's recap what we've learned so far about the best physical body for orgasming. A female body will experience longer orgasms, multiple times, but requires specific physical traits to make orgasming easier, whereas a male body will have a single, shorter orgasm that comes a lot easier and can be any shape or size. But before Mystique declares a winner in this build-a-body battle of the sexes, she should also consider what type of orgasm she wants to have.

Sexual Variety Is the Spice of Life

When it comes to orgasms, there are a large variety to choose from, though slightly fewer for men than women. Both sexes are able to orgasm from anal penetration and nipple play, so we'll consider those fun for everyone. But other than that, men mostly only orgasm via penile stimulation. This can happen several different ways, such as penetrative sex, masturbation, or oral sex, but the male orgasm itself remains mostly the same no matter how you get there. Women, on the other hand, are capable of a large variety of orgasms, such as vaginal orgasms via penetration, clitoral orgasms from clitoris stimulation, and blended orgasms, which is experiencing vaginal and clitoral orgasms simultaneously—the literal definition of double your pleasure, double your fun. Some women are also capable of an untouched orgasm, which involves simply thinking themselves to climax, usually by looking at erotic images. While not exactly a common occurrence, it is one almost no men have been found to be capable of, and also a phenomenon we'll dive into more in Part 3 regarding Mystique's fellow mutant Emma Frost.

All of these orgasms offer different sensations and ways of experiencing sexual pleasure, but the experience is also different for everyone, making it hard to determine which form of orgasm is the best and most desirable overall. Mystique could do some experimentation herself with different body types, but in the real world the best way to find out which kind of orgasm is the best would be to ask someone who has experienced every kind, which is something we can absolutely do.

Plenty of people in the real world have undergone gender-affirming surgery (GAS), which is a procedure predominantly undertaken by transgender individuals to change their physical sex characteristics so that they correspond with their gender identity, which means they have theoretically had the chance to experience a range of ways to orgasm. For example, a trans woman who has undergone vaginoplasty will have potentially experienced sex and orgasm with both a penis and a vagina, and therefore should know definitively which one is better. A 2005 study actually asked participants how they would rate their sexual experiences after undergoing GAS. The study found that the majority of transgender women who had undergone vaginoplasty reported that their orgasms were now more intense, smoother, and longer than they were before they had surgery. At the other end of the spectrum, the same study[55] found that transgender men who had undergone GAS tended to reach orgasm more easily now and described their climax as more powerful and shorter than before surgery. Unfortunately, the participants provided mostly descriptor words regarding orgasming and no one asked them to definitively say which kind of orgasm was the best. Sometimes science fails us.

When all is said and done, it seems that if Mystique does embark on a quest for the perfect orgasm, she is going to have to choose between female orgasms that are intense, smoother, and longer, but harder to achieve; or male orgasms that are easy to come by and more powerful, but shorter in length and supply—and decide which ones she likes the best. To my knowledge there haven't been any studies on the effect that being blue has on a person's ability to orgasm, so Mystique will have to do her own research regarding that area, with which we wish her all the best.

And let's also hope that she is better at choosing her sexual partners than her son Kurt, or do you not know about . . .

Sexual Interlude #2: The Time Nightcrawler Dated His Sister

In the early days of the X-Men, Nightcrawler's origin story was a mystery, but his past came to light in *X-Men Annual #4*, when an anonymous birthday gift exploded in Kurt's face and sent his soul to hell, which has to rank among the worst birthdays of all time. Luckily for Kurt, a bunch of the X-Men traveled to hell after him intent on giving Kurt a ride back to the land of the living. But when they got to hell, they found Nightcrawler on trial for murdering his adopted brother, Stefan, several years earlier. Uh-oh. That seems like a good reason to not get released from hell.

During the middle of Nightcrawler's trial, though, his adopted sister, Jimaine, appeared in Kurt's defense. It's revealed that all three kids, Kurt, Jimaine, and Stefan, were raised together from birth until they were in their twenties, but Kurt hasn't seen Jimaine in years, as he thought she also blamed him for killing their brother (a thing he straight up admits to doing) and had abandoned him.

Kurt is found innocent (even though he absolutely killed his brother), and they are all returned to Earth where Kurt asks his sister where she's been all these years. The answer is . . . not great, as she reveals to him that she's actually been around for quite a while, disguised as a regular human named Amanda Sefton.

Why is that such a big deal? Amanda Sefton is Nightcrawler's girlfriend, and they've been banging for the last few months. So Kurt's sister started dating him when she was fully aware that they were brother and sister and didn't let Kurt in on this important bit of information. Sure, they're not related by blood, but we're explicitly told they had been raised together by the same mom since Kurt was "barely an hour old" and even a jury from hell would rule that makes them siblings. (Shockingly, the next issue is not Kurt going back to hell on new charges for incest.)

In Kurt's defense, he didn't know anything about these hellish dating hijinks so he's probably going to freak out when it's revealed that he was sleeping with his sister for several months without knowing it. Right?

Uh, no. Kurt's reaction when Jimaine reveals her identity is to shout, "OBOY!"

Turns out he's excited to get a cool combination sister/girlfriend as a birthday present, and he kisses her in front of everyone. Then he apologizes for not making out with his sister in a more explicit manner because there are children present:

"I love you, Jimaine. Always have. Always will. I'd be more demonstrative about it but I don't want to set a bad example for Kitty."

For the record, the adults who are present also don't want to see two siblings making out, but Kurt doesn't care about them, or the uncomfortable readers at home, and continues to date his sister for a shockingly long time. Hopefully no one from the Mutant Senate Hearings learns about this, or Xavier's School for Gifted Youngsters is going to find itself surrounded by Sentinels charged with upholding moral standards.

GOING TO FANTASTIC LENGTHS
WITH REED RICHARDS

"The Fantastic Four. Reed Richards, can his whole body stretch? I mean, every part? You know, like his—"
—Brodie to Stan Lee, *Mallrats* (1995)

After taking an experimental rocket into space, Reed Richards and his friends were bombarded with cosmic rays and granted incredible superpowers. Upon arriving back on Earth, Reed found he had the power to stretch and contort his body into incredible lengths and took on the superhero name Mr. Fantastic because stretching is . . . fantastic? Sure. Reed was already considered the smartest man alive, but with these new superpowers he was able to form the Fantastic Four, an unstoppable superhero team, with whom he discovered new universes and stopped multiple alien invasions of Earth. He is a man who has accomplished truly incredible things, which makes it kind of unfair that the question he gets asked most often is whether or not he can use his powers to make his penis, like, really big.

In the movie *Mallrats*, comic book super nerd Brodie gets to meet Stan Lee, the real-life creator of almost every notable Marvel superhero, including Spider-Man, the X-Men, the Fantastic Four, Thor, and Daredevil, to literally only name a few. And with the few minutes he has to talk to his hero and get answers to his most burning questions, Brodie almost immediately asks him if Reed Richards can use his powers to stretch his dick like the rest of his body. In the movie, Brodie doesn't get an answer to his question, which means we will have to find out for ourselves just what lengths Reed can reach with his fantastic fifth member. The short answer is that of course he can make his penis bigger. But the shocking twist is that it might be best if he doesn't.

Before we get into whether or not Reed *should* use his powers to make his dick bigger, let's just confirm that, yes, he absolutely can do this. Due to the fact that Marvel comics are generally not X-rated, we've never actually seen Reed stretch his dick to incredible lengths; he usually saves that ability for extending his arms and legs, maybe even his torso. But his penis is definitely attached to those areas, and according to *Marvel Anatomy*:

> *Reed's body has undergone a complete cellular transmogrification with skin cells, neurons, erythrocytes, fat cells, and even bacteria all displaying the properties of extreme elasticity.*[56]

If every cell in Reed's body is capable of "extreme elasticity" then there's no reason to think this wouldn't apply to his penis. It's not like he was wearing some kind of cosmic radiation–blocking cup that kept his penis from getting superpowers like the rest of his body while he was up in space. As far as we know, Reed's penis is a normal, functioning part of his body and therefore must also be capable of being stretched out like the rest of him. That question is answered, but that opens up the floor to even more questions, like just how big can he stretch that fantastic foreskin of his? Well, *Marvel Anatomy* has an answer to this one as well. Reportedly, "the upper limit of [Reed's] limb extension is estimated at 1,500 feet."

How Big???

Whoa whoa whoa, that's . . . that's too much, right? One thousand, five hundred feet long? That's more dick than anyone wants or knows what to do with. They say some men think with their penis, and if that's true it explains why Reed Richards is literally the smartest man alive. We'll get into the rigidity and erectness of this "limb extension" in a moment, but first we absolutely must take a moment to get some perspective on just how long 1,500 feet is. For starters, the Statue of Liberty is 151 feet high—that's only one-tenth of Mr. Fantastic's stretching limit. That means Reed can stretch his dick to have ten times as much liberty as the statue dedicated to it. The Empire State Building, one of the tallest buildings in the world, is only 1,250 feet high; Reed could extend his penis down the entire length of it with room to spare. The Brooklyn Bridge from tower to tower is 1,595 feet, so if catastrophe struck and the bridge fell, he would be just short of being able to re-create the length of it with his penis. Or maybe people could just take the ferry home. Another great option.

So that's a pretty big penis, especially when you compare it to other penises instead of New York landmarks. After all, the average human penis comes in at about 3.5 inches when flaccid.[57] If Reed can extend his (non-erect) penis to 1,500 feet (approximately 18,000 inches), that means that Reed's flaccid penis is 5,142 times bigger than the average schlong.

You may notice that Reed's penis has been indicated as flaccid in these calculations, and that's with good reason—it would be literally impossible for him to be fully erect at this size. After all, to achieve an erection the penis must be engorged with blood and Reed does not have anywhere near enough blood in his body to make his 1,500-foot penis erect. Though his powers allow for him to stretch his skin and muscle, he is not able to increase the amount of blood in his body at will. Again, according to *Marvel Anatomy*, "Mister Fantastic's body mass averages out to a total of 1.7 cubic feet. This volume cannot be exceeded." Basically, Reed can move and stretch his body to any length and shape he wants, but he only has 1.7 cubic feet of mass to work with, no matter what, which means that despite his potentially giant penis, he only has as much blood available for erections as any other human, making it pretty hard to get, well, hard.

If Reed did want to get all 1,500 feet of his stretchy fellow fully erect, he would need to get a considerable amount of excess blood from somewhere else as he literally does not have it in him to do this. The average penis requires about 4.4 ounces of blood to become fully erect.[58] Since we know that at its largest size, Reed's penis is 5,142 times longer than average, we can infer that it would take about 22,624 ounces of blood to get his member standing at its maximum fantastic potential. For perspective, that's the combined bodily blood mass of about 141 men. That means Reed's coming in a little short in terms of blood volume (but not in anything else).

Rather than starting blood sacrifices to his penis, let's say that Reed doesn't stretch his penis out to its gargantuan length of 1,500 feet, but instead wants to make it as large as possible while engorged with the blood he has in his body, which would probably be more useful to him than a huge flaccid member (unless he needs to tie up some bad guys or something and doesn't have any rope). So, with only the blood available in his body, what's the maximum size he could make his penis while fully erect? Well, the average human male has about 160 ounces of blood in his entire body. You can lose about 50 percent of your body's blood[59] before you start to slip into a coma and die, so let's estimate that, at most, Reed has half his blood volume, or about 80 ounces, available to fill up his pliable fifth member. If an average erection requires 4.4 ounces of blood and Reed has 80 ounces available, that means he has about 18 times more blood available to him than the average penis needs to become erect. The average erect penis is 5.1 inches long, so if we multiply that by 18 we learn that the absolute largest erection Reed Richards could achieve would make his penis about 91.8 inches long, or roughly 7.65 feet. For scale, the tallest players in NBA history were Manute Bol and Gheorghe Mureșan who stood at 7 feet 7 inches. Reed's fully erect penis would be able to look them both in the eye. Which is a hilarious thing to imagine, as long as you're not Reed's wife, who has to deal with this hall of fame monstrosity.

Moving a 1,500-Foot Penis into the Bedroom

We know that Reed's penis is capable of getting as big as Johnny Storm's ego, but would this actually be useful for him? Well, it might be an interesting strategy to break out on the battlefield—I know I wouldn't want to fight a guy coming at me with a seven-foot erect penis. But other, more seasoned warriors may see this intimidating length as an obvious weak point to target, so let's focus on what would happen if Reed loaded up this bad boy in the bedroom, including the problems, and opportunities, that arise from having a super-stretchy penis. One of the first things to consider is Reed's stable body mass. We've already discussed that he cannot increase or decrease the mass of his body with his powers, only stretch or elongate his limbs. This means that if he uses his powers to increase the size of his penis, another part of his body would have to lose mass. If he only makes his penis a little bit bigger this may be fairly unnoticeable, but if he goes crazy with the size increase, the rest of his body will shrink, and his wife Sue Storm may just stop any bedroom session they have going on to insist he go eat something, because he's wasting away in front of her.

If you think this dick-embiggening ability still sounds great or have a fantastic case of penis envy, there is another very important piece of information you have to know about Reed's powers and how they affect his, uh, sturdiness. From our friends at *Marvel Anatomy*:

> *Dr. Richards's bones and muscles remain cohesive during elongation but their rigidity decreases exponentially.*

Uh-oh. An exponential decrease in "rigidity" is not a side effect that anyone who wants to increase their penis size is interested in experiencing. This means that for every inch longer Reed makes his penis, the appendage gets exponentially softer. Forget going 1,500 feet, he would only have to stretch it a few inches before he had a competitor for the world's longest cooked spaghetti noodle. What a terrible trade-off. It's like Reed wished for a huge penis on a cursed monkey paw and ended up with the biggest, limpest member imaginable. Since pretty much the only reason to ever want a larger penis is to impress or please a sexual partner, this decrease in rigidity really puts a damper on the fun of having a massive schlong. But even though a giant, soft penis is of very little use in the bedroom, it's not of no use at all. If Reed wants to try something new (and he's an explorer, so of course he does), he could give soft penetration a go in the bedroom.

Soft penetration[60] (or "the stuffing method," as it's sometimes called) is a sex technique used by couples experiencing erectile dysfunction. The idea is to take a soft, or not fully erect, penis and allow it to penetrate a vagina or anus by stuffing it in. Once inserted it's recommended to use a grinding motion, as opposed to thrusting, to stay inside your partner and have sex. This technique removes the stress of having to achieve an erection to have penetrative sex and frequently results in eventually getting an erection anyway from the previously mentioned grinding experience. So, if Reed's powers do end up giving him a huge, soft penis, he's got options regarding what to do with it (or at least some of it), sexually speaking.

Moreover, there may be ways that Reed could make that deflated balloon of an appendage a little bit harder for his bedroom escapades. As discussed earlier, a penis gets hard when blood flows into it, causing an erection. The nature of Reed's superpowers means his flesh will get less rigid the farther it's stretched, making it extra flaccid, but a substantial blood flow could help make his penis harder and, with a little extra effort, maybe even fully erect. But first he needs to get the blood in there.

The most common way to get the blood flowing into a lower extremity is to be sexually stimulated, either physically or mentally. Considering he's the smartest man on the planet, it seems likely Reed knows the most efficient ways to get himself aroused with his own mind, though this is definitely a use of his super intellect that doesn't get listed on his character stats pages. We worked out earlier that due to his limited blood volume, the largest potential erection he could achieve is over 7 feet tall, but even with a super-brain performing at maximum arousal there's a good chance Reed wouldn't be able to naturally get enough blood pumping to get Mr. Fantastic Jr. fully erect at that size. He could try some blood-flowing stimulants to help out, like man's best friend, Viagra (also known by its generic name sildenafil). There are some misconceptions floating around about what this little blue pill actually does, so to be clear, Viagra is not a guaranteed way to get an erection and has no effect on a person's libido or sex drive; it purely helps with blood flow. What Viagra actually does[61] is block a protein called phosphodiesterase-type 5 (PDE5) from working. This protein tightens up the blood vessels in the penis and makes an erect penis go back to being flaccid. When PDE5 is stopped from working, the blood flows to the penis more easily and can stay for much longer, assuming you're already aroused. If you are aroused, it can be a great way to get a lot of blood to the necessary areas, especially if you've made your penis inhumanly long using the superpowers you got in space. But that might only be relevant to a small number of readers.

The other option Reed could consider for any flaccid issues would be a penis pump. Perhaps most famous for their appearance in an overly long gag in the movie *Austin Powers*, penis pumps have a reputation for being a joke, but that doesn't mean they aren't effective, especially if you only need a temporary boost of blood flow. A penis pump works by using suction to draw blood into the penis, causing it to get erect. The effect of a penis pump is only temporary—it can't permanently lengthen or enlarge anyone's penis—but if you need extra blood flow to your nether regions for a short time, it's an excellent option. If Reed uses his powers to make his penis considerably larger, he may have trouble finding a pump on the market to fit his needs, but considering how much Reed loves to build things there's no doubt he could make himself some kind of Fantasti-Pump to get himself super hard if he insisted on stretching out his penis to unbelievable lengths.

Going to Fantastic Lengths in Real Life

We've discussed Reed's penis at great lengths, including the pros and cons of increasing the size of his dong, but what are the real-life options if someone isn't happy with their junior member (and hasn't been to space to get superpowers recently)? There are some people who try to increase the size of their penis at home with a technique called jelqing,[62] which is kind of the nonsuperhero version of what Reed does. Jelqing is a penis-stretching exercise that involves, well, physically stretching out your penis several times a day to try to make it bigger. Whereas Reed can just straight up stretch his penis out, the idea with jelqing is that the constant stretching will create micro-tears that look engorged as they heal and make the penis look bigger as a result, as long as you keep doing the exercises. Some jelqers take the technique even further and instead of using their hand, they attach weights to their penis to stretch it out (not recommended here), while others use devices designed specifically for jelqing that wrap around the penis like a handle and allow for a smooth jelqing experience (sure, why not). But does jelqing actually work? Some individuals say yes, but science says mostly no. A 2016 study[63] found little to no significant effects on penis length or girth after using traction devices (which is kind of an extreme form of jelqing), but a 2013 study[64] found that these devices did help treat penis deformities. In any case, as long as you're not stretching too hard or for too long, jelqing is a fairly safe technique to try, but if you're too aggressive it can impact your ability to get or stay hard, so, you know, be nice to yourself down there. We don't all bounce back like Reed can.

What about a more permanent solution to get a bigger penis, though? There are a few surgical options, but before we dive into them, it feels worth noting that there are very few people who actually need a larger penis, and even fewer who need to resort to getting surgery on their beloved member. Most doctors agree that the only people who truly need penis enlargement surgery are those with a micropenis (which is a penis that is 7.5 centimeters or shorter when stretched) who experience difficulties having sex or urinating due to their penis size, while other doctors have stated that cosmetic penile surgery should never be done at all.[65] This is because the majority of men looking to get a penile enhancement have an average-sized penis and many of these penis-enlarging surgeries involve complications with few successful results.

So, putting your precious member under the knife in hopes that he'll grow is mostly risk and almost no reward. Keeping all that in mind, let's explore the surgical options . . . for science's sake. If you absolutely must increase your penis size, silicone implants are the way to go.[66] Called the Penuma procedure, it involves crescent-shaped pieces of silicone being inserted under the penile skin to make it look longer and wider. It's kind of like a boob job, but for your penis. It's also the only penis enhancement surgery approved by the FDA and is considered relatively safe. Other enhancement options include fat transfers, which is basically Botox for your dick, and a considerably more extreme procedure where the ligaments of the penis are cut and extended so it hangs lower on the body. This procedure sounds so awful that the only additional detail you need to know about it is that it has just a 30 percent satisfaction rate among those who have had it done, so maybe give jelqing a try first.

But it bears repeating: these procedures are almost never necessary anyway. The main reason some people think they need to resort to extreme surgical procedures to get a bigger penis is because of media influence. In a 2020 review,[67] researchers found that pornography has skewed people's perspectives on how big the average penis is and how large it needs to be to be sexually fulfilling, so chances are if you think your penis is too small, you're probably wrong, statistically speaking.

Because here's the thing about increasing the size of your penis—your partner probably doesn't even want it to be any bigger (and they definitely don't want it to be 7 feet tall, Reed!). A 2006 survey[68] of more than 52,000 heterosexual men and women found that 85 percent of women were perfectly happy with the size of their partner's penis and only 14 percent were interested in their partner having a larger penis. By contrast, 45 percent of men wished they had a larger penis, which indicates that penis enlargement isn't something that women are demanding of men but a concept they are imposing on themselves. In fact, only 6 percent of women surveyed categorized their partner as having a "small" penis, and 94 percent of women thought their partner had an average or large penis. Ninety-four percent! Most women think their partner's penis is a great size. You're good, everyone, stop worrying about your dicks and stop asking Reed Richards how big he can make his. We know it's 1,500 feet and it's long and stringy. Even if it wasn't statistically likely that Sue doesn't want Reed to make his penis bigger, when it's described like that, obviously she would never ask.

If nothing else, be glad that your penis isn't so big that you need surgery to make it smaller to have sex, which is, medically speaking, a thing that has happened. Just ask the seventeen-year-old Florida teen who had the world's first penis reduction surgery on his ten-inch-wide penis[69] (yes, ten inches *wide*). This guy was born with a big but not debilitatingly large penis, but after several priapisms (erections that won't go away) the teen's penis "inflated like a balloon," according to his physician, Dr. Rafael Carrion, who continued his medical assessment to say this about the penis in question:

"It sounds like a man's dream—a tremendously inflated phallus—but unfortunately although it was a generous length, its girth was just massive, especially around the middle. It looked like an American football."

The penis was so wide that the man was unable to have sex with his girlfriend and got himself to the hospital as soon as possible to undergo a penis reduction surgery that Carrion described as similar to "having two side tummy-tucks." The good news is the surgery was a success; the bad news is that he needed it at all and now has surgical scars on his significantly smaller private parts. There's also no word on whether or not this kid wished on a monkey's paw for a huge penis like Reed did. It turns out there are a lot of ways that wish could go wrong. So be careful what you wish for, because bigger isn't always better. And 1,500 feet is just too frigging big.

DAREDEVIL AT THE HEIGHT OF AROUSAL

"I smash fourth walls and bad endings. And sometimes Matt Murdock."
—Jennifer Walters, *She-Hulk*, season 1, episode 9

Daredevil fucks.

Hmm. That was a crude way to start this chapter. I'm so sorry. What I wanted to say is that Daredevil is a vision-impaired superhero who has a robust love life wherein he has sexual intercourse with a large number of women, and unfortunately no other phrase encapsulates his vibes quite as well, because Daredevil does, categorically, fuck.

The Marvel Cinematic Universe gets criticized at times for being a sexless place where heroes are rarely, if ever, intimate or romantic, but even in the sex-barren world of the MCU Matt Murdock has had at least two sexual partners (Elektra and She-Hulk) and been romantically linked to two others (Karen Page and Claire Temple, aka Night Nurse). By MCU standards he is a sexual god, and if you dive into his comic book pages you find he's gone to bed with even more women, including Black Widow, Black Cat, and several others whose names don't start with the word "Black." It seems not even Matt's deeply entrenched Catholic belief that a couple shouldn't have sex before marriage can stop this devil on the streets from being a saint in the sheets.

So, I say again, Daredevil fucks. More so than almost any other fictional character, super or otherwise. But is there a scientific explanation for why Daredevil does so well with the ladies?

Well, a study conducted by the University of Chicago[70] found that people with no impairment to any of their senses had sex 25 percent more often than people who had a sensory dysfunction in some way. Matt is certainly someone who knows a thing or two about sensory impairment, as he is technically blind, but he can also kind of see, and his other senses are also enhanced. He's a complicated guy.

As a refresher, Matt Murdock was born a regular human being, but an accident at a young age led to his eyes being doused with radioactive chemicals, which caused permanent blindness but also granted him superpowers. The exact state of his super senses is described in detail in *Marvel Anatomy*:

> *Daredevil possesses enhanced hearing, smell, taste, and touch, presumably as the result of mutagenic alterations to his brain's parietal lobe triggered by exposure to radioactive material. Specifically, Daredevil's somatosensory cortex—the area of the brain that receives and interprets sensory input—is exceptional in its ability to process signals from Daredevil's enhanced senses, enabling him to assemble a detailed picture of his surroundings despite his lack of sight.*

Basically, those radioactive chemicals cranked Matt's senses up to eleven, or even higher. He can't see in the traditional sense, but his senses of hearing, smell, taste, and touch are so intense that they've basically given him a sixth sense that helps him navigate the physical world, and the dating world, better than the average person. Which makes sense according to science. If people with no sensory impairment have sex 25 percent more often than those with sensory impairment, that implies that more senses equals more sex, so it's only logical that Daredevil, with his heightened senses, would experience an abundance of sexual activity—even factoring in the visual impairment.

So empirical data and science both agree that Matt is having more sex than any of us, but what exactly is all that sex *like* for a man who has enhanced senses? Like most forms of sex, it's probably great, but each sense plays a different role during sex, and there may be a fine line between pain and pleasure when certain senses are ramped up to superhuman levels. It's often said that Matt's senses are "enhanced," but if we're going to figure out just what sex is like for the man without fear, we're going to need to know exactly how enhanced each sense is, and what that means in relation to his sexual function. Let's take a walk in Matt's shoes and break his sex life down by each sense to find out whether his powers will work together for an enhanced sexual experience, or if having superpowers in the bedroom would be super bad.

Whether it's senses or sex, it's always fun to start with oral, so let's begin our sensual journey with Matt's sense of taste.

Taste

Before we discuss how a person's sense of taste affects their sex life, let's look at Matt's tastebuds specifically, to see how they differ from a regular human's. With that in mind, here's everything we know about Matt's sense of taste, again from *Marvel Anatomy*:

> *Through taste, Daredevil can identify almost any substance, including poisons and toxins, at concentrations as low as 20 milligrams.*

The most important thing to take away from this is that we have a definitive scale of Matt's taste threshold and how powerful it is. The second most important thing is that you shouldn't be identifying poisons and toxins with your tongue, no matter what the amount. *Marvel Anatomy* doesn't mention anything about one of Daredevil's powers being a heightened immune system, so maybe stop putting poisons in your mouth, Matt. Anyway, we know that Daredevil can identify substances in concentrations as low as 20 milligrams, and according to dilution tests with salt and sugar,[71] regular humans can only identify substances at about 100 milligram concentrations. Some simple division tells us that Matt's sense of taste is about five times greater than a normal human's, which has good and bad implications. It means when he goes out to a fancy restaurant his meal may taste up to five times better than ours, but there are also thresholds to what is enjoyable. You may like a teaspoon of sugar in your coffee, but if you were suddenly drinking it with Daredevil's mouth it would taste like the equivalent of five spoons of sugar, a flavor too sweet for even the Williest of Wonkas in the world.

How would this equate to sex, though?

There haven't been many studies about the function of taste during the act of sex, so a lot of whether this enhancement would make sex enjoyable for Matt would depend on how he likes the taste of things like perspiration and vaginal excretions (if Daredevil truly is the Man Without Fear, I'm assuming he isn't afraid to perform oral sex on his partner). His powers mean the sensation would be more intense no matter what, but whether this is a positive or a negative would quite literally be a matter of personal taste.

What scientists *have* studied, however, are the effects of natural aphrodisiacs, which are foods and spices that increase your libido and sex drive—and science says Matt may be in for a hell of a time if he ingests these babies.

There are many aphrodisiacs we could analyze here, including powerhouses like ginseng and saffron, but let's talk about nutmeg specifically, if only for the fact that this is a sex book and it's got the word "nut" in it. Hilarious.

In a study on rats at the University of Guelph,[72] researchers found that ingesting nutmeg would consistently increase sexual drive in participants, as well as increase how often they got an erection and lower their refractory period (meaning they can have sex again sooner). Basically, Guelph has a lab full of horny, erection-laden rats who are having as much sex as possible, as quickly as possible. And the more nutmeg ingested, the more sex they wanted to have.

Exactly how much nutmeg are we talking about to make these dirty rats get even dirtier? Scientists generally saw things getting hornier at a dose of 100 mg/kg in the rats. From the *Marvel Encyclopedia*, we know that Daredevil weighs 185 pounds (or about 84 kilograms)—this means it would take about 8,400 milligrams, or a little over half a tablespoon, of nutmeg to achieve aphrodisiac affects in a regular human of his size. Now, in general you won't find a lot of food with that much nutmeg; even most eggnog recipes only call for about 5,000 milligrams altogether, and that's a total nutmeg fest. We regular humans would have to go out of our way to ingest enough nutmeg to feel its spicy effects in our nether regions, but we're all here because Matt Murdock is not a regular human. We've established his sense of taste is five times greater than ours, which means he may only need one fifth of the dose of nutmeg that the rest of us do to feel its effects. This equals only about 1,580 milligrams of nutmeg (well under half a teaspoon) that Matt would need to ingest to start feeling frisky, which is an amount found in a lot of recipes.

Not only could Matt's enhanced sense of taste mean a decidedly more intense oral experience during sex, one of the reasons Matt has more sex than other heroes may be the fact that an incidental amount of things as simple as nutmeg and other aphrodisiacs are increasing his sex drive and giving him constant erections—which means he may be propositioning women for sex more frequently, hopefully while assuring them that it's just a walking stick in his pocket (though he is happy to see them).

Touch

Unfortunately, Marvel has not given us an exact measurement of just how advanced Matt's sense of touch is. All we know is that he's a very sensitive guy who can feel things really well (at least in a physical sense; his emotional feelings are between him and his priest). However, *Marvel Anatomy* tells us that "Daredevil's skin contains ultrasensitive touch receptors . . . so attuned to variations in surface contours that Daredevil can read books just by running his fingertips across the impressions left by the ink on a printed page." Logic tells us that being able to feel more intensely is going to make sex, an activity that already feels pretty great, be even more awesome, but let's check in on the science to be certain.

One way to find out what sex feels like for Daredevil is to find out what sex is like for people in the real world with similarly heightened senses, namely, people who have sensory processing sensitivity (SPS). A person with SPS has "an increased sensitivity of the central nervous system and a deeper cognitive processing of physical, social and emotional stimuli,"[73] which means they feel physical sensations at a deeper level than the majority of the population. This can be a negative in everyday life, as it can cause overstimulation, but a positive in the bedroom, as described in an article by Sarah Lempa, a person diagnosed with the condition.

> [People with SPS] might get irrationally bothered over a scratchy clothing tag, but it's made up for by the undulating waves of pleasure that douse our bodies during intimacy.[74]

Basically, SPS makes bad things feel worse and good things feel really good. It's worth noting that in the *Daredevil* TV series, Matt described his own powers in a very similar vein to Lempa's "scratchy clothing tag" causing discomfort. After his mentor, Stick, made fun of him for sleeping on silk sheets, Matt replied that "cotton feels like sandpaper on my skin." So if Matt's experience with clothing is the same as a person with SPS, it makes sense that his experience with sex is similar as well. Lempa also points out that "sensual touch and orgasm are intense" for those with SPS, and there's no reason for us to think it would be any different for Mr. Hyper Senses himself, Matt Murdock. We established earlier that Matt has had more confirmed sexual partners than anyone else in the MCU. This means Matt is not only having more sex than pretty much anyone elsle in the Marvel universe, he's having more intense orgasms than everyone else, too. Forget being the Devil of Hell's Kitchen; he may just be a saint for not bragging about this, like, all the time.

Sound

When Matt Murdock took his teenage radiation bath in the eyes, it enhanced all his senses, but his hearing seemed to be elevated more than the rest. We've already established that his sense of taste is five times greater than average, but according to *Marvel Anatomy* his sense of hearing is even better.

We're told Matt can hear "a heartbeat from across a busy street," which is quite a feat when most people can't hear a friend shouting their name from that distance, let alone differentiate their circulatory systems. This is probably enough information to figure out how powerful Matt's hearing is. The average width of a street is about 20 feet and an average human can only hear a heartbeat if we put our ear directly against someone's chest, a distance of about 0.33 feet. Dividing these two distances together tells us that Matt's hearing is about sixty times greater than a human's, which might be more problematic than useful, especially in terms of sex.

Research has shown that "linguistic and non-linguistic sounds" (linguistic sounds being words, and non-linguistic sounds being groans, moans, and gasping sounds) are the second most arousing sexual experience for most men.[75] The most arousing sense is visual stimuli, but since he is partially blind Matt can only partially experience this sense, which means sexual sounds are likely what get his devil horns up the most.

But heightened hearing—at least to this degree—may not be beneficial in the bedroom. It's not like it's difficult for the average human to hear the sounds their partner is making during sex, and though Matt may hear some small sounds of sexual pleasure from his partner that others miss, if his partner screams out in bliss during orgasm, it's safe to say the pain is going to override the pleasure of that sensation at sixty times magnification.

If we once again compare Matt to those in the real world with SPS, we find out this is very much true. As Lempa explains, "A sound that is barely perceptible to most people may be very noticeable, and possibly even painful, to an HSP [Highly Sensitive Person]."

Generally speaking, a human shouts at a level of about 80 decibels, which is at the border of being harmfully loud even to normal humans. If Matt's hearing is sixty times greater than the rest of us, then for his own auditory safety he may have to seek out sexual partners that he knows will keep it down in bed, or find someone who enjoys a good ball gag.

Smell

You may not think about your sense of smell much during sex, but you should, because whether you enjoy the Yankee Candle section of the mall or not plays a surprisingly large role in the average person's sex life. For Matt Murdock, it may be the sense that plays the greatest role.

Turning once more to *Marvel Anatomy*, we know that Daredevil can identify a person by scent alone "at a distance of up to 50 feet." Not surprisingly, for us regular humans it's a whole lot less. In an experiment performed at Berkeley University,[76] scientists wanted to determine just how far away a non–super human could identify a smell. To ensure that only the sense of smell was being used, they put blindfolds and noise-canceling headphones on a bunch of students and had them smell things from as far across the room as possible. Ignoring the impossibility that anything you do in university while blindfolded wouldn't end up being a prank, the researchers found that participants could identify a smell from an average maximum distance of about 9.5 feet. If Daredevil can identify a person by smell from 50 feet away, it means his sense of smell is at least five times greater than a human's, and his sex life might be, too.

Through the power of his super nose, Matt can likely pick up two smells that most of us can't—estrogen and testosterone, the sex hormones our bodies release. This is relevant because brain scan studies by the Karolinska Institute in Sweden[77] have shown that the smell of estrogen activates the hypothalamus in heterosexual men, which is the area of the brain responsible for mood and sexual behavior. If you're worried that you think about sex too much, send out a quick prayer for Matt Murdock, who is having the sex area of his brain activated whenever he passes within 50 feet of a woman, which in a tightly packed city like New York would be every minute of the day.

But don't start pitying Matt just yet, because we aren't done dissecting the pros and cons of having a super-sniffer in the bedroom.

As we've mentioned, Matt has a lot of sex, and the science of smell may be able to help explain why. A study at the University of Gothenburg in Sweden found that men with an above average sense of smell have more sexual partners than those with average or no scent capabilities. According to the researchers, this phenomenon, and thus Matt's sexual success, could be due to the fact that we subconsciously use smell to recognize others' emotional states. "A lot of social signals are transported through the olfactory channel, and [men with no sense of smell] are probably missing them," said Ilona Croy, a psychologist at the university and lead author of the study.[78]

If Matt's sense of smell is five times greater than average, then he is picking up on every signal known to man. This would allow him to easily understand exactly what any potential bedmate is feeling emotionally and physically, which might explain why so many ladies are eager to fall into bed with him. He just gets them!

So Matt Murdock, via his heightened sense of smell, is constantly being turned on by sex hormones and has more sexual partners than the average person, but the icing on this sex cake is the fact that a heightened sense of smell actually makes sex more fun. A 2018 study in Germany found that "participants with high olfactory sensitivity reported higher pleasantness of sexual activities."[79] Basically, if you have a really good sense of smell, the act of having sex is more pleasant overall. And Matt has a *really* good sense of smell. Honestly, it's not clear why Matt is so broody at this point. It sounds like his life mostly consists of having way better sex than the rest of us, and more frequently.

But there is one component of this olfactory issue that we have yet to discuss, and that involves the erectile tissue in Matt's nose.

First of all, pretty much everyone has erectile tissue in their nose; this isn't some weird power Matt was given in an adults-only issue of a *What If?* comic. Though we associate erectile tissue most commonly with the penis, it just refers to flesh that can become engorged with blood. If you've ever had a cold with sinus pressure, you've felt your erectile tissue get engorged and cursed its existence (maybe without knowing it) as you struggled to breathe. To be clear, the erectile tissue in your genitals engorges during sexual arousal, but the erectile tissue in your nose engorges as part of congestion and decongestion to help you breathe; it's not about being aroused. *For most people.*

For some unfortunate souls with a condition called Honeymoon Rhinitis,[80] *all* the erectile tissue in their body responds when they get sexually aroused. When these people get turned on, blood starts to flow into their genitals *and* their nose. But this engorgement doesn't have some Pinocchio effect where it makes the nose longer and harder like it does the penis; it usually means the sinuses get inflamed and the sufferer will get a stuffy nose, although in some extreme cases a person with Honeymoon Rhinitis will also experience an uncontrollable bout of sneezing whenever they're aroused, which has to be one of the least sexy things the human body can do when feeling horny.

There's no way to know who will end up suffering from Honeymoon Rhinitis, but considering that Matt Murdock's nasal cavity has "enhanced receptive capacity," there's definitely a chance that his nose would be over-receptive to sexual stimulation. We've also established that Matt likely gets aroused at a rate five times higher than the average man, so Hell's Kitchen better keep itself stocked up on Kleenex, just in case.

Sight

Now, this is a tricky one. It's difficult to determine just how much Matt's sight would affect his sex life because he's blind, but he's also not all that blind, you know. Using his echolocation-like abilities, Matt is able to see the outlines of people and objects, easily navigate the world, and punch all the bad guys he wants, but echolocation doesn't allow him to see everything. For example, he can't look at pictures, tell if his partner's pupils are dilated, or, most tragically, watch dog videos on the internet.

Traditionally, a visual impairment will negatively impact a person's sex life as the visually impaired tend to find it more difficult to become aroused. As discussed in the journal *Sexuality and Disability*, blindness causes issues due to a "lack of the visual stimulation which creates immediate sexual arousal. These problems range from the inability to thumb through *Playboy* magazine to the excitement of looking at the physical attractiveness of one's loved one."[81]

This analysis puts Matt Murdock in a unique place, as he is indeed a man who can't look at a *Playboy* (though I'm not sure many people do any more), but he can partially see the physical attractiveness of his partner, including the majority of her shape and features. The same study also points out that those with visual impairments are more stimulated by the sounds of verbal lovemaking, so listening to pornographic movies or his own partner would likely negate any decrease in arousal Matt may experience due to his blindness. Interestingly, his sight might be the only sense that puts Matt at a net zero in terms of how it affects his sex life.

The Senses Combined

We've looked at each sense individually, but let's combine everything we've learned to figure out just what an average sexual encounter for Matt Murdock might be like.

Let's say Matt leaves the house to go on a date, and on the way to the restaurant he passes by a dozen or so women. With his enhanced sense of smell he is able to pick up on the estrogen in their bodies, which activates his hypothalamus and makes him think about sex the whole way there. As he arrives at the restaurant, he also picks up on the estrogen produced by his date and the thoughts of sex continue. When dinner is served, Matt is still thinking about sex and also ingests a small amount of aphrodisiac, such as nutmeg, which affects him five times more intensely than anyone else who eats the same food, so he is now very aroused, possibly erect, *and* still thinking about sex. Luckily for him, his enhanced sense of smell detects every social cue his partner is putting out, so despite what's happening to his body he's making an incredible emotional connection with his date as he innately understands her moods and desires. They leave the restaurant and go back to his place. As they start to get intimate, Matt becomes even more aroused by the sounds of his lover and the visual aspects of her that he can see. His sense of smell makes sex feel better overall, and his enhanced sense of touch makes the sexual experience more intense, leading to an incredibly powerful orgasm. Unfortunately, his partner also orgasms, loudly, and he is left writhing in pain as his enhanced hearing gets overwhelmed.

As they lie in bed together afterward, his lover falls asleep, but Matt's echolocation ability means he can see the outlines of all the people in the neighboring apartments who are currently having sex *and* hear every sound they're making, leading to him becoming aroused once more. He also smells the estrogen from his lover more intensely than ever since she's right next to him and continues . . . you guessed it . . . thinking about sex. Matt is now being bombarded by so much sexual stimulation that even though he just had sex, he is ready to go again immediately, which happens every time he has sex, and possibly every single night of his life as he lies in bed alone.

This explains why Matt sleeps in a sensory deprivation tank sometimes. It seems like the only way this guy is getting any shut-eye at all.

IN SPACE NO ONE CAN HEAR GREEN LANTERN SCREAM (IN PLEASURE)

"When you nut in space it push you backwards."
—Griffin McElroy, host of *My Brother, My Brother and Me*

Sometimes you don't choose a job, a job chooses you. For most people that sentiment would come off as metaphorical, but for Air Force pilot Hal Jordan this happened quite literally when he was picked up off the street by a bubble of green energy and chosen to be the next member of the Green Lantern Corps, a group of space cops that patrol the galaxy and fight evil with magic rings that can create anything they imagine. The work-life balance of a Green Lantern is such that Hal spends as much time transiting through space as he does living on Earth. Many people would find flying through the vast emptiness of space for days to be a sad, lonely slog, but Hal Jordan is lucky in this regard, as his girlfriend Carol Ferris also has a magic space ring, one that turns her into Star Sapphire, an antihero fueled by the power of love. Now when you put two people who love each other together, sex usually happens. When you put two people who love each other together and both have cosmic power rings, then sex happens *in space*. And doing the dirty deed in a hostile antigravity environment is a whole lot different than getting laid down here on Earth. So let's discuss just what sex would be like for these two if they hooked up in the blackest night of space.

First of all, we have to decide how we want to define "space" as a place to have sex. Both Hal's and Carol's power rings allow them to fly into deep space, but they can also propel themselves into just the upper atmosphere of Earth, and if you're looking to pound it out with your on-again, off-again girlfriend in the sky, the upper atmosphere is where you're going to want to head for the most orgasmic experience. This is because the higher you get, the less oxygen is in the air and, for some people, this drop in O_2 leads to a heightened feeling of arousal and also more intense orgasms.[82] This is one of the reasons people are so eager to have sex on airplanes. It's not the inherently unerotic appeal of those tiny bathrooms, it's because when you're that high up in the air your brain can get less oxygen, which can create feelings of excitement, euphoria, and a generally greater intensification of physical sensations.

The same people who enjoy this oxygen constriction in the sky may also partake in erotic asphyxiation here on the ground, which is intentionally restricting the flow of oxygen during sex by choking or strangulation. Erotic asphyxiation has the distinction of being inherently unsafe, though, and it's not recommended people try it, especially considering the mortality rate from this sex practice is estimated at 250 to 1,000 deaths a year in the United States alone.[83] So if you must know what it's like to limit your oxygen during sex, get you and your significant other a plane ticket and join the Mile High Club for a safe and thrilling sexual time. Or just ask Hal and Carol what it's like, because considering how much those two love to both fight and fly, they have definitely had angry sky sex at least once.

Failure to Launch

But what if these two lovebirds set their sexual sights a little higher, out of the atmosphere and into the depths of space itself? Well, that's where things get a little harder. Actually, scratch that, it's where things get significantly softer. You see, space hates erections. It's a hostile environment not welcoming to human life, and it's especially unwelcoming to the sexual acts that could make more human life. If Hal and Carol want to bone in space, the biggest obstacle will be finding a way to literally get their blood flowing where it needs to go. In space it's very difficult for humans to pump blood into their lower extremities, whether those extremities be legs or sexual organs that are looking to be aroused. Here on Earth, gravity naturally pulls our blood downward, so our hearts aren't accustomed to forcing blood to go into the lower parts of our bodies—it usually just waterfalls down and the heart focuses on pulling it back up to keep circulating. In a zero-gravity environment, though, a person will have pretty normal blood flow in their chest and head, like on Earth, but way less blood will get circulated to the legs (and penis).[84] And with no blood, there can be no erection. But it gets worse than that, because not only does this lack of blood flow make it hard to get hard, it also causes the tissue in the penis to shrivel up the entire time it's hanging out in zero-g. No matter how great your willpower is, that's a crushing blow for any crimefighter.

But that's not to say space erections aren't possible, as some astronauts have reported that they were able to get it up after going up (into space). Russian Cosmonaut Alexander Laveikin confirmed that he masturbated in space easily, while other astronauts have reported having wet dreams and orgasming in their sleep.[85] These instances are the exception to space erections, though, and not the rule, as these men were likely experiencing erections due to "fluid shifts" in their body, which is where bodily fluids move into different compartments due to changes in pressure. Astronaut Mike Mullane has spoken almost too openly about his own fluid shifts and reported that, "A couple of times, I would wake up from sleep periods and I had a boner that I could have drilled through Kryptonite."[86]

If the same thing happened to Green Lantern while he was in space, it would definitely be the most interesting reason for Superman to ask for his help with something. But would Hal's superpowers protect him from these blood-flow issues? Well, his Green Lantern ring allows him to fly through space, but it's unclear if the rings provide their own gravity or just propel their users forward through the abyss. In this way, we might compare the ring to a human astronaut's spacesuit. An astronaut can wear a suit with thrusters on it that allows them to fly through space, but spacesuits don't create gravity and wouldn't help you get a space-erection. When the thrusters on a space suit are inactive, an astronaut still just floats in the merciless abyss. If the same is true for how the Green Lantern ring works, propelling you forward but not providing gravity, then Hal's sexual function might be more doomed than Kyle Rayner's girlfriend (too soon?).

If we admit to there being no gravitational forces on our cosmic couple, though, we must also consider the fact that having sex in space is just physically difficult to do, even with magic rings. According to physicist John Millis, sex in space is not impossible but would be incredibly hampered due to the lack of gravity. "Imagine engaging in sexual activity while skydiving—every push or thrust will propel you in opposite directions," Millis explained.[87] Think about how every time Green Lantern gets hit in a space battle he gets thrown about halfway across the galaxy. Sex can be a battle in its own way, and every thrust would push Hal's girlfriend farther away from him.

The easiest solution to this issue would be to anchor the two lovers together so they don't drift away, physically or emotionally. This is when having a ring that can create anything you can imagine comes in very handy, as Hal could make some kind of energy bands to keep him and Carol together during a deep-space sex romp. Conveniently, there's a real-life object Hal could reference to build such a thing, and that is the 2suit, a garment created by actress Vanna Bonta to allow couples to bonk in space.[88] The 2suit is basically two space suits with internal harnesses that can be velcroed together to keep a couple in each other's arms while doing their sexual business. The suit has even been tested on a zero-gravity flight. The couple wearing the 2suit only kissed while strapped in, but they reported that the suit made them feel "stabilized" and like they could do more if there hadn't been a camera crew filming them. Hal and Carol would similarly have to be on the lookout for any pesky deep-space satellites nearby while they boned in their own green energy band version of the 2suit. You never know what they'll pick up.

But blood flow and lack of gravity aren't the only problems Hal would face in his quest for deep (space) sex; there's also the testosterone issue. Specifically, he wouldn't have much. NASA scientists have found that when astronauts are in space their testosterone levels get drastically low,[89] and Hal spends a lot of time in space, whether he's fighting Sinestro or just traveling to another planet. Scientists haven't exactly figured out why this happens, but testosterone helps maintain a healthy libido, so without it Hal's sex drive will plummet lower than his movie's box office returns. Now, having a girlfriend who literally harnesses the power of love might help him out in this regard, but having the power of "love" doesn't necessarily mean having the power of "sexual enhancement," as you can love someone deeply and still be unable to achieve an erection if there are physical factors holding you back. Those two things are intertwined, but not the same, so if Hal's testosterone levels are too low, even a Green Lantern's willpower wouldn't be able to help his sex drive.

Always Use Protection

Let's say that with their superpowers combined, Hal and Carol are able to get their blood flowing, stick together, and have sex in space. That's great for their relationship, but they're also going to have to use protection, and not just the kind you're thinking of (it doesn't really matter what kind you were actually thinking of, because there are like three different kinds of protection they're gonna need). The first kind is protection against the cold vacuum of space, as temperatures drop to almost absolute zero once a person leaves orbit, which is approximately –459.67 degrees Fahrenheit, or –273.15 degrees Celsius. That's pretty cold, but since they don't die of hypothermia while out in space, we know the shields from their rings can provide protection against the chill of the perpetual night, so they won't be turning into space popsicles anytime soon.

The shields from their rings may protect Hal and Carol from cold, but the pair also has to make sure they have a setting that blocks radiation, because space has *a lot* of radiation and it can mess you up (just look at the Fantastic Four). Specifically, if Hal and Carol have any interest in having kids now or in the future, they're going to need to suit up to avoid any fertility issues. The human body can go temporarily sterile after being exposed to about 1,500 milli-Sieverts (mSv) of radiation.[90] For a little perspective, NASA estimates a trip to Mars and back would expose the human body to about 1,070 mSv of radiation. Now that's less than the amount needed to cause sterilization, but those numbers relate to humans on a rocket ship with layers of radiation-blocking metals around them, not two humans just rawdogging it through space fueled by literal willpower like Green Lantern and Star Sapphire, so they'll have to be careful out there.

But the siren call of space sex doesn't just bring with it the risk of infertility, there's also the risk of fertility. No one really knows what would happen if a human got pregnant in space, but we know it would probably be bad, which has led NASA to ban sex in space altogether.[91] Officially speaking, no sex has ever occurred above Earth's atmosphere. At least not between humans. The United States and Russia have had "limited success" with bringing invertebrates and insects into space to conceive, but they have yet to see a mammal, and definitely not a human, successfully produce any offspring. The main concerns with space pregnancy are radiation and the lack of gravity. As mentioned, there's a lot of radiation in space, coming from stars, nebulas, and even exploding planets (RIP Krypton). Even if the radiation in space isn't enough to make Green Lantern sterile, it's still enough to severely impact a fetus and would likely cause birth defects, mutation, or miscarriage if Carol got pregnant. If a fetus somehow got through the radiation unharmed, though, there's still no telling what the lack of gravity they were grown in would do to them. Scientists and astronauts speculate a child born in space would have a severely malformed bone structure and be incredibly weak.[92] And even if their skeleton somehow formed normally, they would be in a kind of reverse-Superman situation as they would have no resistance to gravity and likely wouldn't even be able to stand up if they ever came to Earth. The good news for our superhero couple is that both the Green Lantern and Star Sapphire rings are known to block radiation when necessary, so hopefully that shielding is always on and extends to any child they may conceive on a space romp so they don't have to worry about either becoming sterile or having a space baby that can never walk on Earth. Then again, these are comic book characters and that sounds like a super badass origin story for their kid, so we won't discount it just yet.

The third kind of protection Hal and Carol would need for their space sexcapades is just straight up sex protection such as condoms to ensure they don't have messed-up space babies, but more importantly to stop the spread of herpes and other viruses. And they'll want to use them every time they have sex, even if they think they aren't currently sick or infected with any diseases, because here's a crazy thing a lot of people don't know, maybe not even Hal Jordan: going into space makes you sick, but it also makes you sick *again*. A 2019 report from NASA revealed that flying into space can cause dormant viruses in your body to reactivate and become contagious.[93] Specifically, they found that chickenpox, shingles, and four different types of herpes that go dormant in people's bodies can become active again if you go to space. And this isn't some random incident that happened to an outlier astronaut once. NASA studied the astronauts on the International Space Station and found more than half of them had the herpes viruses reactivated in their system after going into space. So this phenomenon is not only possible but common. It happens to *most* astronauts. Thankfully, only a few space-farers reported any symptoms to go along with their rebooted viral buddies, but they were all still capable of infecting others once the viruses weren't dormant.

NASA is trying to figure out the cause of this virus reactivation, but they haven't made much progress yet. Their best guess is that it's caused by stress, that pesky emotion that gets blamed for most bodily maladies that science doesn't have an answer for. Regardless, if Hal and Carol are gonna knock space boots it's best that they use protection, because they literally don't know what they're going to find coming out of their bodies while they're out there. Hopefully the fear demon Parallax that inhabited Hal and destroyed the entire Green Lantern Corps isn't one of those viruses that can just suddenly reactivate. That would really kill the mood.

At the end of the day, the allure of making love in the private depths of space probably isn't strong enough to overcome the difficulties in literally doing it, which has to be embarrassing when your girlfriend is powered by love, but what can you do. To accomplish this great feat, Hal and Carol would have to overcome a lack of blood flow, gravity, and sexual arousal all while protecting themselves against cold, radiation, pregnancy, and space diseases, which is probably asking too much. Hal's got incredible willpower, but if he and Carol want to avoid their darkest night together, the couple should just find a bed on Earth and go about boning in gravity like the rest of us.

In fact, we know that Hal Jordan has had sex while on another planet before, but he'd probably prefer if we didn't talk about . . .

Sexual Interlude #3: The Time Green Lantern Dated a Fourteen-Year-Old Girl (Who Was a Full-Grown Woman)

Hal Jordan is generally considered a pretty stand-up guy. As the main Green Lantern on Earth, he's a paradigm of willpower, fearlessness, and high moral standards, which is what made it so weird when Hal started dating a fourteen-year-old member of the Green Lantern Corps for a while.

Her name was Arisia, and she was an alien who came to Earth to help fight off the ridiculous number of villains we have on our planet. By her own admission she was fourteen years old in "Earth years" and in love with Hal Jordan, and since that made her a teenager to Hal, who is from Earth, he made a point of calling her things like "little sister" and making sure he was never left in a room alone with her, as it was clear that Arisia was in love with Hal to an almost obsessive degree, despite their age difference. When another Green Lantern confronted Arisia about her feelings for Hal, she revealed that she even had a plan to basically trap Hal into loving her back and said:

> *"I'll never give up! I'll get older and we have to spend a lot of time together now as fellow Green Lanterns! I still have hopes! . . . Let him see how independent I am! Then he'll stop thinking of me as a little girl!"* [94]

Honestly, pointing out that they work together does make this a little weird, as there's a certain hypocrisy in saying a teenager is old enough to fight killer space aliens but not old enough to be smooched on the lips. Hal stands his ground against her constant flirting and eventually takes her aside and tells her to stop flirting with him before it gets him in trouble and to go after boys her own age. Arisia argues that she really loves him and they can be together, but Hal stands his ground and tells her, "You're still a teenager in my eyes and I don't date teenagers!" which is absolutely the right thing to do! Way to go, Hal! After being shot down, Arisia gives up and runs away in tears.

So, that's that, then—Hal broke a little girl's heart, but his integrity is fully intact. Nice work. Well, at least it was until the next issue when Hal and Arisia get knocked out and trapped in a cave together for a while, at which point Arisia uses her Green Lantern ring to age her body into that of a fully grown woman in a matter of hours! Which is . . . a choice.

Physically Arisia looks older now—her legs are longer, her face is more defined, and her boobs have popped, but that doesn't change the fact that she's still mentally and emotionally only fourteen, does it? Well, if you asked Hal, he couldn't tell you. He's pretty flustered by the whole thing, seemingly unfamiliar with what the space laws say about fourteen-year-old grown women. Arisia says they can be together now since she is an adult, but Hal explains to her that even if this was okay (which it's not!), he's not going to date anyone right now, as his girlfriend, Carol, has recently died. And on this point he is very firm, and sad . . . for about three more pages. Which is when the rest of the Green Lantern Corps comes to rescue them and finds the two of them making out in the cave. Wow.

Despite Green Lantern's superpower basically being willpower, he's unable to resist this fourteen-year-old girl for more than an hour now that she's got developed breasts and long legs. So much for morality, righteousness, and promises that you don't date teenagers. Because they don't just make out in a cave; the two start dating, for like, a while, and have the audacity to act like the rest of the team are being assholes for questioning their relationship and absolutely just trying to protect them. Green Lanterns are supposed to have no fear, but Hal should probably be afraid of going to jail for statutory rape, especially when he and Arisia start sleeping together several issues later. So, in conclusion: Hal's happy dating his child-woman, Arisia's happy dating her grown man, and the readers at home are left wondering whether they have to turn these comics in to the cops because they might technically be child porn.

Part 3

MIND OVER MATTRESS

Psychological Issues That Affect Heroes in the Bedroom

DOES PARADISE ISLAND LIVE UP TO ITS NAME?

"You don't sleep with women?"
—Wonder Woman to Steve Trevor, *Wonder Woman* (2017)

Since her creation in 1941 Wonder Woman has undoubtedly been the most famous female superhero on the planet. She's starred in block-buster movies, fought Nazis, gone to space, graced magazine covers, made countless media appearances in comics, cartoons, and video games, and was even made an official ambassador of the United Nations, in both the fictional world and in real life. Obviously, she's led a rich life, but has she led a rich sex life? We don't really know. Despite her outstanding body (of work), there has been very little official exploration into the sex life of Wonder Woman or the Amazon warriors who raised her in Themyscira (aka Paradise Island), an island inhabited only with women. This unique cultural situation brings up a lot of questions about the society and sexual complex-ity of the Amazons who have continued to uphold their no-boys-allowed policy for centuries. After all, what does a world without men look like, sex-ually? Do only some Amazons have sexual relationships with each other or does an island inhabited by only women make everyone a lesbian by default? Can a society without men survive without a means of sexual reproduction? And most importantly, why is bondage such a huge part of their lives?

To answer these questions about Wonder Woman and the Amazons of Paradise Island, we first have to explore the life of their creator, a man who has the rare distinction of having a more interesting and well-documented sex life than the bondage-loving superheroes he created.

The Man, the Myth, the Marston

Born in 1893, William Moulton Marston (also known by the pen name Charles Moulton) is best known for being the creator of Wonder Woman, but she wasn't the only thing he made. Marston was a man of multitudes who also invented the first lie detector test. *Seriously.* After Marston's wife pointed out to him one day that "[w]hen she got mad or excited, her blood pressure seemed to climb," he invented a blood pressure test to see if she was right, which became one of the major components of the modern polygraph machine[95] and later inspired him to create Wonder Woman's lasso of truth. So if you love those videos where celebrities take lie detector tests, you can thank this guy. But inventing was just Marston's side hustle; before getting into comics he predominantly worked as a psychologist to some slight renown. His 1928 book titled *Emotions of Normal People* was famous for being an early defender of many sexual taboos and included several pro-bondage–themed chapters with titles including "Dominance," "Submission," "Compliance," and, the fan favorite, "Dominance and Compliance."[96]

William Marston wasn't just famous for his psychological stance on the beauty of bondage, or inventing the lie detector test, or creating Wonder Woman (though damn, that is a lot of things to be known for—cool it, man); he is perhaps equally famous for being in a publicly known polyamorous relationship with his wife, Elizabeth Holloway Marston, and their partner, Olive Byrne, in the 1920s and '30s. By all accounts the three were very happy together, and though Byrne couldn't legally marry either of the Marstons, she wore wide-band bracelets on each arm signifying her "marriage" to them both, which Marston later incorporated into the design of Wonder Woman herself.[97] The two women even continued to live together after William's death in 1947, creating a home not unlike the all-female island that he had created in his comics.

So William Marston was a man who loved sexual taboos, women, and machines that could tell if you're lying. Taking all of these things into account, it makes sense that he invented a female hero who hailed from an island of women and wielded a lasso that makes you tell the truth. What about the bondage, though, you're probably saying. You haven't talked about the bondage! Well, to get to the bondage we have to look at the earliest Wonder Woman comics, which also give us our first glimpse into what the sexual relationships may be like on Paradise Island.

Bondage in Comics

In the original comics by Marston from the 1940s, Wonder Woman's weakness was that if she was tied up by a man, she would lose her superpowers and become helpless. Subsequently, Wonder Woman got tied up *a lot*, empirically more often than any other hero. In his book *Wonder Woman Unbound: The Curious History of the World's Most Famous Heroine*,[98] author Tim Hanley looked at how often Batman and Robin got tied up in their comics compared to how frequently Wonder Woman found herself in chains during the 1940s and the numbers tell quite the story. Batman and Robin, combined, were only tied up in about 1 percent of the panels in Batman, despite the boy wonder's penchant for being kidnapped, whereas Wonder Woman was tied up a whopping 11 percent of the time in her comics. That's more than ten times as much bondage for the world's most prominent female superhero. And that's just counting the times Wonder Woman herself was tied up. When the parameters were expanded to include all instances of bondage, including side characters and villains, the total amount of bondage jumped to 27 percent. That's over a quarter of every issue devoted to tying people up.

And we aren't just talking about Wonder Woman getting her hands lightly tied together; these comics, which were essentially children's books, had some explicitly sexual posing and rope play happening, including an issue where Wonder Woman has a bridle placed in her mouth while she is tied to a tree; an issue where she is hogtied with her legs, hands, and neck all roped together; and a final issue where she is bodily chained up, collared, and forced to wear a full leather face mask before she is thrown in a vat of water.

This amount of bondage definitely wasn't the norm in comics back in the day, and it didn't take long for people to notice how much Marston enjoyed chaining up his Amazonian princess and start asking him to officially scale it back a little. In 1943 he even received the following letter from Max Gaines, the President of All-American Comics, which published Wonder Woman at the time.

Dear Doc:

Attached is a copy of a letter which came in yesterday's mail. I'd like to discuss this with you next time you come in.

This is one of the things I've been afraid of (without quite being able to put my finger on it) in my discussions with you regarding Miss Frank's suggestions to eliminate chains.

Miss Roubicek hastily dashed off this morning the enclosed list of methods which can be used to keep women confined or enclosed without the use of chains. Each one of these can be varied in many ways—enabling us, as I told you in our conference last week, to cut down the use of chains by at least 50 to 75% without at all interfering with the excitement of the story or the sales of the books.[99]

There's a lot to unpack in this letter, mainly the fact that Marston had been asked by his bosses multiple times to cut down on the bondage, or at the very least mix it up and not just stick to chains, and had so far refused. And that Gaines's assistant, Miss Roubicek, is an absolute trooper who walked into work that day and was told to come up with a list of ways to "keep women confined or enclosed without the use of chains" and didn't call the cops or anything. I can't say I'd do the same, at least not without a pay raise. What might be even more incredible, though, is that even after multiple letters and talks like this from his boss, Marston "refused to change the series in any way."[100] He just loved bondage, you guys. But to his credit, his commitment to tying ladies up wasn't just about drawing enticing sexual imagery; he also had something to say about how participating in bondage can lead to happy, healthy relationships, as we see between the Amazons on Paradise Island.

Despite constantly chaining up his own heroine, William Marston actually believed that women were the superior sex and that the real world would be a peaceful place if men would only submit to women. According to Hanley, "the bondage imagery that made up more than a quarter of Wonder Woman was actually an elaborate series of metaphors about submission," but you had to dig down to truly understand them. You see, there were two types of bondage in Marston's Wonder Woman. The first, and more prevalent, involved Wonder Woman being tied up against her will. Despite losing her powers when this happened, Wonder Woman would always triumph in the end after breaking free and regaining her power, which was intended as an allegory for women in real life and how they would not be held down by men indefinitely. The second type of bondage was the consensual "bondage games" that took place on Paradise Island among the Amazons, which seemed to spark true joy in all parties involved. Many issues included sequences where the Amazons would dress up in costumes and tie each other up to celebrate different holidays, and in other issues women were seen walking through the background wearing chains while shouting with full sincerity, "Oh yes, we love it!" about the situation. The large difference between these two representations of bondage is that while men tie Wonder Woman up as an act of oppression, on Paradise Island bondage is portrayed as an act of trust meant to make others feel safe and loved. According to Hanley:

The Amazons incorporated bondage into their society as an expression of
trust to emphasize that their utopia was based on kinship with a hierarchy

of submission. The intent of bondage was never to hurt, ridicule, or shame someone, and there were rules of safety and care.

While these bondage games were never shown to be explicitly sexual (again, it was a children's comic), if we assume these games progressed in a sexual way off-panel we gain some insights into what the adult relationships were like between the Amazons on Themyscira.

Bondage in Real Life

Even though men tying Wonder Woman up against her will was depicted more frequently in the comics, and has obvious sexual implications, the type of bondage Marston depicted happening between the Amazons on Paradise Island is more similar to the kind experienced in real-life sexual relationships. Or at least, in healthy, consensual relationships. A sexual relationship that incorporates bondage usually involves some sort of BDSM play (BDSM standing for Bondage and Discipline, Dominance and Submission, Sadism, and Masochism). That's a lot of letters and words, but the acronym is better explained by the department of psychology at St. Francis Xavier University, as follows:

> *B/D stands for bondage and discipline, which refers to the act of using restraints, both physical and psychological. D/S signifies domination and submission and describes one person taking control while another gives over control. Finally, S/M includes two complementary categories: sadism, deriving pleasure from the pain or humiliation of others, and masochism, deriving pleasure from one's own pain or humiliation.*[101]

Among those participating in BDSM are usually a dominant, who does the restraining, and a submissive, who gets restrained, and while on the surface this may seem like a relationship with a power imbalance toward the dominant partner, many practitioners of BDSM believe that the submissive partner actually holds more power in a relationship. According to participants in a study conducted by St. Francis Xavier University, "[s]everal dominants and submissives stated that subs have most or all of the power because they are typically the ones who set the boundaries. One dominant stated, 'Well, they set the boundaries. They put themselves at your mercy and under your power, but they set the boundaries. You do not do something to them that they don't want done to them.'"[102] In the end, the dominant member of the relationship does not actually need to be all-controlling; it is only the illusion of the dominant having all the power that is required for BDSM to be enjoyable.

Participants in the study who identified as submissives expressed a feeling of "absolute freedom in relinquishing control," but they also emphasized that "they want to give up that control to someone they can trust and they want to have fun doing it." This interpretation of BDSM supports Marston's depiction of bondage on Paradise Island as being a fun and freeing experience when it occurs between people who trust and care for each other. In one early issue, Wonder Woman discusses that level of care as she ties up a henchman and says, "On Paradise Island where we play many binding games this is considered the safest method of tying a girl's arms!" clearly showing that the women she plays bondage games with are well cared for by her—so much so that she carries those safety lessons into her crime-fighting life.

So we know the Amazons play "bondage games" with each other, but are they partaking in sexual relationships with each other as well? We'll discuss Diana's unique sexual circumstances a little bit later, but as for the rest of the women on Themyscira, yeah, a bunch of them are definitely lesbians. Maybe even all of them, depending on who you ask.

Love Island

In 2015, an issue of Sensation Comics[103] featured Wonder Woman officiating a same-sex wedding on Earth, in which she says to Superman, "My country is all women. To us, it's not 'gay' marriage. It's just marriage." And before this, Bob Kanigher, who took over writing Wonder Woman after Marston, "stated outright that all of the Amazons were lesbians,"[104] a claim he had deeply insinuated by having Wonder Woman and her companions make reference to "Suffering Sappho!" at least "2.5 times an issue," Sappho being an ancient Greek poet known as a symbol of love and desire between women. In fact, the English words *sapphic* and *lesbian* are derived from her name and that of her home island of Lesbos, respectively. Basically, if you think Sappho is great, you're probably a woman who loves women.

This tells us that at least some, and possibly all, of the women on Paradise Island are lesbians involved in sexual relationships with other women. We also know that they enjoy partaking in bondage games, which Marston believed led to great feelings of satisfaction and fulfillment for everyone involved—and modern-day science tells us that he was basically right.

Participants in the previously mentioned St. Francis Xavier study stated "that the level of connection, intimacy, trust, and communication that BDSM play fosters was greater than that which was typically achieved in a more conventional relationship," while other researchers have found that BDSM relationships typically lead to personal empowerment, excitement, and improved communication between partners that is more likely to lead to an "optimal sexual experience"[105] for those involved. And who among us isn't trying to optimize our own sexual experiences? We already discussed that a healthy BDSM relationship requires trust and care, and what goes hand in hand with that is open communication about what you like and don't like, sexually speaking. So even if you're using a regular rope and not a lasso of truth to tie up your partner, they're likely still being completely honest with you about what they want in the bedroom and how they feel. Which is a conversation that couples in non-BDSM relationships are less likely to have. What this all boils down to is that our BDSM-loving Amazon warriors are more likely to clearly communicate with their partners about what they like in the bedroom and get it, thus having a truly optimized sexual experience. Honestly, it sounds like these Sapphos aren't suffering at all.

We can say with a fair amount of certainty that most of the Amazons of Themyscira are in sexual relationships, but we can't say for certain that all of them are, because we still haven't talked about the most famous Amazon of all time, Wonder Woman.

The 800-Year-Old Virgin

We established in the previous section that all of the Amazons in Themyscira are likely lesbians, which is defined as women who are exclusively attracted to other women, but Wonder Woman famously had a sexual relationship with a man, Steve Trevor. This may indicate that the Amazons are not lesbian by nature but by circumstance as they live on an all-female island, or Diana being a sexual outlier might be explained by the fact that she is very different from all the other Amazons in terms of her birth, superpowers, and her dating options on Themyscira. In the *Wonder Woman* film we meet a version of Diana who is 800 years old and has "read all twelve volumes of Clio's treatises on bodily pleasure," which sound like a good read but unfortunately don't exist here in the real world (I checked). Despite being highly educated in sexual theory, though, Diana had never met a man before Steve Trevor crashed his plane on Themyscira. That leads us to only two possible conclusions about her sex life while living on the island: either she had had sexual encounters before, and if so they would have had to have been with other women; or she never had any type of sexual relationship on Paradise Island, and it's been given the wrong name.

At first glance it seems unlikely that in 800 years Diana would have never indulged in any kind of sexual relationship or experimentation with her fellow Amazons, especially while living on a tiny island with not a lot of activities (or people) to do, but there is a complication for Diana: she's the only Amazon ever born and raised in Themyscira. In a lot of ways, growing up on an island inhabited with only women would be a positive in life, as studies have shown that children raised in same-sex households "fare as well as, or better than, children with parents of the opposite sex,"[106] leading to children that are generally more tolerant and have healthier relationships with their parents. But that fact brings us to Diana's problem: she *only* has parents. Generally speaking, Diana is considered the daughter of all the Amazons who live on Themyscira as they all helped raise her. This may mean that the rest of the Amazons on the island see her in a child-like or familial role and would be hesitant to partake in a sexual relationship with her, even after 800 years together. So Wonder Woman could very well have been a virgin when she left Themyscira. This would explain why she's so eager to leave the island with Steve and why she sleeps with him just a few days later in the middle of a war. This girl's been hard up for a while.

But there may be a more urgent reason for Wonder Woman to leave the island and sleep with Steve Trevor. She says she is leaving to save mankind from war, but she may also have left to help save her own people from dying off. We've discussed how the good women of Themyscira are likely in satisfying sexual relationships with each other, but if we assume the Amazons are all cisgender women it means they basically have no way of procreating together, which is actually kind of a problem.

The Extinction of the Amazons

Marston may have created an island paradise for these warrior women to flourish in, but unfortunately the society he designed is not self-sustaining. In her first movie Wonder Woman tells Steve Trevor that on Themyscira they're taught "men are essential for procreation, but when it comes to pleasure, unnecessary." This gives a bit more credibility to the theory that all the Amazons partake in lesbian relationships, which is great for sexual satisfaction, but definitely an issue when it comes to their longevity.

If "men are essential for procreation" but banned from their island, that's a real problem for the Amazons as a race. These women may not age but they still die in battle, frequently. In a single fight in *Justice League* (2017), the villain Steppenwolf kills at least a dozen Amazon warriors, each one representing a huge percentage of their population being lost.

After enough battles they would be wiped out completely, unless of course they find a way to start reproducing among themselves, even without men, which could actually be possible.

Here's the thing about the Amazons as a race: they're predominantly asexual in nature. Not in terms of personal attraction, but in terms of reproduction. A species is considered asexual if their offspring is produced by a single parent with no sexual component involved or member of the opposite sex contributing DNA. Well, in the DC movies the Amazons were created by Zeus singlehandedly, giving them all only one parent (except for Diana, who is the daughter of Zeus and Hippolyta). But Diana's comic book origin long held that she was formed from clay by her mother and brought to life by a lightning strike, which means all the Amazons were in some way born of asexual reproduction, and this might just be their saving grace.

In the scientific world, asexual reproduction is known as parthenogenesis, which comes from two Greek words that translate to "virgin creation," a wildly wonderful coincidence for our Greek warrior women who may require parthenogenesis to perpetuate their species. Assuming they're out of that special baby-lightning clay that made Diana, there's still a chance the Amazons could start to reproduce asexually on the island like several other species before them.

Scientists have discovered that a range of species have accidentally developed the ability to reproduce asexually in specific scenarios, such as when the females are kept in captivity with no males to mate with. If this sounds familiar, well, it basically describes the living conditions of Themyscira, and it's also kind of what happened in *Jurassic Park*, except whereas the dinosaurs were bred to be female and then changed their sex to become male and started mating, the animal ladies we're talking about remain strong, independent women and just get pregnant all by themselves. In the real world we've seen this phenomenon in several different species. In 2019, a female water dragon at the Smithsonian's National Zoo began producing eggs and healthy offspring[107] even though she had no male counterpart to mate with, and similar occurrences have been seen in swellsharks at the National Aquarium and even in the California condor.

One species who can reproduce asexually is already named after these great Greek gals. The Amazon molly is a freshwater fish found in Texas that naturally evolved to reproduce asexually, which means it just kind of gets pregnant one day and has a bunch of babies. But not just any babies—every child born of an Amazon molly is female and a genetic clone of its mother. This has led to the Amazon molly becoming an all-female species, and the perfect animal mentor for the women of Paradise Island. If lizards, fish, and birds are all reproducing asexually, maybe there's hope for the Amazons as well.

We may not have Clio's twelve volumes on bodily pleasure, but we've learned quite a bit on our own about the sex lives of Amazons. We know that Diana left her home to experiment with men because every woman she knew was basically her aunt. And we know that the rest of the Amazons are partaking in satisfying sexual relationships with each other that involve bondage games that give them a sense of freedom, which is especially nice when you're trapped on a tiny island. But Paradise might not last forever, as the Amazon race can't survive without a means of reproduction. If the Amazons continue to insist on not allowing men on the island, even for procreation, then let's hope they can learn a thing or two from mother nature and start getting pregnant on their own before their species dies off. After all, if the Amazon molly can do it, maybe any Amazon can.

WHY GOOD BATS LIKE BAD GIRLS

"You like strong women. I've done my homework. Or do I need skin-tight vinyl and a whip?"
—Chase Meridian, *Batman Forever* (1995)

There are a lot of ways to describe Batman. He is vengeance. He is the night. He is . . . single? This is mostly true. Though he has dated many women, both as Bruce Wayne and Batman, the Dark Knight isn't famous for having a consistent, steady relationship like most of his super-colleagues. In almost every comic book continuity you'll find Superman with Lois Lane, the Flash with Iris West, or Aquaman with Mera, but Batman doesn't have that one woman he ends up with in every dimension across all of space and time. Most versions of Batman are either casually dating someone or just plain single, too busy raising a slew of orphans and defending Gotham to have a love life. So Batman may not have a true love out there, but when we look over Batman's dating history it becomes obvious that he certainly has a type: Batman likes bad girls.

Whether it's cat burglar Selina Kyle, League of Assassins heir Talia al Ghul, or the murderous Phantasm Andrea Beaumont, Batman definitely has a tendency to hang his cowl up with ladies of questionable moral integrity. That's not to say he only dates women on the wrong side of the law; he has also had relationships with reporter Vicki Vale, the Amazon warrior Wonder Woman, and assistant district attorney Rachel Dawes, but these have been much shorter flings in Bruce's life. He almost always ends up back with a woman he knows he should be slapping a set of Bat-cuffs on (whether that be in jail or the bedroom is up to him).

So why does our Dark Knight, who is so laser focused on justice and the law, spend so much romantic energy on the baddest girls who cross his path? The answer to that may lie in both science and psychology.

Misattribution of Arousal

The first explanation for Batman's morally skewed dating choices is that his crime-fighting life is causing a misattribution of arousal,[108] which would mean he's not actually attracted to these women—his body is just overly exhilarated during their interactions and making him think that he is. Misattribution of arousal is a phenomenon where people find themselves in an aroused state while doing something exhilarating (like, say, swinging across the rooftops of Gotham) and then mistake that feeling as attraction to the person they're with. Many people (and possibly bats) mislabel their responses to fear and excitement as romantic arousal if they experience these sensations with a person they could potentially be attracted to, like a relationship version of thinking you're hungry when you're really just bored. After all, the body's physical responses to fear and excitement include increased blood pressure, shortness of breath, and a rush of endorphins, which can feel similar to arousal.

The most famous study regarding misattribution of arousal took place in 1974[109] when researchers had a conventionally attractive woman wait on the opposite side of two different bridges—a shaky suspension bridge and a sturdy reinforced bridge—and conduct a survey of male participants after they walked across. The study found that the (presumably heterosexual) participants who crossed the shaky suspension bridge and experienced a sensation of fear considered the woman more attractive than the participants who crossed the reinforced bridge and remained fear-free. Applying these findings to our high-flying crimefighter, it's plausible that Batman simply thinks femme fatales like Catwoman and Talia are more arousing than other women because he only encounters them during high-adrenaline battles and chases, leading to an endorphin rush that mimics attraction. This same misattribution of arousal would also occur in the opposite direction, with the women Batman courts finding him especially arousing while they are doing something exhilarating with him. It may even solve the mystery of why so many women are attracted to Batman despite only being able to see the lower half of his face. Unless the women of Gotham have a chin fetish I don't know about, there's something else going on here. The misattribution of arousal theory also explains why Batman pushes these women away with little protest at the end of each adventure. As the adrenaline wears off, the attraction toward them fades and Batman is left with the question of whether he can truly be with someone who breaks the law so openly, to which the answer is always no. So he slinks back to his Batcave, perpetually alone.

A Chance at Redemption

Batman's attraction to bad girls likely can't just be explained by a physical response to excitement, though. After all, this guy has layers upon layers of mental issues to process, which means there is definitely some psychological reason for Batman's dastardly dating choices, the most obvious of which is that Batman just wants to save people. In his book *Batman and Psychology: A Dark and Stormy Knight*, author and psychologist Dr. Travis Langley theorizes that Batman is attracted to women like Catwoman and Talia because they pose a challenge to him, not just physically and mentally, but in his attempts to reform them. There hasn't been a wealth of real-world analysis about the allure of bad girls to well-behaved boys like Batman, but there has been plenty to say in the psychological community about why good girls like bad boys.

This relationship dynamic is usually sought out by a woman who has a desire to save or redeem a man and help him find his full potential, giving her a sense of achievement and accomplishment if she succeeds in reforming him. The same is likely true for Batman. Catwoman and Talia both represent women on the wrong side of the law who are capable of being reformed. Talia constantly battles between her desire to help her eco-terrorist father, Ra's al Ghul, destroy the world and rebuild it with more order, and her competing desire to join with Batman to fix a broken world as it stands. Catwoman's crimes consist almost entirely of stealing from the rich, but with Batman's influence over the years she shifts to using her stolen wealth altruistically to help the poor people of Gotham in a more Robin Hood–esque way, and even helps Batman fight crime on occasion. If Batman's goal is to reform these women, these shifts in moral conscience count as an absolute win. And according to Dr. Langley, the appeal of a bad boy or girl isn't just the chance at redeeming them, but the value that can be found in the act as well:

> *We value the things we work harder to get. Procuring a collector's item after months of meticulous searching makes it a greater prize than if you'd ordered it online within three minutes of first Googling. Things that come easily to us, we undervalue. The more we suffer for something without sufficient external justification, the more we increase its perceived value so we don't feel like idiots for putting up with it.* [110]

When Batman first met Catwoman, she was a jewel thief known only as the Cat and displayed no virtuous qualities, trying instead to convince Batman to join her in her life of crime. In exchange, Batman threatened to "spank" her (seriously)[111] if she didn't behave while he arrested her, thus beginning a seventy-five-year span of flirtatious banter between the Bat and the Cat. The attraction between the two was instantaneous, but the relationship would become more rewarding to Batman every time he managed to convince her to turn away from her criminal life and help him stop a heinous crime or save an innocent person. Because it took years to change her, the value of their relationship seems much higher.

Opposites Don't Attract

But Batman isn't attracted to every sexy villainess he meets. He appears to need his love interests to walk the line between good and evil, never straying too far in either direction. If a woman falls too far toward the "good" side, as we see in characters like Vicki Vale or even Wonder Woman, the relationships tend to fizzle out before they even begin, and if a woman is too evil Batman will never show any sexual interest in her at all. It's not like he's ever tried to start up a romance with bad girls like Harley Quinn or Poison Ivy (outside of some hormonal mind manipulation)—these women are fairly ruthless killers (and sometimes dating each other) and therefore outside Batman's scope for a potential romantic partner. They're also not enough like him, as the women that Bruce is attracted to are versions of Batman himself. As Dr. Langley explained:

> Is Batman attracted to these women for their similarities to himself or for their differences? . . . Despite the popularity of the "opposites attract" notion and whatever anecdotal contradictions spring into your mind, researchers have been broadly unable to support the notion. . . . We prefer others as a function of how similar they are to ourselves.

It makes sense, then, that Bruce is attracted to women who straddle the line between good and evil—that's his MO, too. Don't forget that despite all his desires to see justice done, Batman is himself a vigilante and technically a criminal, working outside the law in a violent crusade against crime. The women he is most attracted to reflect this same level of moral line walking—they are dangerous and strong and want to create change in the world through unconventional and often illegal means, whether it's Talia destroying a corrupt world to build a better one, or Catwoman robbing a millionaire to redistribute his wealth. Though he's often forced to stop their plans, Batman almost always sees the moral validity in them in some way—an obvious reflection of himself and how he is trying to change the world through unconventional means. In some ways he believes if he can save and redeem these women, who are very much like him, he can save and redeem himself.

The notion that these women are a reflection of Batman was even posited by Batman's co-creator, Bob Kane. In his autobiography, *Batman & Me*, Kane briefly touched on the similarities between Batman and Catwoman in particular:

> *Bill and I decided to create a somewhat friendly foe who committed crimes, but was also a romantic interest in Batman's rather sterile life. She was a kind of female Batman, except that she was a villainess and Batman was a hero. We figured that there would be this cat and mouse, cat and bat byplay between them—he would try and reform her and bring her over to the side of law and order. But she was never a murderer or entirely evil like the Joker.*[112]

Kane's desire was to have Batman and Catwoman continue their romantic cat and mouse game indefinitely. They could work together and have adventures, but they could never truly be in a relationship, as their different views on the law would constantly come between them. What he couldn't predict coming between them, though, was the Comics Code Authority, which almost broke the Bat and the Cat up for good.

Cockblocked by the Comics Code Authority

Launched in 1954, the Comics Code Authority was a censorship movement that strictly defined what could and couldn't be included on a comic book page, created as a response to the backlash started by historical stick-in-the-mud Fredric Wertham's book *Seduction of the Innocent*, which said that comic books were the cause of juvenile delinquency. Despite Kane's desire for Catwoman to be a "female Batman," according to the Code, which governed what could now be included in comic books, she wasn't enough like him by a long shot, specifically for breaking three sacred laws of the Comics Code Authority, which included:

- If crime is depicted it shall be as a sordid and unpleasant activity.
- Criminals shall not be presented so as to be rendered glamorous or to occupy a position which creates a desire for emulation.
- In every instance good shall triumph over evil and the criminal punished for his misdeeds.[113]

Because of these new rules, Catwoman ended up disappearing from Batman comics for twelve years, since a Catwoman who isn't committing crimes, looking glamorous, and getting away with it isn't a Catwoman at all. While she was gone, DC made a concerted effort to give Batman more wholesome girlfriends, including reporter Vicki Vale and original Batwoman Kathy Kane, but neither Batman, nor readers, were interested in the Dark Knight dating any ladies firmly on the right side of the law. These new relationships lacked both chemistry and conflict, and he never threatened to spank one of them even once. Thankfully, Catwoman was able to return to the comics after becoming wildly popular from her appearances on the 1966 *Batman* TV show starring Adam West. The show only had to adhere to broadcast standards, not the Comics Code Authority, so it could let the villainess be more evil, glamorous, and flirtatious than ever, and also showed that Bruce and Selina's tempestuous relationship worked just as well on the screen as it did on paper.

If DC had been determined to keep Catwoman around in the comics for all those years, they could have just ended the relationship between the two and let Batman send her to jail as the Comics Code Authority dictated he had to, but that's never been a skill Batman has been particularly good at. Part of the couple's appeal is that Batman always has to let the beautiful Catwoman go, and in this way he's a lot like the justice system he loves so much.

"Pretty people get away with more," explains Dr. Langley. "Researchers have found that jurors and mock jurors will consider good-looking defendants less dangerous, believe attractive plaintiffs more sincere, and recommend that they receive lesser sentences."

This means Batman may be stuck in a perpetual feedback loop with the legally challenged women in his life. As soon as he chases them across rooftops, he'll feel his adrenaline spike from the chase, causing a misattribution of arousal, then find himself so attracted to their genuine beauty that he mirrors the justice system itself and just lets them go.

This would again be an easy problem to avoid by simply dating women who aren't involved in criminal activity, but this brings us to perhaps the most interesting aspect of Batman's sex life: he's the only superhero who dates under his superhero alter ego, and, according to some psychologists, it's actually the healthier way to form a relationship.

An Equitable Relationship

In *The Psychology of Superheroes*, Dr. Christopher Peterson and Dr. Nansook Park discuss the major psychological perspectives on personal relationships, the first being equity theory, which "proposes that close relationships—friendships or romances—are established and persist to the degree that both people involved believe that what they are getting out of the relationship is proportionate to what they are putting into it."[114] They also posit that the only way for a superhero to have an equitable relationship is with another superhero. After all, if a superhero dates a regular human, there is a massive inequity caused by the fact that one partner is living a secret life and the other isn't, making it impossible for there to be a true level of intimacy and trust in the relationship, even after their secret identity is revealed. Clark Kent may eventually reveal to Lois Lane that he is Superman, but this can't change the fact that their relationship was imbalanced from the start, with Clark's admission revealing that he has been lying to Lois throughout their entire relationship and is only now being truly honest with her. Bruce is able to avoid this relationship inequity by predominantly dating women he meets as Batman and removing most of the imbalance caused by having a secret identity. After all, when he's dating someone like Catwoman, she may not know that his real name is Bruce Wayne, but she also doesn't think it says "Batman" on his driver's license (okay, maybe it does, but it definitely doesn't say Batman on his second driver's license). Selina may not know who Batman really is, but she is fully aware from day one that he has another identity. This is a stark contrast to most heroes who date civilians that end up being blindsided deep into the relationship when they find out their significant others are superheroes, usually right before they get thrown off a building by a villain or something.

It's also likely that Bruce prefers these women because he can truly be himself with them. Not just because they know he spends his nights superheroing around Gotham, but because Bruce considers his true self to be Batman and Bruce Wayne to be the alter ego. Anyone who dates Bruce Wayne is dating a persona that he puts on like a mask. If a potential romantic partner asks him his name and he answers, "I'm Batman" (as he loves to do), he considers that the truth.

At the end of the day, we'll never know for sure if Batman likes bad girls because he mistakenly thinks they're more attractive, wants to reform them, or sees himself reflected in their actions. But we do know that dating someone as Batman lets him be himself and creates a relationship with greater equity, which explains why he is so inclined to only date women he meets while out in the superhero world. It's also true that the majority of women he meets as Batman are criminals, but that just means we need more female superheroes in the world, not only for equal representation but to pad out Batman's dating options so he can finally meet a semi-nice girl and settle down.

And anyway, Bruce may like dating bad girls, but it's nothing compared to what his friend Superman has gotten up to in the bedroom. Let's not forget about. . . .

Sexual Interlude #4: Superman's Porn Career

To learn about Superman's brief foray into the world of porn, we must begrudgingly open up the pages of *Action Comics #592*, a tale of sex, Sleez, and mind control made by highly revered writer/artist John Byrne, who maybe could have used some oversight every now and then, just saying.

This story begins with Big Barda, a former warrior of infamous DC supervillain Darkseid, who finds herself in a bit of a bind when she is attacked and subsequently mind controlled by a character named Sleez after he gets ahold of her Mega-Rod (this is not a euphemism but the name of her actual weapon, promise). To paint a picture for you, Sleez looks like a three-foot pile of mud that is decomposing. He describes himself as "driven from my native world because great Darkseid judged me too disgusting even for the blackest corner of Apokolips." After looking at Sleez, it's hard to say that Darkseid was wrong. Sleez is a gross little dude.

Case in point: Sleez then mind-controls Barda into doing sexy dances for him in the sewer for two days, which he records and sells to a porn producer named Grossman (because of course that's his name). Standard villain plot. Moving on.

Shortly after this, Superman shows up for pretty unrelated reasons and frees Barda from Sleez's mind control. However, Barda thinks Superman's rescue is "too convenient" (much like the audience reading the comic) and starts to beat him up, assuming he's a trick created by Sleez. Barda weakens him enough that Sleez is able to trap Barda and Superman in a giant hole (man, a lot of things suddenly seem sexual when you're dealing with a character named Sleez who makes super-porn) and mind-controls them both.

The next big twist in this story is Darkseid showing up at the doorstep of Barda's husband, Mister Miracle, with a VHS tape of Barda's sexy dancing. Mister Miracle is rightfully shook by seeing this footage of his wife but Darkseid, new to the sketchy porn distribution industry, just leaves without any explanation, like Tuxedo Mask at the end of a Sailor Moon battle.

In the next scene we find Sleez meeting with Grossman again and find out that the first tape of Barda is on track to make them a million dollars in video sales. At this point Sleez reveals that he also has Superman under mind control now, and the upstanding pair decide to shoot a full porn movie, starring their mind-controlled super duo. Perhaps an even bigger twist is the next reveal that Sleez is only making these porn movies because he needs money to build an army, and this is the best way he can think of to do so. A mind-controlled Superman could rob every bank on the planet in about thirty seconds, and literally no one alive could stop him, but sure, Sleez, there's also money in porn if you're into that sort of thing (Sleez is very much into that sort of thing).

Anyway, soon we arrive at a film set where Superman and Barda, surrounded by lights and video cameras, are making out in bed with Barda dressed only in her underwear (Superman is technically also in his underwear, but that's just because he wears his on the outside of his costume). They are interrupted, not by a rescuer, but by Grossman complaining that their acting is terrible and "Superman's got all the sex appeal of a side of beef." Sleez agrees and, since they're making a quality production here, tries to use his mind-control powers to pull more emotions out of his stars. Just as Supes and Barda start making out more passionately, Mister Miracle breaks through a skylight and brings this horrific nonsense to a much-desired end. Speaking of much-desired ends, Sleez blows himself up with sewer gas to avoid being captured and is hopefully never spoken of again.

Superman and Barda then stand around awkwardly, saying they can't remember what happened, perhaps to make readers who are incapable of forgetting such a thing jealous. They never tell us what happened to the footage from their film session, and we'll probably never find out. But if either one ever needs to make a quick million dollars, at least they have some content for an OnlyFans account.

EMMA FROST'S ORGASM ATTACK

"Of course I'm a threat. Why? Did you think for a moment that I wasn't?"
—Emma Frost, *Generation X*, volume 1, number 23

Emma Frost, also known as the White Queen, is a fascinating character in the X-Men universe. Over the years she has gone from a villain to a hero, known for her intelligence, no-nonsense attitude, and barely-there costumes. She also has the rare distinction of having two unique mutant powers, bringing both diamond skin and powerful psychic abilities to the battlefield. The diamond skin is pretty cool, but her telepathic powers offer a far greater range of interesting abilities, including things you've never even dreamed of. For example, as a psychic Emma can alter people's thoughts and perceptions, a power that she has used for good, evil, and everything in between, like the time she made a crowd of people all orgasm simultaneously.

This act of sexually dubious consent happened in *New X-Men #118*, when a large group of protestors gathered outside Xavier's School for Gifted Youngsters and demanded that the mutants inside move out of the neighborhood, at which point Emma Frost stormed out of the school and diffused the situation by causing everyone in the crowd to start moaning in pleasure and then fall to the ground with huge smiles on their faces. At first it appeared that Emma may have put the protestors into comas, until she explained:

I pushed their Bliss Buttons, Jean. They'll wake up utterly ashamed of themselves. Don't say another word.[115]

So Emma didn't just use her powers to make the protestors feel happy, but hit a supposed "Bliss Button" in their brains to make them all orgasm simultaneously (possibly assisted by her costumes that are held together by double-sided tape and hope). This technique seemed to work well enough for crowd dispersal in this instance, as the protestors all left, but it may not be the greatest long-term strategy. Emma basically put up a sign on the front of the school saying "Free Orgasms If You Yell at Me." Just feels like a few of these guys are going to show up the next day shouting even louder, is all I'm saying.

But how was Emma able to do this? Unlike her famous X-Men counterpart Jean Grey, Emma doesn't have telekinesis; her powers are purely telepathic. This means she's unable to manipulate the bodies of these protestors in any way, so she has made them orgasm purely through thought. Which leads us to our next logical question: Is it possible to make a human orgasm with no physical stimulation? Do we in fact have a "bliss button" in our minds capable of being triggered? And if so, please draw where it is on a map so we can all find it.

There is no singular answer to this question, but research has shown us that there are several possible ways to experience a hands-free orgasm for those who don't have a powerful psychic nearby who gives out orgasms to people who piss her off.

I Think (Off), Therefore I Am

The real-life experience closest to Emma Frost's aforementioned mind-induced orgasm is a technique sometimes referred to as "thinking off" but can also be called a "spontaneous orgasm," an "energy orgasm," or "just frigging awesome" by those capable of achieving them. Thinking off is the ability to give yourself an orgasm just by thinking about it and while you may not have heard of such a thing, doctors and scientists have been aware of this phenomenon for quite a while. In 1896, Dr. T. J. McGillicuddy, after accepting his award for the funnest name to say, published "Functional Disorders of the Nervous System in Women," wherein he warned women against experiencing "involuntary orgasms" from erotic thoughts as they could "cause melancholia and mental weakness."[116] If you're thinking that Dr. McGillicuddy doesn't sound like he knows what a woman's orgasm actually feels like, well, you're probably right. Spontaneous orgasm is an ability almost exclusively seen in women, which means McGillicuddy's warnings might not have been in the interest of protecting women, but were instead spurred on by jealousy that he couldn't have one himself. In fact, famous sexologist Alfred Kinsey conducted a study of thousands of men in 1948 and found only two who "could reach climax by deliberate concentration of thought on erotic situations," but a few years later the same researchers surveyed 2,727 women and found 54 that reported being able to orgasm from "fantasy alone."[117]

Kinsey's findings were based on self-reporting surveys, though, and there was no way at the time of the studies to know whether what these women (and two men) were experiencing could actually be defined as orgasms or were just wildly pleasant daydreams. Years later, however, scientists started turning on their science machines to determine if what these women were experiencing in their minds were indeed orgasms, and they discovered that yep, those are orgasms all right!

A 2022 report by the International Society for Sexual Medicine extensively studied one woman who claimed to be capable of orgasm through thought alone and without genital stimulation. To verify her claims the scientists took blood samples when the woman was at rest, as well as before, during, and after several "thinking" sessions in the lab during which she claimed to orgasm. The scientists found that every time she conducted a mind orgasm it was followed by hugely elevated levels of prolactin in her blood, a hormone that is released during orgasm (you may recall our good friend prolactin from an earlier chapter on the Flash where we determined that he could orgasm 7,500 times a day if he wanted to). The researchers concluded that the subject's orgasms were "not 'faked' or partial orgasms, but rather reflect a top-down induction of a real subjective orgasmic state that includes objective hormonal changes."[118] So, unlike 60 percent of women in the world, she wasn't faking it.[119]

This coincided with a larger study done by researchers at Rutgers University on ten women who also reported being able to "think off." To determine what was happening in their bodies and how, the women were hooked up to monitoring devices and then reached orgasm first by masturbation and then by merely looking at "erotic imagery." Researchers found that in both experiments, the women had a "steep rise and abrupt post-orgasm drop-off in heart rate and systolic blood pressure,"[120] indicating a true orgasm had occurred each time. They also performed brain scans on the women that showed when they simply thought about stimulation of their breasts and genitals, the corresponding sensory areas of their brain would light up despite not being touched. For a group of ladies with no known mutant abilities, this is an incredible display of mind over matter. And if just thinking about stimulation can cause actual stimulation in some women, it may explain exactly what Emma did to make a group of people orgasm without being touched.

Turning (Wet) Dreams into Reality

If "thinking off" was the technique that Emma employed on the crowd of protestors, though, it would likely only work on women since so few men are capable of doing it—at least while they're awake. While it's true that very few men are able to think themselves into orgasming while conscious, it's also true that 83 percent of men experience a spontaneous orgasm at least once in their life during a wet dream (also called a nocturnal emission, if you like a more clinical turn of phrase). So most men are capable of experiencing an untouched orgasm, just not while they're awake, which is weird. It feels like if our brains can make us orgasm without being touched while we're sleeping, they should be able to make us orgasm the same way while we're awake. But life's not fair, is the thing you have to remember. It's also a little-known fact that women experience wet dreams as well. Studies have shown that up to 40 percent of women[121] will experience wet dreams in their life, but the actual number may be higher as women are more likely to sleep through a wet dream or forget one even happened. They're certainly easier to forget when you don't wake up sticky and with an increasingly high laundry bill. But even though anyone can experience a wet dream, it's still far more likely to happen to someone with a penis as one of the functions of those nocturnal emissions is to force the body to expel any old or dying sperm and make way for new swimmers in the fleet.

We've determined that there is a way that Emma Frost could make someone orgasm just by manipulating their mind, but if only 2 percent of women and almost no men are capable of "thinking off" willingly, it's hard to say if Emma could make them do it. Though there are some teachers of this particular sexual art who say the skill can be taught, most people just don't seem to be wired to be able to do it, certainly not to the degree that Emma would have a 100 percent mind-blowing orgasm success rate for an entire crowd of protestors. If Emma is instead somehow triggering whatever happens to our bodies during wet dreams, she will have a much greater chance of successfully getting people off, but still not everybody. We'll have to "work out" if there could be another way.

Exercising Your Brain

This brings us to our next hands-free orgasm option that Emma may activate in an individual. Let's talk about the "coregasm," an orgasm experienced during exercise and perhaps the best reason to start going back to the gym. A coregasm occurs during certain workouts that activate the same muscles our bodies use to orgasm. Exercises that have been known to induce orgasm are resistance training, running, hiking, and biking, with ab exercises like sit-ups and crunches reporting by far the most instances of climax.[122] What's even better about the coregasm is that it's much more common than being able to think yourself off and almost equally achievable among the sexes. In a 2021 study, about 10 percent of women and 8 percent of men[123] surveyed said they had experienced an orgasm while exercising at least once, so if ten X-Men entered the Danger Room to work out, there's a good chance one of them would walk out having experienced an orgasm. No wonder they spend so much time in there. Overall, then, coregasms are a better orgasm-inducing possibility for Emma Frost to engage on a crowd than telepathic "thinking off," but it's still far from a perfect option. With her mind-control powers, Emma could certainly force a crowd of people to vigorously contract their genital muscles or start doing crunches to get off, but it would still be unlikely to simultaneously cause orgasm in a whole crowd of people.

So science has offered us two imperfect explanations for how Emma O-faced an entire group of people, but is there any guaranteed way to send an entire crowd into orgasmic bliss? Well, there might be, but you won't like it (even if you think you would definitely like it). A final theory for this occurrence is that Emma Frost indeed knows about a "bliss button" buried deep inside of our brains that science is only just learning about but also having difficulty studying because it can literally only be reached through brain surgery (yeah, this is the part you won't like). In 2013, neurosurgeons at Notre Dame Hospital reported that they had induced "orgasmic ecstasy" in a patient several times using only electrodes planted deep inside her brain.[124] This was shocking to all involved as the goal of the procedure hadn't actually been anything like that.

The patient suffered from epilepsy, and surgeons were attempting to map her brain using subdural electrodes to figure out what was causing her seizures, but ended up accidentally causing several orgasmic events in their patient instead. Inducing orgasm in this case also caused the patient to experience a forty-five-second seizure afterward, which actually corresponds perfectly with what happened to the crowd when Emma sent out her orgasm blast and would explain why all the protestors fell down and passed out afterward. Either Emma gave them the best orgasm of their lives, or the "bliss button" she was pressing in their brains did a lot more to them than she bargained for. The doctors at Notre Dame who reported the seizure/orgasms concluded that creating orgasmic ecstasy in a person "involves the unilateral activation of a network comprising the amygdala, hippocampus, the parahippocampal gyrus, the temporal pole, and the anterior inferior insula," which is a fancy way to say that it is indeed possible to directly stimulate the brain into having an orgasm that will knock you off your feet. And if there's one thing that Emma Frost is good at, it's cutting giant pieces out of her costumes. But if there are two things she's good at, it's the costume thing and stimulating people. Especially ones who interrupt her class.

THE MISEDUCATION OF CAPTAIN AMERICA

"I had a date."

—Steve Rogers, *Captain America: The First Avenger* (2011)

Throughout this book we've discussed how different superpowers have caused weird and unique sex lives for the superheroes that have them, from Reed Richards's superlong penis to Mystique's ability to shape-shift her way into the perfect orgasm. But Captain America stands alone among the pantheon of heroes as a man whose superpowers didn't affect his sex life in any way. After all, you can't affect something that doesn't exist.

Steve Rogers is in the unique position of being a man who is sexualized but never sexed in his heroic outings, despite being portrayed by Sexiest Man Alive recipient Chris Evans in the Marvel films. There's no good reason why modern-day Steve Rogers with his moral integrity and his Dorito-shaped physique remained single, but it's at least obvious why he wasn't a heartthrob back in the 1940s. When we meet Steve Rogers in both the comics and movies, he is an unfathomably scrawny young man with no sexual prospects, which may have been for the best because he was so plagued with illnesses that the physical exertion of having sex might have actually killed him. According to his military application in *Captain America: The First Avenger*,[125] Steve suffered from all of the following maladies before the ripe young age of twenty-five:

- asthma
- scarlet fever
- rheumatic fever
- sinusitis
- high blood pressure
- palpitations or pounding in heart
- chronic or frequent colds
- heart trouble
- a family history of diabetes, cancer, and tuberculosis

Honestly, it's astonishing that Steve could leave the house, let alone apply multiple times to join the army. It's no wonder the military told him to get some superpowers or get the hell out every time. After undergoing a government experiment to give him said superpowers, things admittedly started to pick up in the romance department for our now incredibly ripped and exceedingly handsome super soldier. Suddenly all kinds of women started to pay attention to Steve, including nurses, soldiers, and USO dancers. But even with his newfound attractiveness, Steve never appeared wildly comfortable in the dating world as he clumsily interacted with most women he met. He also doesn't seem particularly well informed about anything regarding sex, going so far as to mistake "fondue" for a sex act instead of a delicious way to eat bread and cheese.

Steve does become briefly involved with Special Agent Peggy Carter, who would end up being Steve's main love interest throughout the films, but their relationship consisted of only a single kiss in 1945 before Steve found himself abruptly frozen under several feet of ice in the Arctic Ocean, not to be thawed out until 2012. And if Steve thought dating in 1945 was hard, he discovered that dating in 2012 was near impossible, bordering on the criminal. In modern times, Steve's main love interest is Agent Sharon Carter, a woman we find out later is the niece of Peggy Carter, his ex-girlfriend. Dating two women in the same family is kind of gross on its own, but it gets even worse when Steve later time travels back to the 1940s to marry Peggy, which means technically Sharon was also *his* niece when he made out with her, adding new levels of gross to Steve's limited dating history. Honestly, it's starting to make sense why Old-Steve refused to tell Sam about his marriage when he gets back to present day in *Avengers: Endgame*—who knows what other weird stuff this guy got up to during his second trip through time. He's probably his own grandpa or something.

But why is Steve Rogers so terrible at dating? By his own admission, "it's kind of hard to find someone with shared life experience" in the present day, as there aren't a lot of people who are simultaneously ninety-five and twenty-seven years old, unless we count Steve's childhood friend Bucky Barnes, aka the Winter Soldier. Despite their promises to be with each other "until the end of the line," a romantic relationship between Steve and Bucky never developed, leaving Steve's dating options in the modern day to be women who didn't personally experience World War II, which can certainly be a relationship barrier. Dating culture also changes significantly over time, especially when that time is sixty-seven years. When Steve tried to enter the dating scene in 2012 he likely went through culture shocks so powerful even his shield couldn't protect him. But what exactly are those differences? Let's do what Steve did with a plane full of bombs and dive straight into exactly what dating and sex culture were like when Steve went into the ice in 1945.

Steve's Got a Lot to Learn

The first thing to consider about Steve's dating life in the early twentieth century is the state of sex education at the time, or the lack thereof. Steve Rogers was born in 1918, meaning he went to school in the 1920s and '30s, and during that time only about 20 to 40 percent[126] of schools offered any type of sex education at all, and the other 60 to 80 percent of kids had to learn about sex from their parents (who also didn't have sex education), from schoolyard gossip, or just figure it out on their own. And even if you attended one of the few schools that taught sex education, it wasn't exactly the treasure trove of useful information that most youth have access to today.

Back then sex education was presented as scientifically as possible so as not to titillate the young masses, with a focus on sex being a natural act primarily performed as a means of procreation. For this reason, there were no pictures of humans used in school sex education; children were instead shown animals in any depictions of intercourse.[127] The idea was that by showing how the animal kingdom got its groove on, children could kind of get the gist of what sex was without being exposed to imagery that might make parents or teachers uncomfortable. This scientific approach wasn't without its flaws, though, as it removed the uniquely human aspects from the act of sex. For example, no animals have sex in the missionary position and would look wildly strange depicted in that way, so there's a chance this educational system led an entire generation (including Steve Rogers) into believing doggy style to be the default pose. Whether that's a positive or negative of the system can be decided by the reader's personal preferences.

But sex education wasn't just delivered by teachers. Much like today, a lot of educational materials came in the form of short films, each of which had a unique and particular lesson they were trying to instill in youth. For example, the American Social Hygiene Association's video *The Gift of Life* was an explicit warning against boys masturbating, calling it a "solitary vice" that "may seriously hinder a boy's progress towards vigorous manhood" and "is a selfish, childish, stupid habit."[128] Teenage boys throughout history would likely disagree, but this anti-masturbation message was repeated through many educational materials nonetheless, which might explain why this time frame was known as the Depression era.

Of course, no sexual education is complete without learning about the dangers of sexually transmitted infections, and if you think adults sat children down and explained these risks in a scientific and informative way in the 1920s, you'd be wrong. They absolutely just showed them another movie. The most famous STI-related cinema experience was 1914's *Damaged Goods*, a short film that follows a man who has unsafe sex with a prostitute the night before his wedding, contracts syphilis, passes the disease onto his newborn baby, and then kills himself. You know, standard kid stuff. Despite the dark subject material, the film was a hit with almost everyone who saw it, with one critic calling it a "masterpiece" and another saying that "every American boy . . . should be made to see it."[129] The film was so popular that new versions were released in 1914, 1919, and 1937, which means the *Damaged Goods* film franchise has more reboots than Captain America himself.

Though it was shown in some schools, *Damaged Goods* was actually made as a warning to soldiers against contracting syphilis from prostitutes while overseas in World War I and II. Statistically speaking, Steve Rogers was more likely to see the film while serving in the military than attending school, but this was the norm for a lot of soldiers. During World War II, more than half a million young men received sex education from the US military as the army was desperate to slow down the spread of venereal disease that was costing them valuable manpower. In World War II alone, almost 100,000 potential draftees were rejected from service for testing positive for syphilis[130] (the one disease Steve didn't have), representing a huge potential fighting force lost due to preventable venereal disease. In response to this epidemic, the military began releasing films, posters, and educational materials warning about the dangers of syphilis, how it's contracted, and how using a condom can help prevent the spread of disease. The military even started coming up with catchy slogans, with one pro-condom film proclaiming, "Don't forget—put it on before you put it in."

Speaking of which, if you ever wondered what Steve Rogers carried around in all those pouches on his uniform, there's a good chance at least one of them was full of army-issued condoms. In keeping with their ongoing mission to stop those pesky venereal diseases in their tracks, the US military issued condoms to soldiers during World War II, which means Steve would be used to having these pocket-sized sex shields around since they were likely included in every ration kit he ever received. Civilians also purchased them in droves back home, forcing production to ramp up to three million condoms a day[131] at times, but you'd be hard-pressed to find anyone talking about them, as their uses were more implied than openly stated.

The word "condom" would never even appear on early product packaging; instead they were referred to by generic names like "hygienic rubber product" or "genuine latex sold for prevention of disease" until eventually "prophylactic" became the common name, a term that originally meant any benign item from the pharmacy, such as toothbrushes, that has since become interchangeable with the word condom. Though it was known that condoms could help prevent pregnancy, in the 1940s they were predominantly marketed as a measure to prevent venereal disease. In fact, sex education in schools and the military almost never included lessons on birth control despite the existence of condoms and basic IUDs at the time, most likely because getting a girl pregnant wouldn't stop a soldier from fighting in the war like a disease would. So, you know, priorities.

Sex Myths of the 1940s

School and the military are what we might call the "official" sources from which Steve Rogers could have learned about sex in the 1940s, but we must also consider that a lot of sex information at the time was gleaned from myths and misinformation shared among friends as fact. Much like today, boys at the time liked to gossip about sex, but unlike today they were unable to fact-check the ridiculous claims that were spread around the schoolyard or trenches. For example, there's the persisting myth that some believe to this day that a woman can't get pregnant the first time she has sex. This, combined with a lack of education about birth control, led to many couples not using condoms the first time they slept together, resulting in unwanted pregnancies and some women being accused of cheating.

But this was not the only sexual misconception that floated around social circles of the time. Other more ridiculous myths that Steve may have heard included the belief that period blood contained poisonous toxins or that tampons removed a woman's virginity.[132] And then we have the most famous war-era sex myth of them all: that grafting monkey testicles onto a man's scrotum could cure impotence and increase a man's libido. That may sound bananas, but the craziest part about this myth was that it wasn't just gossip—people were actually trying it.

Pioneered in 1920 by Dr. Serge Abrahamovitch Voronoff, monkey-testicle transplant surgery was "hugely popular," and by the 1930s thousands of people had undergone this new "miracle" surgery, with almost all recipients being incredibly wealthy.[133] The surgery involved grafting a thin slice of a baboon's or chimpanzee's testicle onto a man's scrotum, like a primate-powered booster pack for your penis. The reported side effects of the surgery ranged from increased memory to enhanced libido, and even claims of a longer and more youthful life. And people believed it. Demand for monkey testicles was so high that Dr. Voronoff had to open a "monkey farm" to maintain his supply of transplant materials. Though the common masses couldn't afford to have their testicles rearranged with monkey parts, they certainly heard about the procedures, as jokes about monkey glands started appearing everywhere, including Marx Brothers movies, novelty mugs, and newspaper cartoons.

By the 1940s, the surgeries were branded as bogus and fell out of favor, but there may be nothing funnier in history than the fact that thousands of rich old men were walking around with monkey testicles in their scrotums that didn't even cure their impotence. Then again, it probably wasn't just old men who gave the surgery a try. Steve didn't become Captain America until 1943 and considering the long list of maladies he suffered from growing up, it's not a stretch to think he may have looked into the monkey testicle transplants himself. After all, we know from his eagerness to take the super-soldier serum that he's open to experimental procedures on his body. Honestly, if Steve could have afforded it there's a good chance he would have ended up as Captain Monkey Balls instead of Captain America. (Sorry, language—he would have been "Captain Monkey Testicles," obviously.)

With all this in mind, it becomes easy to understand why Steve Rogers had trouble stepping out of the ice and into the dating pool in 2012. He was absolutely right; it's hard to find "someone with shared life experience" when you're a man whose sex education consisted only of sex images of animals, terrifying films about how syphilis kills babies, no information about birth control, and being told that monkey testicles are a sexual cure-all. But these are just the things Steve would have believed from 1945 when he went into the ice; we also have to consider everything he missed while he was frozen.

Steve Missed the Entire Sexual Revolution

As previously mentioned, when Steve went into the ice, syphilis was running rampant, in America and the trenches, and would later be described by doctors as the "AIDS of the late 1930s and early 1940s." But almost as soon as Steve went under, things began to change.[134] The same year Steve went into the ice, the United States started mass-producing penicillin, which not only treats but cures almost all forms of syphilis. Penicillin was such an effective treatment that the syphilis death rate fell by 75 percent and the syphilis incidence rate fell by 95 percent between 1947 and 1957. And guess what happens when all the men come back from war just as a cure becomes available for the only major venereal disease at the time? People have a lot of sex. The availability of penicillin launched the modern sexual era, and it hit maximum throttle in the 1960s with the introduction of the birth control pill, which meant that it was now possible to have sex without getting sick *or* pregnant. You can almost hear Steve watching all this happen under the ice and screaming "Come on!"

Interestingly, though, a lot of the social staples of dating haven't changed since Steve took his ice nap—at least in terms of what couples do on dates. In the 1930s, the most popular date activities were drive-in movies and going out dancing, which both remain very good options in today's world, though you may have to settle for a sit-down theater and a very different dance experience than Steve lived through.[135] In the modern day, going out dancing almost always involves a dark, crowded nightclub filled with sweaty club-goers packed together like sardines as they rock out to pounding music. In the 1930s, going dancing involved a live band and a lot more room on the dance floor, but also a lot more partners.

Between World War I and II, dating was more of a popularity contest than it was about going steady or being locked down in a relationship. Dance floors were an important part of this culture, and it was common for women to show up and leave with different men or dance with a different guy every time a song changed. This explains why we see Steve's best friend Bucky Barnes take two women dancing in 1943 before he heads off to war, and also why Bucky asks Peggy Carter if she wants to dance despite her obvious interest in Steve. At the time, dancing with multiple people over the course of the night was the norm, and couples only exclusively danced together if they were already engaged. So Bucky may be a handsome flirt, but he's not a jerk. At least he wasn't before the Soviets put him into a brainwashing machine; that made him a little cranky.

Now that we've covered everything Steve Rogers does and doesn't know about sex and dating, let's imagine just how Steve would do on a hypothetical date after waking up in 2012 (with a woman who hopefully won't turn out to be his niece).

We know Steve believes the internet is "so helpful" with adjusting to modern life, so he likely met his date on a dating app of some kind after sorting through what had to be hundreds if not thousands of responses, because really, who isn't swiping right on Captain America? After taking his date to the movies, and trying not to have a heart attack about the fact that a tub of popcorn that cost a nickel in the 1940s is now upward of $8, he may suggest they go dancing where he will abandon his date for a new partner on every song change. If they somehow end up back together by the end of the night, Steve could very well be persuaded to come upstairs, but only if he'd gone to the pharmacy to pick up some "prophylactics" to avoid getting a venereal disease he may not know has been all but eliminated from the world thanks to penicillin. And the night wouldn't be complete without Steve apologizing that he couldn't afford the monkey testicle surgery, but he thinks he can manage without it. And then there is the sex itself. Well, Steve's body being in peak physical condition almost guarantees that intercourse would be exhilarating (though possibly only in doggy-style position). But if his sex education also included the belief that masturbation is evil, it's possible he hasn't had a proper orgasm for more than sixty years, so a person may be able to go for a ride with Captain America, but don't expect it to be a long one, at least not at first.

Steve Rogers may not be great at dating modern women, but that doesn't mean all old-fashioned men have the same problem. For example, do you know about . . .

Sexual Interlude #5: The Time Dr. Strange's Girlfriend Cheated on Him with Benjamin Franklin

Dr. Stephen Strange has been on some wild adventures. He's gone to hell to fight the devil; he's accidentally pulled every Spider-Man onto one Earth; heck, he was even a walking, talking corpse once. But nothing will ever be more humiliating than the time his girlfriend cheated on him with Benjamin Franklin. Yeah, *that* Benjamin Franklin.

Our story starts in *Dr. Strange #18*, where we find Stephen and his girlfriend Clea time traveling around to learn about the history of the occult in America in a plot more akin to Dr. Who than Dr. Strange. The couple arrives in 1775 because Dr. Strange is dying to meet Benjamin Franklin. He can't wait. In fact, he's so excited about it that he can't stop telling Clea all about just how great Benjamin Franklin was:

> "Franklin was perhaps colonial America's **greatest man**—in an **era** of great men. He was a **genius** who dedicated himself to improving the **general standard of living**—a genius for the **common man**. He was the **first** man to understand **electricity**. He invented **bi-focal glasses**, a new kind of **stove**, and a **hundred other** useful things. He was **also**, I'm told, quite the **ladies' man**."[136]

Oh man, Dr. Strange, you sure are hyping this guy up to your girlfriend, sure are making him sound pretty great. Making him sound like a guy a woman would only ever have one chance of hooking up with while time traveling. And you know he's a ladies' man? That's something you are definitively aware of? Well, I'm sure you won't just leave your girlfriend with him after he was hitting on her then. You definitely won't insist she go hang out in his cabin alone with him for hours, right?

Good reader, he did all of those things.

Shortly after meeting Ben Franklin, the ship they're all sailing on is attacked by a sorcerer named Stygyro, a villain whose name has such a bad mouthfeel he hasn't appeared in a comic since 1977. While Dr. Strange goes to fight the bad guy, he tells Clea to stay with Benjamin "Ladies Man" Franklin in his cabin to keep them safe. Benjamin Franklin then shows his gratitude to Dr. Strange for saving his life by proceeding to seduce his girl-friend. As soon as they're alone, Franklin pours them both a glass of whis-key and proceeds to sweep Clea off her feet. After only five quick panels of flirting, Clea finds herself unable to resist the combination of Franklin's receding hairline, jowls, and spectacles, and she lies down in his bed while he snuffs out the candles and works on making his next great discovery.

We never get to find out Dr. Strange's reaction to this incident as the whole time-traveling adventure turns out to be an illusion, but all things considered, it seems obvious that if he found out Clea slept with Benjamin Franklin he would have been wildly jealous . . . of Clea.

Part 4

SECRET ORIGINS

Pregnancy and Childbirth Among the Superpowered

WOLVERINE'S IMMORTAL SPERM

"I'm the best there is at what I do, but what I do best isn't very nice."
—Wolverine, *X-Men Origins: Wolverine* (2009)

Wolverine wants you to believe that he's a pretty simple guy. He prides himself in being a man who likes beer, cutting things up with his claws, and being left alone, except one of those things is empirically a lie, as Wolverine is basically the opposite of a loner. He's been friends with so many people he can't even remember them all, and not just because of his crippling amnesia (but it certainly doesn't help). This man has been a member of at least eleven different superhero teams, mentors dozens of young mutants, and also hooks up with as many women as possible. So, he's not as simple a man as he claims to be—and neither are his powers.

Whereas most mutants have one main superpower, Wolverine's a little overachiever imbued with at least three separate, unrelated mutant abilities, including enhanced senses, retractable bone claws, and, of course, his incredible healing factor, which allows him to heal from almost anything (except maybe a broken heart). But he can definitely heal from physical injuries like bullet wounds or Sentinel blasts. He even survived the detonation of an atomic bomb one time. Some theorize that Wolverine's healing factor is so powerful he may be functionally immortal, a theory propped up by the fact that he was born in the late nineteenth century and is still vigorously clawing his way around the Marvel universe despite dying hundreds of times in dozens of different ways. But if Wolverine is immortal, does that mean every part of his body is as well? Including the little Logans swimming around in his testicles?

It's not as ridiculous a question as it may seem at first. After all, in the X-Men universe, mutant abilities develop at a genetic level, caused by a mutation in the X-Gene that gives you some kind of power or ability (or blue skin way more often than you'd expect). The job of sperm is to transmit a person's genetic material, which would include the X-Gene. That's not to say that every sperm would have the incredible abilities of the mutant they're born from; sperm are a very small, basic form of life, so they're not capable of shooting optic blasts out of their eyes (because they don't have eyes) or reading people's minds (because they also don't have minds) or anything cool like that, but Wolverine's healing ability presents a rare power that a simple organism like a sperm may be able to inherit. Unlike most mutant abilities, his healing power is automatic, meaning Wolverine doesn't have to activate it or think about using it; his body just starts healing itself if he's hurt. Sperm are also a living entity that are capable of being injured or dying, so would Wolverine's sperm inherit his healing ability and be able to heal themselves automatically like the rest of Wolverine's body does? And if so, what does that mean for his own body chemistry, the women he has had sex with, and any potential offspring?

In previous chapters I've relied on scientific studies to answer my questions about superhero sexual anatomy, but I was let down in this instance and couldn't find a single piece of research among the annals of academia on the repercussions of having immortal sperm. Shame on you, science. What are you even doing all day? So, to answer these important questions about the power of Wolverine's little bubs, I've assembled my own super team of specialists, and, in honor of Wolverine, I even made sure they were Canadian. Therefore, I must take a moment to say a special thanks to Dr. Jesse Ory, male fertility and sexual health specialist at Dalhousie University, and Dr. Josh White, male infertility and sexual health specialist at the University of Calgary, who generously took it upon themselves to work out the limitations of Logan's super semen with me.

The X-Gene Marks the Spot

Before we determine the consequences of expelling undying little X-SeMen all over the place, we must first confirm that Wolverine's sperm could even inherit his healing ability. To do that we need to figure out where in his genome Wolverine's healing ability comes from and if those genes pass on through the sperm. Unless you've got a sample of Wolverine's DNA to study, this is almost impossible to know for certain, but we can make a very educated guess based on the fact that, in the comics, Wolverine has a son named Daken who has the same mutant abilities as his father, including retractable claws and a healing factor. This simple fact tells us that Wolverine's sperm definitely carries the genetic code for his healing factor, since he passed it along to his son. It also makes it really easy to figure out whether a kid is yours or not. Most sons just inherit their father's eyes or something, but if a kid shows up with bone claws and immortality Logan can probably skip the trip to the paternity court and say that one's his.

Because his son inherited the same powers, we know that Wolverine's sperm carry his X-Gene. Now the real question is, would these sperm also inherit Wolverine's X-Gene healing factor themselves and be functionally immortal? According to Dr. Ory, no, only half of them would:

> Half the sperm will have [his healing ability] and half of them won't, because a regular human cell has two sets of chromosomes, but when sperm are made they only have a single set. You get a single set of chromosomes from the man and a single set of chromosomes from the woman and then they combine and you get a human . . . But [with sperm] they get split in half, so you have half your sperm with the Y chromosome only, and half with the X chromosome only.[137]

In other words, half of Wolverine's sperm would inherit his healing ability and be essentially immortal, and the other half wouldn't, and we even know how to tell which is which. Sperm each carry a single set of chromosomes, either X or Y, and a male child has an XY pairing of chromosomes (as opposed to a female who has an XX pairing). Wolverine's son had to have been conceived from a sperm with a Y chromosome and since he inherited the same mutant abilities as his father, Wolverine's X-Gene must also be found on his Y chromosome, so all the sperm that carry Logan's Y chromosome basically can't die. This also means that any of Logan's offspring that inherit the self-healing, maybe-immortal ability would be biologically male. (There's no word on whether the sperm in question also have weird triangle-shaped hair like Wolverine does, but maybe we'll figure that out in the next book.)

An Abundance of Sperm

It might sound cool that Wolverine is constantly generating a tiny immortal army inside his body, but it's actually kind of a problem because sperm are very much supposed to die eventually. In fact, a lot of the function of the male reproductive system kind of counts on that happening. In most men the testicles make about 1,500 sperm per second[138] to replace the ones that are dying off or getting expelled from the body in ejaculate, and this production *never stops*. Even if someone doesn't masturbate or have sex, new sperm just keep being made no matter how much they currently have in testicular storage.

For example, someone who has had a vasectomy (an operation to cut the tubes that carry sperm to the testicles) can no longer ejaculate sperm, but their body will still keep creating new sperm every day for the rest of their lives.[139] In males without a mutant healing factor (so, everyone except, like, three people), sperm only live in the testicles for about seventy-four days, after which the sperm cells die off and get reabsorbed by the body. This keeps the amount of sperm a person has in their body at any given time at a reasonable level. In most people. But Wolverine isn't most people. So what happens if half of Wolverine's sperm never die and his body also never stops making them? According to our experts, that overflow of sperm would be bursting out of him more often than his adamantium claws.

"Because he's producing all of that sperm and things are getting engorged . . . if he's not busting a nut pretty regularly, he's gonna be so miserable," says Dr. White, speaking with a notable empathy toward the X-Man's predicament.

According to Dr. Ory, the only way to relieve the pressure in Wolverine's testicles caused by the overabundance of sperm is to "either be having sex all the time or masturbating all the time," which at least wouldn't be too difficult for him, all things considered. We discussed in an earlier chapter that the Flash's refractory period (the amount of time after orgasm until the body can orgasm again) would be approximately 0.102 seconds due to his accelerated healing and super speed. Wolverine lacks super speed, but his healing ability is second to none, which means his refractory period would be wildly shorter than the thirty minutes it takes the average male to get it back up. That doesn't mean it would be fun to be forced to frequently masturbate to relieve the tension in your testicles, and it would definitely make for some awkward conversations about why Wolverine abruptly leaves the room all the time, but the alternative is also not great. According to Dr. Ory, if Wolverine doesn't ejaculate frequently to lower his sperm count, he would likely be constantly "leaking sperm," and he would "probably have wet dreams all the time."

Wet dreams (or "nocturnal emissions," if you're fancy) happen when you ejaculate during sleep. They're more common in teenagers but also happen to adults, and they almost definitely happen to Wolverine. According to Dr. Ory, "in regular people, if you don't masturbate or have sex for a long time you'll have a wet dream," which is the body's way of expelling excess sperm and semen while you sleep. If half of Wolverine's sperm never die or get reabsorbed into his body, then he will have far more excess sperm that needs to come out than the average person, and a way higher laundry bill when it's time to clean his sheets.

We now know a bit about what's going on internally with our friend Logan: half his sperm aren't dying and he's perpetually uncomfortable about it, which might explain why the dude's so grumpy all the time. But if half of Wolverine's sperm won't die, he's going to have bigger problems than fitting those blue balls into his spandex pants. Like, what the hell happens when he has sex?

Well, Dr. White believes that with his immortal sperm Wolverine would "be the ultimate impregnator" and may even be the best chance for the survival of the mutant race, but we'll get into that in a minute. First let's talk about how Wolverine's new code name might just be the Fertile Crescent.

Quality Semenship

In regular humans, most of the sperm found in semen is, well, not great. In an average semen sample a large percentage of sperm are either dead, not moving, or have abnormalities that will impair their mobility. In fact, a regular human is considered "fertile" if only 40 percent of their sperm are capable of moving at all,[140] which is a failing grade on literally any other test. In Wolverine's case, we know that at least 50 percent of his sperm would retain his healing ability and be in literally perfect health for perhaps all of time. The other 50 percent would be mortal but made in a pristine pair of testicles in a body with a healing factor, making it very likely that almost 100 percent of his sperm would be alive, healthy, and ready to swim their tails off upon ejaculation. So what does that mean for Logan's sex life?

When taking into account just how powerful and healthy Wolverine's sperm would be, Dr. Ory is willing to guess that Wolverine's "probably got a 100 percent pregnancy rate" when he has unprotected sex with a woman. Which is a recipe for a huge child-support bill if Wolverine doesn't take precautions.

To understand why Wolverine's super sperm are so potent, we need to understand some things about regular human pregnancy. First, it's pretty much only possible to get someone pregnant during ovulation, which is when a mature egg is released from the ovaries and travels down the fallopian tube to be fertilized. Once there, the egg has anywhere from twelve to twenty-four hours to get fertilized, but even if someone has unprotected sex during this window there's still only about a 10 to 33 percent chance of getting pregnant.[141] This is mainly due to the fact that for the non-Wolverines out there, about 99 percent of sperm either die or get lost on their way to the egg—they are very small, after all, and their journey to Egg Town is about the same distance that Frodo traveled to get the one ring to Mount Doom, with just as many obstacles along the way.

First, the sperm have to be strong enough to get through the mucus around the opening of the cervix that is designed to trap unhealthy sperm, then they swim up either the left or right uterine tubes. Unfortunately for the sperm, the human body doesn't put all its eggs in one basket, so only one side releases an egg every month, which means 50 percent of the fellowship of sperm simply go the wrong way and hit an eggless dead end. Half the sperm take the correct path to Egg Town but still have to find their way through the extremely narrow openings of the uterine tube. It's only then that a sperm may reach the egg. On average, there are around 300 *million* sperm who start this journey, and only about 200 will ever reach the egg—that's a 0.00006 percent completion rate for the sperm. But again, that's in a regular human. Dr. Ory feels confident that Wolverine's sperm are "swimming super fast, they're fully healthy, all the sperm are perfectly shaped, [and] there's no abnormalities at all," so they have an exponentially better chance of going all the way. This means almost all of Logan's little guys would make it through the cervix; half of them would still swim up the wrong uterine tube as they wouldn't have any better sense of direction than a regular sperm; and about 50 percent of Wolverine's sperm would ultimately arrive at the egg, compared to way less than 1 percent for the regular humans, which is why Wolverine can add "ultimate impregnator" to his list of superpowers. Well, maybe.

This super fertility could be an example of too much of a good thing, as there's a very real chance that Wolverine's sperm could be so powerful it would result in no viable pregnancy occurring at all. Normal human conception (and mutant, as far as we know) occurs when a single sperm cell enters an egg and fertilizes it. After an egg is fertilized the shell becomes hard and cemented to prevent more sperm from breaking through. But it is possible, even in regular humans, for two sperm to have a photo finish race and enter the egg at the exact same time. This is referred to as polyspermy and is estimated to account for around 1 percent of all fertilizations.[142] Unfortunately, this usually results in an excess of chromosomes and too much genetic material for the egg to fertilize normally, and so the embryo doesn't usually survive. Real-world studies have found that in couples who have suffered through multiple miscarriages, it's common for the male to have a sperm count that is significantly higher than average, increasing the likelihood of polyspermy.[143]

But a sperm count that is high for a human would be considered low for Wolverine. Let's consider, if the average human has about 200 sperm that successfully reach the egg and Logan likely has about 150 million little bubs arriving at the same time, that egg is about to experience the reproductive version of meeting an army of Wolverines in a berserker rage and get absolutely decimated. For Wolverine the likelihood of polyspermy happening is exponentially higher than in humans, almost to the point of certainty, meaning that Wolverine's sperm is likely too powerful to get a woman pregnant. At first.

Internal Loitering

Wolverine's sperm may be too eager and numerous to fertilize the first egg they come across, but there will be more eggs in their tiny little futures as the ovaries release a new one every twenty-eight days or so. In normal humans this isn't helpful since sperm that make it into the vagina can only live for about five days, after which they die and fertilization isn't possible.[144] But as I may have mentioned, Wolverine's sperm retain his healing ability and won't die, so they can just wait around inside the fallopian tubes for as long as it takes for another egg to come along to get fertilized. Which means it doesn't matter at what point in your ovulation cycle you have sex with Wolverine—his sperm will still be there even a month later, eager to pop out their claws and tear into the egg like it's a beer to be cracked open.

The first egg these sperm come across would likely succumb to polyspermy, as too many cooks are trying to get into the kitchen, so to speak, but over the next month Wolverine's sperm would keep swimming out to different areas of the body, moving in less concentrated groups and making it less likely that the next egg, or even the one after that, would be overwhelmed with their presence. If enough sperm wander away from where the egg is released, a viable pregnancy is possible. And these boys are known to roam. Even regular human sperm have been known to wander their way right out of the female reproductive system and into the fluid surrounding the internal organs, never once stopping to ask for directions.[145] Sperm just kind of keep swimming until they die, except Wolverine's don't die, so, much like Dory in *Finding Nemo*, they would just keep swimming. It's very likely, then, that a bunch of Wolverine's sperm would end up floating around endlessly in the body of anyone he had unprotected sex with, and you don't want these wandering wigglers inside you forever.

Left to their own devices, the immortal sperm could get all the way down the fallopian tubes and into the ovaries where the nonmature eggs hang out before they're released during ovulation. Thankfully, a nonmature egg can't be fertilized by a sperm, so a woman wouldn't suddenly find herself exploding with thousands of fertilized eggs in her ovaries if they got in, but these little immortal tadpoles waiting right outside the door makes it more likely that an egg would be fertilized immediately upon maturing. Dr. White worries this would cause "a whole bunch of ectopic pregnancies," which are bad. A normal pregnancy develops after a fertilized egg travels through the fallopian tubes and attaches to the lining of the uterus. An ectopic pregnancy happens when a fertilized egg gets impatient and implants outside the uterus, usually in the fallopian tube, but sometimes also in the ovary or elsewhere in the abdomen, none of which are a great place for a potential baby-to-be. The uterus is literally the only place an embryo will have the room it needs to grow, so if the egg implants anywhere else it usually can't survive and will cause a slew of health problems for the birth parent, such as a ruptured fallopian tube, which requires emergency medical care and can even lead to death. This isn't great news for Wolverine's lovers. They already risked their lives sleeping next to a man who might accidentally eviscerate them during a nightmare, and now they might also die from having sex with him. It's starting to make sense why he doesn't date many women for long.

Return of the Living Sperm

Throughout this chapter we've maintained that Wolverine's sperm are functionally immortal and incapable of dying, but let's push that assumption aside and discuss the possibility that his sperm would still be able to die, much like Wolverine himself. After all, Wolverine is a living being who needs air and nutrients (and beer) to survive, and has also been killed many times, whether by explosion or drowning or laser blast. By most accounts he technically dies during these events, but his healing factor allows him to come back to life when the environment is no longer hostile; in other words, he will start breathing again when he's pulled into the air after drowning, or his body will regenerate after the deadly radiation that killed him clears. And the same is likely true of his sperm.

Sperm require nutrients to live, specifically fructose, which they get from the semen around them, and die from hunger without it. This could very well mean that Wolverine's sperm would actually die from a fructose shortage about five days after ejaculation, as they would for a regular human. If the sperm did die from a lack of nutrients, they would likely go into stasis and only come back to life when new nutrients were introduced into the environment. These nutrients could come from Wolverine's own ejaculate if he has unprotected sex with the same woman twice, or they could come from *any other semen that enters the vagina*. It turns out sperm aren't picky eaters and will take fructose from wherever they can, even semen that wasn't meant for them. According to Dr. White, sperm can act a lot like Wolverine himself, a lone soldier fighting to survive by any means necessary, even if it means killing the other sperm around them.

> What [sperm] do, though, is they will use up the resources and then there isn't enough fructose and the other nutrients that the other sperm needs, so they're not directly killing [each other] but they're not leaving enough scraps for the rest. [It's] every sperm for itself.

It's hard to imagine that any battle between regular human sperm and Wolverine's all-star swim team would end in anything other than victory for Wolverine and his boys. This means there's a very real possibility that several weeks or even months after sleeping with Wolverine, a woman could have sex with a different man, that man's semen could revive Wolverine's super sperm inside her, and she could get pregnant with Wolverine's child months after sleeping with him. Talk about days of future past.

Considering the fact that Wolverine's sperm either live forever or can be revived indefinitely inside the body, it feels accurate to say that Wolverine would have an almost 100 percent success rate when trying to impregnate a partner. Dr. White even theorizes that Wolverine could be the ultimate savior of the mutant race in an apocalypse scenario as he would be able to impregnate pretty much any fertile person left in the world and, as seen with his son Daken, those children would likely inherit his mutant powers, including his healing ability, creating a world full of nearly unkillable mutants with weird hair. And science backs this up (the part about the mutations, not the hair). According to a 2017 Icelandic study, older men are more likely to pass genetic mutations onto their children,[146] and there aren't many people out there older than Wolverine, meaning most, if not all, of his children would be mutants. These kids would also have Wolverine's enhanced sense of smell, so let's hope for their sake that this apocalypse includes showers somehow. We also determined earlier that Wolverine's X-Gene is almost certainly on his Y chromosome, so any mutant children he has would be biologically male, which isn't great for population growth. But when your children can't die, population *growth* isn't exactly necessary.

Unless there's an apocalyptic need for super babies to save the mutant race, Wolverine probably doesn't want to get every woman he sleeps with pregnant, though. The child-support payments alone would be scary enough to make a man run back to Canada. But can the "ultimate impregnator" have sex without getting someone pregnant, or are these super sperm truly unstoppable?

The Birth Control Battle

For most men who no longer wish to have children but do wish to keep having sex on the regular, a vasectomy is an excellent option. A simple surgery cuts or seals the tube that carries the sperm into the penis and removes almost any chance of pregnancy occurring. Unfortunately, despite his love for things that go "snikt," this isn't an option for Wolverine because his healing factor would reverse the effects of this surgery almost immediately (if it could even happen at all, since he would likely heal from a surgical incision too fast for it to even be attempted).

Wolverine may then be tempted to try the pull-out method of contraception, which happens when you take the penis out of the vagina just before ejaculation to prevent pregnancy. Even in regular humans this isn't an overly effective form of birth control and would be an especially bad choice for Wolverine, considering he would likely be able to impregnate someone with pre-cum alone. For the record, pre-cum (the liquid that leaks out of the penis when aroused) doesn't inherently contain sperm, but both pre-cum and semen travel down the urethra to be ejected, so even though they don't come out at the same time, pre-cum has been known to pick up any sperm lingering around in the urethra from the last time the person ejaculated.[147] A 2011 study found that 37 percent of pre-cum samples contained a significant amount of sperm.[148] In Wolverine's case we've already established he may be leaking sperm constantly due to his high sperm production, so any unprotected genital contact at all is likely to cause a future little Wolverine in nine months' time. Thus, the pull-out method is out as a form of contraceptive.

What would be effective against the mighty force of Wolverine's sperm, though, is a simple condom to keep the sperm from ever making it inside the vagina in the first place. Condoms are about 98 percent effective, so wearing one would stop almost all of Wolverine's potential pregnancies from happening. As a second line of defense, Wolverine's partner could also use birth control, almost guaranteeing there would be no conception even if some sperm got past the condom's defenses. In this case the best choices for Wolverine's partner would be either an intrauterine device (IUD) or the birth control pill. An IUD creates a hostile environment in the uterus, so even if Wolverine's sperm successfully fertilized an egg, it wouldn't be able to implant on the uterine wall and mature. Or they can use the birth control pill, which works by stopping ovulation, meaning the eggs in the ovaries never mature and don't get released. Since immature eggs can't be fertilized, this would also keep Wolverine's sperm in check. We already learned that Wolverine's sperm can potentially live forever inside another person, though, so if his partner removed the IUD or they stopped taking their pills, pregnancy would still happen almost instantly, perhaps even years after intercourse. To avoid being impregnated by Wolverine, these methods would have to be used continuously, perhaps for the rest of your life. Which means Wolverine truly is the best there is at what he does, and what he should do is always wear a condom.

We've learned a lot about the limitations of Logan's lower extremities today, but here's the most horrifying part: we might know more about Wolverine's testicles than Logan himself. Considering the extreme memory loss that Wolverine suffers from he may be completely unaware that his sperm are immortal. And he likely doesn't know that those same sperm are capable of impregnating or possibly killing every woman he has sex with. And he probably has no idea that his undying swimmers could be responsible for saving the entire mutant race someday. That's a lot of things to not know about yourself, even for Wolverine. But even if he has lost all of his memories and doesn't know anything about his immortal little Logans, there's one thing he will always know for certain—his balls hurt and he's grumpy about it.

SUPERGIRL'S FORTRESS OF SOLITUDE

"I'm the Girl of Steel. I don't bend, I don't break."
—Kara Danvers, *Supergirl*, season 2, episode 17

Superman has one of the most tragic backstories in comics. As a baby, his home planet Krypton was about explode so he was sent to Earth, raised by Jonathan and Martha Kent in Kansas, and grew up never knowing his real parents or his people because they were all space dust. So sad, right? Except years later we learn his teenage cousin Kara also survived the destruction of Krypton and, after getting stuck in the time-stopping Phantom Zone for twenty years, landed on Earth with all the same powers as Clark. Unlike Clark, though, Kara wasn't a baby when Krypton exploded; she was a teenager who watched everyone she loved die in a fiery planetary explosion and still turned out to be a kind, optimistic young woman. So clearly one of her powers is being able to cope with inexplicable tragedy. Which is a power she's going to need when Superman sits down to talk with her about sex. Namely that, here on Earth, neither of them can have any.

You may be familiar with Superman's inability to have sexual intercourse from Larry Niven's famous satirical essay, "Man of Steel, Woman of Kleenex," which outlined exactly what would happen if Superman attempted to have sex with his girlfriend, Lois Lane. (Spoiler: Lois ends up super dead.) Highlights of Niven's essay include his belief that during orgasm "Superman would literally crush [Lois's] body in his arms, while simultaneously ripping her open from crotch to sternum" and concludes that because of his enhanced Kryptonian muscles, "Kal-El's semen would emerge with the muzzle velocity of a machine gun bullet" and shoot straight through Lois's body.[149] Great Krypton, what a mood killer!

Since Niven's essay explored Superman's sexual difficulties almost too thoroughly (and is widely available online), let's accept that Clark could not in good conscience attempt intercourse with a human being and flip our attention to the other side of the Kryptonian sex coin, his cousin Supergirl.

Unlike Superman, Kara's never really had a long-term love interest, which is surprising because you'd think she would be pretty lonely and trying to find companionship after the whole death-of-her-entire-race thing. The few guys she has been involved with were almost all regular humans, with the exception of that time she dated Comet the Super-Horse (for the love of God, don't ask). But would she have any luck actually bedding one of these fragile male Earthlings, or is she going to win the illustrious "I have the saddest life" title from Superman and be physically alone forever?

Before we figure any of that out, just a side note to keep us all from feeling weird about this: though Supergirl is typically depicted as about sixteen years old in the comics, she is in her mid-twenties in both the DCEU movie *The Flash* and the 2015 live-action *Supergirl* television series . . . and in this book. Glad that's out of the way—now let's figure out if this twenty-something demigod can get her sexual groove on with a puny human.

First, we must make the highly unlikely assumption that Supergirl's sexual physiology is the same as that of a human woman, even though Kryptonians are complete aliens. In reality Supergirl is as likely to lay physical eggs as she is to have a human-like vagina, but since comic books are about as far from reality as we can get, we'll assume all her bits match up with human female sex organs. Now we have to figure out all the ways she can enjoy them.

If Kara just wants to masturbate, there shouldn't really be much standing, or lying, in her way. Yes, her genitals would have the consistency of steel, but so does the rest of her body, making manual stimulation as easy and straightforward for her as it is for humans. Finding sex toys strong enough to please her might be a little bit more difficult. In our earlier chapter about the Flash, we discussed research done at Idaho State University to find the most powerful vibrator on the market. All the vibrators they studied were deemed "effective" at both vaginal and clitoral stimulation, with the weakest vibrator clocking in at an acceleration of just 8 m/s^2. The top performer had an acceleration of 311 m/s^2, making it almost forty times more powerful than the weakest option,[150] and hopefully capable of bringing our girl of steel to climax. But even if that's not powerful enough, she can always rely on herself.

The next step in the sexual ladder that Kara might land on is oral sex. Oral sex doesn't necessarily involve penetration, so it should be easy enough for her to attempt with a human partner, but the key word here would be attempt, as success in this venture really relies on just how steel-like Kara's body is, how receptive her skin is to comparatively weak stimulation, and, honestly, how many jaw exercises her partner's been doing. Hopefully a lot. But even if this venture doesn't end in an orgasm for Kara, it's at least safe for a human to try it, as long as Kara remembers to lie still and keep her super legs from closing in any kind of crushing motion on her partner's head.

The same level of safety can't be guaranteed if Kara wants to try penetrative sex with one of her frail Earth boyfriends, though, as there are numerous ways this venture can go badly. Is there any way her super vagina could play nice with a regular human penis without resorting to setting up some red sunlamps that take away her powers (though they would set a pretty cool mood in the bedroom)? To figure that out, let's look at everything that might stop this sex train from leaving the station, starting with the hymen.

Girl of Steel, Hymen of...?

The hymen is a thin membrane that circles the vaginal opening, and is wildly misunderstood. Despite popular belief to the contrary, the hymen does not cover the opening of the vagina but is more like a flesh donut that circles the entrance. There's also the longstanding belief that if you have no hymen it means you're not a virgin, an idea about as fictional as the superheroes we're discussing. While the hymen certainly can be torn during sex, it's also weaker than Clark Kent's powers of disguise and wears away from literally any physical activity. The hymen can deteriorate from everyday activities such as playing sports, masturbating, or even just walking around. So, a person could have no visible hymen at all and indeed still be a virgin.

But does Supergirl's incredible strength mean she has a hymen made of steel protecting her *cough* Fortress of Solitude?

The answer is probably, but it wouldn't really deter her from having sex. First of all, Kara may have arrived on Earth with no hymen at all, and not because she didn't have time to pack it in the rush of escaping an exploding planet. Supergirl and Superman get their powers from Earth's yellow sun, but back on Krypton they had no superpowers at all. Since Kara arrived on Earth when she was already a teenager, her hymen may have worn away from everyday activity before she ever arrived.

If her hymen was still intact upon landing on Earth, though, it's logical that exposure to Earth's yellow sun made this tissue incredibly strong, just like the rest of Kara's body. But this still wouldn't really affect Kara's penetrative-sex-having abilities. Even a super hymen can be stretched or torn by intense athletic activity (like fighting Darkseid or getting thrown into the Earth's core). The hymen can also be ruptured manually, which means Supergirl could simply use her own super strength to stretch her super hymen to have (hopefully) super sex. Since the tissue doesn't grow back, she'd only have to do so once, and boom—she's hymen-free forever.

Hitting a Vaginal Wall

So we know the hymen is not a hindrance to Supergirl having sex. Her potential for physical human interaction has officially made it past the tip. But now we get to Supergirl's vaginal walls, which are strong enough to squeeze a piece of coal into a diamond (which is great for her bank account, but not so great for her partner's erection).

A regular human vagina is made of soft flesh that has some give, allowing for sexual penetration. Because of Kara's super strength her body has the consistency of steel, which means attempting sex with her would be like trying to penetrate a steel vice. Something's gotta give, and if her partner is a regular human, it probably won't be the steel, especially when we factor in the sizes involved of the two opposing forces. On average a woman's vaginal opening is 2.62 centimeters wide,[151] while the average diameter of an erect penis is 3.89 centimeters wide.[152] The simplest math can tell us that this is a problem.

If the default state of Supergirl's vagina is steel-like and too small for a human penis to penetrate, this means Kara's best chance of having an enjoyable human interaction is to find a little extra room down there. Generally, the vagina relaxes and expands during arousal and/or manual penetration, so Supergirl may be able to manually loosen herself up enough for sex with a human man and his terrifyingly fragile penis. But there's no guarantee that she could *maintain* this level of relaxation once intercourse began. If the sex is bad (and let's face it, the first time is almost guaranteed to be) and she doesn't remain aroused . . . well, Supergirl's steely vaginal walls could tighten back up to 2.62 centimeters, which is bad news for any 3.89-centimeter-wide penis inside her at the time.

Is that it for Supergirl's sex life, then? Should she just put up a "Danger, Do Not Enter" sign on her underwear and get some cats? Maybe give Comet the Super-Horse a call? Not yet. There may be a light at the end of the vaginal tunnel, as Supergirl still has a chance to have penetrative sex, and it all relies on the power of her brain. A great deal of vaginal muscle control comes from the brain, which means a person can choose to tighten or relax these muscles, as opposed to being an involuntary response they have no control over. This is true in most human girls and should be equally, if not more, true in Supergirls, so if Kara's super strength extends to her brain power she would have better control of her vaginal muscles and walls than most.

So Supergirl's ability to have penetrative sex really relies on her having super control over her muscles, which is a power she absolutely must have. Especially considering how many insane abilities Superman has displayed over the years, including super ventriloquism, super imagination, super amnesia-causing kisses, super foreign-language interpretation, and super ability to make tiny versions of himself come out of his fingers (weird that this one doesn't come up more often). Superman's even been shown to be able to stop his own heart and breathing for long periods to appear dead, so surely Supergirl, who has the same powers, would have the brain power to relax her vaginal walls enough for sex. It's not like she wouldn't have the motivation to try—after all, Supergirls just wanna have fun.

A Steel Trap

Let's say Kara is able to focus during sex and mentally relax her vaginal walls; that means we've gotten past the tip and the initial penetration. But what happens as Kara nears completion? An orgasm is generally thought to make a person's mind go blissfully blank and cause them to briefly lose control over certain bodily reactions. A little involuntary twitching or clamping down isn't a huge deal for a human (it can even feel enjoyable), but when you're strong enough to punch through a planet every muscle spasm suddenly becomes a deadly weapon. Does that mean Kara risks showing thanks to her sexual partner by castrating them as they bring her to orgasm?

This scenario may sound similar to the real-life myth of penis captivus. If you think that is a medical term for a penis becoming stuck in a vagina during sex (and are also thinking, *no, no, no, no, no—please don't let that be real*), then congratulations, you're right on both counts. Though there are indeed half a dozen amusing stories of penis captivus happening in the past century (the best involving couples being brought into hospitals stuck together and stacked on a single gurney), none of these cases have been documented medically or officially diagnosed. In the medical community, penis captivus is generally held as a hilarious but exceedingly rare phenomenon of little concern and almost all information on the condition is based on rumor and hearsay. Those doctors who believe it could occur at all say it would only last a few seconds, not minutes or hours as people like to believe.[153] So if that's something you've ever worried about, you can act like Kara's vagina and just relax now.

Even if penis captivus isn't likely to happen to Kara (or the general public), logic still suggests that in the throes of orgasm Supergirl might lose control and contract her considerably powerful muscles around the penis inside of her—to great detriment. But this concern is also unfounded because the vagina wants this sex to happen as much as Kara does and actually expands to make things easier for everyone involved—including during orgasm. Sexual arousal leads to swelling in the vagina, causing it to become elongated and tented, either to improve the chance of pregnancy or just to accommodate penetration; doctors aren't sure. Whatever the reason, the inner two thirds of the vagina actually open up even more than usual during orgasm, creating a safe space for any visiting sexual organs.[154] Though it's true that some muscles tighten during orgasm, it's primarily the uterine muscles that are doing the contracting. Thankfully the uterus contracting bears no threat of strangling any precious body parts inside it as it sits above the vagina and is a no-fly zone for the penis. Vaginal contractions also happen, but it's exceedingly rare for them to be so intense as to make them painful as opposed to pleasurable for all involved.

So, contrary to what we might expect, Supergirl experiencing an orgasm would actually make it *less* likely for a penis to find itself on the wrong end of her super strength. Which means the best bet for Kara's sexual partner to ensure their penis's safety is to do everything they can to make her orgasm. And you better hope she's not faking it.

Born Under a Yellow Sun

Since we know Kara is likely capable of getting down and dirty with a measly human, the next question to answer is whether she is able to get pregnant from a human sperm and build herself a family here on Earth, if she so chooses. Her cousin Clark has had surprising success in this regard, as Lois Lane has given birth to their biological son Jonathan Kent in both the comics and the CW series *Superman and Lois*. This must be confounding to Larry Niven, who posited in "Man of Steel, Woman of Kleenex" that even if Lois Lane was safely impregnated with Kryptonian sperm by artificial insemination the results would still be disastrous because "when [the baby] starts to kick . . . he will kick his way out into open air, killing himself and his mother." This obviously assumes that the child would inherit Clark's super strength while in the womb, in which case Niven would be right; a human Lois could very easily be killed by a god-like baby inside of her. So how did this pregnancy come to term?

In some continuities this death sentence is avoided by Lois spending her pregnancy in Kandor, a Kryptonian city far away from Earth that has no yellow sun, thereby removing the superpowers of any Kryptonians who live, or are currently gestating, there. This is one viable explanation, but it's also possible that Lois carried her baby to term right here on Earth through the power of just having skin. Kryptonians receive their powers from our yellow sun and get especially powerful and rejuvenated when they are in direct sunlight, but a Kryptonian fetus in a womb has no chance to work on their tan and would likely remain powerless until birth, as UV light can only penetrate about 1 to 4 millimeters deep into the human body. A fetus is shielded by about 80 millimeters of skin and tissue, meaning there will likely be no ultraviolet rays—and thus, superpowers—in Lois's womb.[155] We see an example of what happens to a shielded Kryptonian on Earth in *The Flash* movie where we meet a Supergirl who has had all of her powers stripped away simply by being kept underground and out of direct sunlight while she has been on Earth. By this logic it makes sense that Lois's baby would remain powerless until birth since no UV rays could reach them, though it's probably smart to avoid any trips to the beach or a tanning booth during pregnancy, just in case.

So it's possible for a human woman and Kryptonian man to procreate, which is good for Lois and Clark, but what about Kara? Would a human sperm have any chance of penetrating a powerhouse Kryptonian egg or are those sperm going to crash into that egg like a brick wall? According to Dr. Jesse Ory, whom we met in our previous chapter about Wolverine's superpowered swimmers, the answer to this question lies in the source of Supergirl's strength (her literal strength, not like the power of love or something like that) and whether her powers are cellular or muscular in nature. "To really understand it you have to know the cellular basis of her strength. Is it just muscles . . . because if it's just muscles, then yes, they are not super eggs that have this, like, impenetrable barrier," says Dr. Ory.[156]

It turns out that human eggs are not made of muscle; they're made up of cells. Specifically, an egg is surrounded by a cellular barrier that a sperm has to be able to break down to fertilize the egg, so if Supergirl's strength is purely muscular in nature and her cells are normal, she should have no problem being impregnated from a human sperm. And we know that at least part of her strength is muscular. According to *DC Comics: Anatomy of a Metahuman*, Kryptonians are naturally stronger than humans because Krypton's gravitational pull was far greater than Earth's. This is similar to how the moon has a much weaker gravitation pull than Earth, allowing humans to jump almost twice as high up there and pick up objects that we could never lift on Earth's surface. But even though some of her strength can be attributed to her muscles, there is undeniably super stuff happening at the cellular level of Kara's body as well.

After all, the gravitation pull alone doesn't explain just how ridiculously strong Kryptonians are on Earth. Even *DC Comics: Anatomy of a Metahuman* states "there is more to Superman's strength than a simple gravitational disparity" and cites a Kryptonian's "unusual cell structure" as an explanation for their ability to absorb yellow sun radiation and process that energy as fuel for their superpowers.[157]

It becomes even more obvious that Supergirl's powers can't just be muscular in nature when we consider that she doesn't only have super strength, she also has X-ray vision, freeze breath, heat vision, flight, and possibly, like her cousin, the ability to shoot tiny versions of herself out of her fingers. If all of these powers could come from just being super jacked, a lot of people would be hitting the gym more regularly.

"It's not all muscle," agrees Dr. Ory. "There is something with their cellular structure that is probably super strong . . . a male Kryptonian could get a female human pregnant, but I don't think the reverse would be true, because how would the sperm get through the shell of that egg to fertilize it?"

This means that even though Kara can probably have sex with a human, her Kryptonian eggs are likely too powerful to be penetrated and fertilized by a human sperm. If she isn't trying to get pregnant, this is great news because it means she doesn't have to worry about birth control. If she is trying to get pregnant, well, she's probably going to have to turn those red sunlamps back on to take away her superpowers. Dr. Ory theorizes that if her powers are removed, conception with a human sperm is indeed possible. "If the sperm got through that outer shell, the rest should happen normally. There shouldn't be any problem."

Bottom line: Supergirl's hymen and orgasm pose little to no threat to her ability to have penetrative sex. But her vaginal muscles are so strong that the only way she can participate in sex with a human is to go all mind over matter on herself to relax her vaginal walls. If she can do this to the point where penetration is possible, it's unlikely her partner would suffer any ill effects from intercourse or orgasm, but she wouldn't be able to get pregnant by her partner unless her powers were temporarily removed. At least she can have sex, though, which is great news for Supergirl (even if it does mean she lost that "most tragic backstory" award) because if she couldn't have sex with humans that would limit her possible sexual partners to Comet the Super-Horse (we're not talking about it!) or other Kryptonians. And the only other Kryptonian she knows is her cousin, and they would never date, right?

Right?

Sexual Interlude #6: The Time Superman Tried to Marry His Cousin

Let's go back to a simpler time, when comics were campy, wholesome, and light-hearted. Like *Action Comics #289*, which tells the totally normal story of Superman trying to marry his teenage cousin Supergirl.

Released in 1962 and aptly titled "Superman's Super-Courtship," this fantastic tale does not get any saner through the detailed telling of it. The story starts with Supergirl asking Superman if he'll ever get married, to which he says no, he's too busy protecting the Earth. To which us Earthlings say, awesome! But Supergirl decides she must meddle in her cousin's life and proceeds to sneakily set Superman up on disastrous dates with famous women in history (oh yeah, there's casual time travel in this story; just go with it).

Anyway . . . following a particularly terrible date, Supergirl admits that she's been trying to set Superman up with a wife and apologizes for meddling with his life. And then this light-hearted story takes the creepiest U-turn ever when we learn that Superman actually isn't as opposed to marriage as he previously said. It's just that he totally, definitely wants to marry his underage cousin and explains the following to her while gently holding Supergirl's chin and tilting her head back:

> "If I ever **did** marry it would be to someone super and loveable like . . . **you**! We can't marry because we're cousins! Though cousins **can** marry on certain countries here on Earth . . . we're both from the planet **Krypton** where the marriage of cousins was **unlawful**!"[158]

So Superman basically just said if it wasn't against the law, he'd totally marry his teenage cousin. Lucky for him he lives in a comic book where all his crazy cousin-marrying fantasies can come true. Supergirl ends up being disturbingly supportive of the idea of them getting married and finds Superman the craziest loophole of all time to justify it. She opens a portal to an alternate dimension and finds a grown-up copy of herself, not related to Superman, and suggests he go marry her. Like, right now!

Instead of laughing and saying he was just joking around and that would be weird, Superman jumps at the chance to fulfill his cousin-marrying fantasy and flies off to the alternate reality faster than you can say, "You're supposed to be a hero, Superman!"

And wouldn't you know it, his alt-cousin is totally into it and agrees to marry him on the spot. They almost live happily ever after, too, but then the couple learns that the other Supergirl can't survive on our Earth. Since Superman promised to stay and protect us, he comes back to our dimension alone, leaving behind that random Supergirl clone whose life is now in shambles after having a brief taste of love.

It all ends with Superman heartbroken and Supergirl a guilt-ridden mess for having caused it all, but at least that means the moral of this story (and the only sane thing about it) is that you shouldn't try to marry your underage cousin. It just ends bad.

BATMAN HATES GUNS BECAUSE
HE SHOOTS BLANKS

"Tim Drake—or is it Wayne now? Adopted by Daddy Warbucks then?"
—Captain Boomerang to Tim Drake/Wayne, *Red Robin* #15

atman isn't the loner he wants you to think he is. Sure, the Dark
Knight likes to give the impression that he's a solitary warrior, taking on the dark underbelly of Gotham's criminals by himself and
swearing to uphold justice as the city's lone protector. He likes to brood
in a corner alone and tell the Justice League he doesn't work on a team,
or chase Catwoman across rooftops all night with no mention of having
anyone waiting for him at home. But the truth is that Batman rarely ever
works alone, because he has anywhere from one to four children living with
him at any given time, including Robins and former Robins named Dick
Grayson, Jason Todd, Tim Drake, and Damian Wayne.

Upon hearing about this overflow of children, one might think that
Bruce is throwing his "batarang" around with the ladies too much without wearing bat-protection, but the truth is most of those aforementioned
kids are around because he collects orphaned children the way some people collect Pokémon cards. Of the four Robins previously mentioned, only
Damian Wayne is biologically related to Bruce and even he wasn't conceived by normal means. Bruce's DNA was stolen by Talia al Ghul who

used it to grow Damian in an artificial womb. Which means that despite the fact that he has a literal child army running around the Batcave, Bruce has never naturally fathered a child. And there's a good chance that's because being Batman has taken such a toll on his body that it's made him physically unable to be a father (you could argue it's also made him emotionally unable to be a father, but that's a different discussion).

After all, Batman's lived a wild life. He's a world-class martial artist, he dresses as a bat to fight crime, he's the world's greatest detective, and sometimes he even goes to space to battle aliens. Those things are all categorically cool, but they're also things that are lowering his sperm count dramatically, which means if he did want to have a child with someone, his Batgun would be shooting blanks. (Not that he would use a gun, since he hates them, but you get the metaphor.) So let's take a look at just what Batman's been doing that decreases the population of his testicular Batcave.

Let's Get Physical

There are a lot of things that can lower a person's sperm count (most of them being things Batman has absolutely done, which we'll get into), but some of the things are just unfair, like exercising too much. Now to be clear, exercising regularly and maintaining a healthy body mass index is good for you and your sperm count, so please don't read this and then sit down and stop moving, because your little swimmers will, too. But studies have found that high-intensity exercise over a long period of time can lead to decreases in sperm density, motility, and morphology.[159] So working out too hard can make you have fewer sperm that don't swim well and look funny. In the same study, the worst culprit for sperm reduction was using a treadmill for too long and too hard, and people's sperm counts only got lower the longer they kept "overtraining." Considering Batman is basically a living weapon and one of the world's greatest martial artists, it's fair to assume he's working out a lot, and probably not skipping cardio day—and that's going to affect how many Bat-sperm his testicles can generate. The good news in this case is that the study also found that cutting back on intense exercise will bring a person's sperm quality and quantity back to the same level as before they started rocking out too hard at the gym. But Bruce isn't exactly known for taking things in life at a moderate and normal pace, so it might take a talking-to from Alfred about the Wayne legacy or something to actually get him to cool it with the high-intensity workouts.

But too much exercise is far from Bruce's only semen-killing issue. There are also the head injuries to consider. Oh, the head injuries! Batman's cowl may be reinforced to protect him, but that doesn't change the fact that he has taken some hella bad hits to the noggin over the years. Whether it's falling off a skyscraper to land on a car in *The Dark Knight* or getting fully shot in the head by the Riddler in *Batman Forever* or fracturing his skull in a fight with Catwoman in the comics, his head's taken some blows that his testicles are definitely feeling. It turns out that people who suffer from traumatic brain injuries or concussions can see surprising side effects in their sex lives, such as:

- changes in sexual desire
- difficulty becoming sexually aroused or maintaining an erection
- difficulty reaching orgasm
- decreased sperm production[160]

It's theorized that the low sperm count in people with head injuries is due to damage in the areas of the brain that stimulate production of sex hormones. But no matter what the reason, the fact remains that if you get hit in the head a lot, or even just once really hard, there's a good chance it will be detrimental to your sex life in general, your sperm count specifically, and your ability to get your Dark Knight rising, so to speak, creating a terrible trio of reproductive issues. So that's two strikes against Bruce's potential to have any more Bat-kids running around his belfry.

The third obstacle in the way of Batman's semen production is the Batman costume itself. Even though he's promised never to take a life, his vigilante wardrobe choices are killing millions of Bat-sperm every day.

According to a 2016 study in the journal *Human Reproduction*, wearing tight-fitting underwear can drastically lower your sperm count.[161] Admittedly, the study was looking at the difference between people who wear boxers as opposed to briefs, not boxers versus spandex/Kevlar combination briefs, but the conclusion reached was that any underwear that holds your testicles close to your body, instead of letting them dangle, will lower your sperm count. The reason for this spermicidal difference in underwear is because the testicles need to be a little cooler than the rest of the body to make the best sperm. While wearing boxers, the testicles can hang below the torso, staying about four to six degrees cooler than the rest of the body. But when you slap on a pair of briefs, the testicles get mashed into the rest of the body and heat up, which can harm sperm production, even if you wear the briefs on the outside of your outfit like Batman does. The testicles can also be heated up by sitting for long periods, like when you're working for hours at the Batcomputer, so Batman may want to consider loosening up his utility belt and investing in a standing desk while he's solving mysteries in the Batcave.

Toxins, Herbicides, and Heavy Metals

But there are even more problems that Batman's job is creating for his testicles, because exposure to toxins, such as herbicides and heavy metals, can also affect a person's sperm count.[162] We know Batman's definitely worked with herbicides while fighting Poison Ivy, and studies show that prolonged exposure to pretty much all of them can reduce sperm count and motility. As for heavy metals, we also know that Batman works with lead pretty frequently. This is the only substance that his good friend Superman can't see through with his X-ray vision, and even though Bruce trusts the big blue Boy Scout almost implicitly, he also enjoys his privacy and has been known to line his cave, office, and personal belongings in lead. Just to be safe. But he totally trusts you, Clark, for real. The bad news for Bruce is that lead is one of the worst villains to his personal Batcave, as it not only reduces sperm concentration but also causes testicular damage. But it's all worth it if Clark can't peek at his birthday presents, I guess.

Interestingly, though, Joker Gas, the toxin that Batman is perhaps exposed to the most, may be causing no harmful aftereffects (at least not to his testicles). The exact formula for Joker Gas has never been released, but it's safe to assume that at least one of the components is nitrous oxide, also known as laughing gas, most commonly used in medical procedures. And according to a report by Stanford University, even lengthy exposure to nitrous oxide has no effect on sperm production or increase in sperm abnormalities.[163] So even if Batman got dosed with Joker Gas, his testicles are safe, which is one reason to smile (the second reason to smile is the Joker Gas itself, but that's more of an involuntary thing).

The Radiation Situation

So far, Batman's sperm are fighting an uphill battle against exercise, head injuries, tight costumes, and toxins, but we haven't even gotten to sperm's arch-nemesis yet, so let's talk about radiation. As it so happens, radiation is an absolute juggernaut in the fight against sperm, and it may be the first opponent that Batman can't defeat. We discussed in an earlier chapter how humans exposed to radiation have a surprisingly low risk of having children with mutations or abnormalities, but we can't forget that that same radiation can absolutely cause temporary or permanent sterility in the testicles. In the real world, radiation therapy in cancer patients commonly kills sperm cells and the stem cells that make sperm, resulting in slow sperm production for years after treatment or even permanent infertility in patients. Now, Batman hasn't had cancer, but he has been exposed to a specific radioactive material for long periods of time. Yeah, we're talking about Kryptonite.

In *Batman v. Superman: Dawn of Justice* (2016), we see Batman using Kryptonite smoke bombs and yielding a Kryptonite spear in his fight against

Superman, while in the comics and cartoon shows, he owns a Kryptonite ring to be used in emergencies to fight a mind-controlled Superman or any evil Kryptonian who may try to start shit on Earth. No matter what universe we're talking about, Batman almost assuredly has a rock so radioactive it can kill the strongest person on the planet in a matter of minutes, and he's just carrying it around as though nothing bad could happen because he's Batman. Well, something very bad could happen from being exposed to Kryptonite, and we can figure out just how bad it might be.

Radiation dosage is measured in rems, and we're told in an issue of *Superman* from 1990 that the radiation emitted by Kryptonite is 75 rems.[164] So, is that bad for Bruce's little Bat-mites? According to the Committee on the Biological Effects of Ionizing Radiation, the testes can become temporarily sterile with a dose of just 15 rems of radiation, and Kryptonite emits five times that amount, so, yeah, it's probably bad. Just ask Lex Luthor, who wore a Kryptonite ring for years to keep Superman away from him and then had to have his hand amputated because the radiation from the Kryptonite had given him cancer. That's pretty terrible, but there is some good news. It turns out that permanently sterilizing the testicles would take a dose of about 350 rems of radiation at once,[165] which is well above Kryptonite's output. So if Bruce gets rid of his Kryptonian deterrent ring, his sperm count could slowly ramp back up in a few years, but he'll probably never get it super high unless he plans to stop all the other sperm-killing activities he loves, like wearing the tight costumes, exercising, and getting head injuries.

But there are other forms of radiation besides Kryptonite. We should also talk about X-rays for a moment, specifically the ones that come out of Superman's eyes. For the average person, an X-ray involves being exposed to a dose of radiation in a hospital that is supposedly small but still makes the doctors and nurses hide in another room, so probably isn't great for you. But Batman may be the only person who gets x-rayed more by his best friend than by a machine, and that's a good thing because Superman is actually providing a clean X-ray service that must be a relief to Batman's balls, as explained in *DC Comics: Anatomy of a Metahuman*:

While [Superman] has the ability to see through all materials except lead, the term "X-Ray vision" is actually a misnomer, considering that the objects he scans are not irradiated.[166]

It turns out Superman's X-ray vision doesn't use radiation at all but just allows him to sense the decay of particles within matter and observe an object's layers in that way. This at least means that Batman isn't getting a dose of radiation every time Superman uses his X-ray vision around him. Now, if only he can stop exercising and getting hit on the head, get a looser costume, avoid exposure to toxins, and never pull out his Kryptonite ring again, he may just have a chance of getting his sperm count up and having a biological child with someone. But let's be real, it's easier for Batman to just adopt. At this point the orphanage is probably offering some kind of punch card where he gets the tenth sidekick free, and everyone loves a deal, even Batman.

Part 5

DO IT LIKE AN ANIMAL

Insect and Animal Powers in the Bedroom

TEENAGE MUTANT PENIS TURTLES

"She's so hot I can feel my shell tightening."
—Michelangelo, *Teenage Mutant Ninja Turtles* (2014)

The Teenage Mutant Ninja Turtles are fun guys. They run around in the shadows of New York fighting Shredder, eating pizza, skateboarding, and making immature jokes, because even though they're giant turtles, they're also teenagers. But the teenage years aren't just for goofing around, they're also when most young men experience a sexual awakening. As puberty arrives, they start to notice their bodies changing, not because of radioactive ooze (in most cases) but because of hormones, and the ninja turtles are no different.

In almost every iteration of the turtle franchise, our heroes appear to be in the throes of puberty yet none of our ninja teens have ever had a long-term relationship, which means that overwhelmingly the turtles have pretty negligible sex lives (unless we count the fact that Donatello does machines, but that's a different essay entirely). But why the lack of love for our mean green heroes? The bestiality-adjacent implications of a human and giant turtle hooking up could be one reason to keep April O'Neil from engaging in a relationship with one of the turtles, but there have been multiple other mutant turtles introduced to the canon, including Mona Lisa and Venus de Milo, and yet they've never done more than kiss one of the boys on the cheek and then disappear. Perhaps this lack of

romantic interest is because the turtles are in their mid-teens and not looking for anything serious at the moment? But eventually they will age into
the Twenty-Something Mutant Ninja Turtles, which is when we will find
out why they were never given love interests: because when they become
interested in having sex, the ninja turtles will be absolutely terrifying, in
ways that I'm obligated to explore with you right now.

Now, the Teenage Mutant Ninja Turtles did not start out as teenagers,
mutants, or ninjas. Leonardo, Michelangelo, Raphael, and Donatello were
born as regular turtles who were exposed to Mutagen, a chemical ooze that
mixes a creature's DNA with the last living thing it touched, when they
were babies. In the case of the turtles, they were last touched by the human
who kept them as pets and were thus mutated into turtle-human hybrids.
Physically, the turtles seem to have retained most of their animal characteristics other than the fact that they can walk upright, so as we discuss the
horrifying potential sex lives of these sewer-dwelling heroes we'll assume
that their sexual organs and habits are the same as their unmutated turtle
brethren out in nature. If you're wondering just what those turtle mating
habits are like, then I'M SO SORRY THIS IS GOING TO BE HORRIBLE—I
HOPE YOU STILL LOVE THE NINJA TURTLES AFTER THIS!

Sexual Awakening in the Sewers

Okay, well, let's start off easy and talk about turtle puberty and when it
happens. To know exactly what age the ninja turtles would reach sexual
maturity and be ready to start knocking shells, we'd have to know exactly
what species of turtle they are, and unfortunately there isn't a lot of consensus in the TMNT continuity in that regard. In some cartoons they are
theorized to be diamondback terrapins; some say common box turtles;
others say red-eared sliders. Basically, the only thing every iteration of the
turtles can agree on is that they are, in fact, turtles. Luckily for us, all these
species reach sexual maturity when they are anywhere from two to five
years old. Thanks to their very catchy name, we know for sure that the

ninja turtles are teenagers, so we can say they've definitely reached sexual puberty. In fact, in turtle years our green heroes are full-on adults, which is nice because it makes it less weird to talk about their sex lives (but also, they're turtles—who cares). Therefore, we can confirm that the ninja turtles are sexually mature, though they are immature in almost every other way. This means that if their creators gave them any form of serious love interest, they'd be physically capable and interested in having sex, which would be very unfortunate for their potential lovers, mostly due to their giant, terrifying penises.

Size Matters

Now you may be saying, what penises? You've probably seen your fair share of TMNT cartoons and movies and I bet you've never once seen a penis anywhere on a ninja turtle (unless you're partaking in some interesting internet searches, but that's your own business). You may have even examined a non-ninja turtle in real life and come away thinking, nope, no penis there. And it's true, regular turtles have no visible penis most of the time, which means their cartoon counterparts are actually anatomically correct as far as turtles go. But don't let their smooth shells fool you. Turtles are, in fact, very well endowed, and their penises are also ninjas—hard to spot until they're right on top of you.

Instead of letting their nunchucks hang out, exposed and vulnerable like most species do, turtles fold their penises up and keep them safely tucked inside their shells, only popping them out when they're needed for mating. When they do unsheathe those bad boys, you'll absolutely know it because they're hard to miss, hard to forget, and also just plain hard (and long). A turtle's flaccid penis is so long that it has to be folded up in order to be hidden away in its shell, but a turtle's fully erect penis is about 50 percent longer and 75 percent wider than that, which translates to a hard penis that's about half the length of its body.[167] Half the length! For a diamondback terrapin, that equals a penis that's about two and a half inches long. For a six-foot-two anthropomorphic ninja turtle, that equals a penis that's about 2 feet 8 inches high. Yeah, high. You see, turtle penises curve up the length of their body and since the ninja turtles stand upright, their giant penises are going to be shooting straight for the moon. In an earlier section we talked about how Reed Richards, a man who went to space to get super stretching powers, can stretch his erect penis to be about 7 feet and 7 inches. The ninja turtles, using only the attributes Mother Nature graced them with, have penises almost half that enormous size.

Oh, and this is where the body horror is turned up to eleven. Their penises aren't just big—they've also got a blossoming head at the end that they can open and close at will. A kind description of their penises would compare them to a big, flared-open orchid[168] but a more accurate description is that they look like the head of the Demogorgon in *Stranger Things*, a haunting demonic monster that makes you grateful the turtles wear those giant trench coats all the time when they're in public. And we should be even more grateful that they've never had a love interest who's had to face one of these beasts in the bedroom, especially considering the people the turtles are canonically most interested in are regular humans like April O'Neil and Shredder's daughter Karai. There is literally nothing those women could do with a three-foot-long, blossoming penis other than run away as quickly as possible.

What's even more haunting than the appearance of their penis, though, is what they do with it. In the wild, turtles get their mega penises out whenever they're about to mate with a female turtle, and the mating process . . . isn't great. First, they climb on top of their potential girlfriend, then use their claws to latch on to her shell in a ninja-esque death grip that can be physically damaging to both parties. Once he's in place, the male turtle's penis emerges and penetrates the female to initiate sex, an act that scientists have described as "kind of like watching two boulders with flippers getting it on," which is probably a letdown for anyone who ran one of the internet searches for turtle penises I mentioned earlier.[169]

If boulder-sex is something you want to watch happen for yourself, though, you won't exactly have to rush to the beach to catch it before it's over, as turtles have been known to hold this mating position for up to twenty-four hours. Talk about turtle power. This explains how four turtles are consistently able to defeat dozens of enemies in battle every week without getting tired. Even more impressive than their stamina (or terrifying, depending on your point of view) is that other male turtles sometimes try to knock the first male off to take his place on top of the female. Considering the combative nature of our four favorite turtles, and how they are all sometimes interested in the same girl, this seems like something they might very well do in a romantic setting, even though they definitely shouldn't, as it's both rude and a mood killer. At least buy a girl a pizza first.

Multipurpose Penises

So that's the story of the giant penises that a potential turtle love interest would have to deal with if they were to ever have sex. But wait, our penis journey isn't over, as it turns out sex is not the only time turtles reveal their rocking manhoods; they will also literally let their penises come out to play. Scientists have found that turtles in the wild will "expose their impressive genitals for fun, or when bored."[170] That means when Leonardo, Michelangelo, Raphael, and Donatello don't have anything to do down in the sewer they may just shoot their penises out and partake in literal dick-measuring competitions. Considering those penises come out erect and almost 3 feet long, it feels like dick-sword fights would also absolutely happen in the turtle lair at some point, hopefully not when April's visiting or they will never see that girl again. She might be a tough-as-nails journalist, but even scientists who study turtles full time have described their penis displays as startling and not for the faint of heart. As one turtle researcher observed:

Sometimes males will distend their organ neither while mating, nor while in the presence of females. Usually while bathing or drinking, the turtle will submerge the front half of his body, rise up on his back legs, and drop his organ through the cloaca. It is a sight to behold, and one that can startle both novice and experienced herpetoculturalists alike.[171]

Okay, weird, but that's not even the final reason that turtles unsheathe their giant personal weapons. They've also been known to shoot them out in displays of aggression to intimidate their enemies. And guess what the ninja turtles have? A ton of enemies! So when the evil Shredder attacks, these turtle boys are gonna cut him no slack by coming at him with their three-foot-high penises that open and close at the end like a demon's mouth while shouting "Cowabunga!" at the top of their lungs. I'm guessing the Foot Clan hasn't exactly trained for this scenario and would be immediately surrendering.

At the end of the day, it's clearly for the best that the writers of the Teenage Mutant Ninja Turtles chose to make our green heroes perpetually single so we don't have to think about these extreme turtle appendages in battle or the bedroom, and wonder how any potential relationship with one of them might work. That's a secret of the ooze that they're welcome to keep to themselves. But at least our unbetrothed boys can still have penis-sword fights in the sewer. Honestly, it sounds kind of fun.

GETTING IN TOO DEEP WITH THE DEEP

"I like you, too, you know that, let's not rush into anything too fast."
—The Deep to a dolphin, *The Boys*, season 1, episode 4

We've discussed the sex lives of a lot of superheroes in this book and considered a range of super sex-adjacent topics like vampire erections, immortal sperm regeneration, and vaginas of steel. But at the end of the day, despite combining these theories with scientific facts, most of these discussions are purely hypothetical because we know very little about the actual sex lives of most superheroes. Despite these characters being played by some of the most beautiful actors on the planet, most superhero media is a surprisingly sexless affair. Heck, it took the Marvel Cinematic Universe thirteen years to show a single sex scene, and that was in 2021's *Eternals* between two characters who (spoiler) ended up being robots and weren't even human.

This lack of information regarding the fine details of the sex lives of superheroes has led to a lot of guess work in this book about what Marvel and DC superheroes are actually like when it comes to sex. But there's one group of heroes we don't have to speculate about because we know exactly what they do in the bedroom, or in space, or underwater, or whatever other weird place they want to have sex. I'm talking about the characters from Amazon's *The Boys*, who have pretty much every aspect of their sex lives depicted on screen in shocking and graphic detail. Whether it's

Homelander having laser sex with Stormfront, a shrinking man accidentally exploding his boyfriend's penis off, or a bunch of characters attending
an orgy called Herogasm, *The Boys* don't leave a lot to the sexual imagination. And no one encapsulates this fact better than Kevin Moskowitz, also
known as the Deep, who brings a whole new meaning to the phrase "sleep
with the fishes." A clear parody of Aquaman, the Deep is able to breathe
underwater and talk to fish; unlike Aquaman, though, he also has sex with
those fish. It's, like, his thing. We already know everything about the sex
lives of the characters on the show, but we don't know about the sex lives
of the Deep's aquatic sexual partners, which, frankly, might be the weirdest
of them all.

Riding the Dolphin

Let's start with season 1, episode 4 of *The Boys*, when the Deep tried to
commit a rare good deed and free a dolphin from an aquarium, though he
had some clear sexual ulterior motives for doing so. As the Deep escapes in
a getaway van with the dolphin, he is bombarded with sexual requests from
the marine mammal, which the Deep is unable to act on at the moment as
he's currently driving toward the ocean. The Deep insists that they don't
have to rush into anything too fast but eventually concedes to touch "it"
(the dolphin's penis) because the animal will not stop insisting they have
sex. It might sound over the top for a dolphin to be that aggressive about
having sex with a human, but it turns out it's actually the most realistic
part of the whole scene. You see, dolphins love to fuck. If you're near a dolphin while reading this, it probably wants to have sex right now, so avoid
eye contact with it and just keep reading.

While most animals only mate for procreation, there are four lucky
species out there that have sex for pleasure, and those evolutionary lottery
winners are pigs, bonobos, humans, and, of course, dolphins. And boy do
they have sex. Technically dolphins have a mating season, but it doesn't
really matter because they fuck all year round, in a variety of different

ways, including some that are too gross and graphic even for a show as sexually explicit as *The Boys*.

For example, female dolphins have a clitoris with erectile tissue and nerve bundles that scientists think makes them capable of orgasm, but male dolphins are *definitely* capable of orgasm, as they have been known to masturbate with eels or dead fish heads wrapped around their penis for stimulation.[172] They're able to hold on to these sex accessories thanks to their prehensile penis, which has been described as "absurdly dexterous" and able to "swivel, grab and grope, much like a human hand."[173] Forget the Deep, it's starting to sound like the dolphins are the ones who actually have super powers in this scenario.

It also might seem ridiculous that a dolphin would be attracted to a human and proposition him for sex, but it's not at all unprecedented. Back in 2002, a dolphin named Georges caused an uproar in Weymouth, England, when he became "sexually aggressive" with people who were swimming in the harbor and tried to mate with several divers.[174] After a few months, Georges eventually moved back out to open water, but never forgot the sweet siren call of the people of Weymouth, as this sexual deviant came back to menace the population every year for nearly a decade. To help with the situation, the town called in Ric O'Barry, the trainer of TV's Flipper, who wasn't surprised by the dolphin's interest in the human form. "When dolphins get sexually excited," said O'Barry in an interview with CNN about Georges, "they try to isolate a swimmer, normally female. They do this by circling around the individual and gradually move them away from the beach, boat or crowd of people." It may not be very flattering to consider that dolphins will have sex with pretty much anything, whether that be a human or a decapitated fish head, but it does make it wildly possible that the dolphin the Deep is rescuing sincerely wants to have sex with him. And the fact that the Deep is a guy also wouldn't matter, because dolphins are also open-minded as hell.

Researchers have found that male dolphins in the wild are frequently found to be gay or bisexual, with some only mating with male partners and others mating with males and females, so it's completely in character that this dolphin would be attracted to the Deep as a potential mate, despite him being human and male. Unfortunately, the Deep never has a chance to further his relationship with this dolphin as it is thrown through the windshield of his van, then run over by a truck and killed in a scene that manages to be both tragic and hilarious, but if the Deep *had* managed to have sex with his flippered friend, he might have ended up with more than he bargained for.

Male dolphins have been known to go absolutely hog wild when they have sex, especially with other males. Dolphins will stimulate same-sex partners with every part of their body, including their snout, flippers, tails, and genitals—so anything they can rub against their partner, they will. But they don't stop at rubbing. Male dolphins will also have anal sex with each other and penetrate each other's blowholes as a sexual act.[175] Basically, they will use every hole and appendage they have for a fully immersive sexual experience that would put most of us to shame.

But there's one catch to their aquatic sexual free-for-all: it doesn't last for long. Dolphins have a more intense sex drive than humans, but for the most part they get in and then get out almost immediately. Dolphins don't engage in foreplay; instead, they get erect almost instantly and then have sex for about ten seconds before ejaculating.[176] That's plenty of time if you're the Flash, but for any other human or superhuman, that's gonna be a pretty unsatisfying sexual experience. As mentioned, though, dolphins *love* sex and have a short refractory period that allows them to ejaculate several times an hour, so they can get flipping again pretty quickly, but they'll still only last about ten seconds. They're here for a good time, not a long time. So if the Deep wants to get with an aquatic lover, a dolphin might not be right for him, but that's okay, because we know that he's already branched out with other gilled guys and gals.

Eating Out

Which brings us to Timothy and Ambrosius, the Deep's other aquatic love interests, both of whom are octopi. Timothy is a palm-sized octopus that lives in an aquarium next to the Deep's bed, which we learn is not an accidental placement. On the show we see the Deep's relationship with Timothy is only verbal but highly sexually charged, as the Deep enjoys speaking directly to Timothy and making eye contact with him in his aquarium while he watches the Deep have sex with his human wife.

This blossoming relationship is brought to an abrupt end when Homelander forces the Deep to eat Timothy alive, and not in a fun, sexual way, but in a sad and upsetting way, as many things are that happen on *The Boys*. The Deep tells us that Timothy is begging for his life as he eats him, but oddly enough this fate is no worse than what he would experience out in the ocean, as many male octopi are killed and eaten by their female suitors, either before or after sex. In fact, most males are so scared of females that they will put a rock between them while copulating as a form of defense, or hide in a small adjacent den from a girl and just stick out their reproductive arm to have sex with her, like a human jutting out just a leg from underneath the covers for a monster to grab.[177] Now the Deep never actually has sex with Timothy, perhaps because male octopi are picky when it comes to lovers, but luckily for the Deep, female octopi will have sex with pretty much anyone. Enter Ambrosius, a female octopus and the Deep's first (verified) aquatic lover.

Octopussy

The Deep meets Ambrosius at Herogasm, a giant orgy for superhumans, but instead of having sex with one of the dozens of humans who offers, the Deep heads straight for Ambrosius's aquarium and they immediately begin to bone. It's interesting to note that the Deep's ability to talk to sea creatures means that, unlike pretty much any other act of bestiality, their relationship is fully consensual, and I leave it up to you, dear reader, to decide if that makes the things they do better or worse. What it does mean, though, is that Ambrosius can tell the Deep all about octopus mating habits, which would make him more informed than most scientists studying this field, as the sex lives of fewer than 10 percent of octopus species have even been studied by humans.

What we do know is that octopi don't seem to have sex for fun like dolphins and humans, but other than that, the Deep and Ambrosius might be pretty compatible. In the ocean, Ambrosius's sexual escapades would involve finding a male with a large ligula. This is a special reproductive arm on the male octopus that doesn't have suckers, and acts more like a penis, as the ligula has erectile tissue and gets larger during mating. The ligula also releases sperm, but not in the same way a penis does. Instead of releasing semen, the male's ligula releases a spermatophore inside the female, which is basically a capsule of sperm that the female stores in her body until she is ready to fertilize her eggs.[178] Pretty normal so far. Oh, almost forgot, the male has to insert his penis right next to her eye because her ovaries are in her head. Which means when they have sex, the Deep would have to penetrate Ambrosius right near her brain, unless of course they have oral sex.

Octopus ladies do indeed have a mouth, but it's on the underside of their body and they don't use it during sex, with good reason. It's the only part on their entire body that is hard and unforgiving, as the mouth surrounds their beak, which is made of keratin, the same material our fingernails are made of. But even if the Deep wants to risk getting his penis clawed up by her beak, it's important to know that octopus mouths also secrete a venom that can nausea, vomiting, and sometimes death in humans.[179] There's no information on what that venom would specifically do to a penis upon contact, but logic tells us it would be nothing good. This means that the Deep and Ambrosius will need to have a long talk about how exactly this sexual relationship is going to work in regards to specific holes. They'll also need to discuss just how long they want to go at it, because while humans have intercourse for about three to seven minutes on average, octopi mate for three to four *hours*, so Ambrosius might find herself slightly unsatisfied when she finds out her partner can go deep, but not long.

Probably the greatest factor standing in the way of their relationship (aside from being a human and an octopus) is that an octopus dies after having sex. Now, they don't die immediately, they're more like Padme in the *Star Wars* prequels—after they have kids they just kind of lose their will to live. Called senescence, this part of the octopus life cycle is like a form of underwater dementia that happens after mating, when the octopus stops eating and then either starves to death or is eaten by a prey animal that takes advantage of their weakened state.[180] Before the Deep eats Timothy, the octopus begs for his life and says he has kids. If this is true then the Deep can take some comfort in the fact that Timothy wasn't long for this world anyway, as senescence would overtake him shortly after the birth of his children, causing him to die within the month. However, Ambrosius is a different story, because instead of killing her, her relationship with the Deep might just be saving her life. A male octopus will die shortly after he mates, but a female octopus will only succumb to senescence after her eggs are fertilized and cared for. Since the Deep is a human and can't fertilize her eggs, it's very possible that Ambrosius can have a sex life with him that won't trigger her going into a death spiral that eventually kills her. Honestly, this might be the first life the Deep has ever saved. But it's also still really gross.

We've looked at the sexual history of the Deep and various marine life, from dolphin to octopi, male to female, and learned that he may not be very heroic, but he's definitely had a super weird sex life thus far. And there's also no telling what the future will hold for the character. Perhaps he'll do the most shocking thing of all and settle down with a single partner, or only have sex with humans going forward, but that seems unlikely. After all, the Deep knows better than anyone that there are plenty of fish in the sea, and he wants to bang them all.

Since we're on the topic of humans having sex with animals, let's talk about . . .

Sexual Interlude #7: The Time Loki Gave Birth to a Horse

Name: Sleipnir
Occupation: Steed to the Throne of Asgard
Known Relatives: Svaðilfari (father), Loki (mother)
—Marvel Pets Handbook[181]

As the god of mischief, Loki's gotten himself into a few interesting situations over the years. We've seen Loki die one to three times (depending on who you ask), impersonate his own father to claim the throne of Asgard, and even fall in love with a version of himself from another dimension in an impressive display of narcissism. And that just covers what he's done in the MCU. As a figure in Norse mythology, Loki has more than eight hundred years of wild adventures under his belt, and none are as crazy as the time he gave birth to a horse (while he was also a horse).

The story goes like this: one day Loki convinced the gods of Asgard to make a deal wherein they would give a stonemason the sun, the moon, and the goddess Freya herself if he could build the wall around Asgard in three seasons with the help of "no man." This seemed like a pretty good deal to the Asgardians because there was no way one guy could build a wall that fast alone, *but* they failed to specify that the stonemason couldn't use his horse to help him. And his horse just happened to be Svaðilfari, who was like the Thor of horses and could move huge amounts of stone and rock every day and just ruled at building walls. As the deadline got close, the wall was looking pretty good, which was bad news for Loki as this deal was his idea.

Since the gods absolutely didn't want to pay this guy, they told Loki that if he didn't stop the builder from finishing the wall on time, they would kill our favorite god of mischief. Very much wanting to live, Loki then either made the ultimate sacrifice play or took this as his chance to finally indulge in his long-hidden horse desires, turning himself into a sexy mare to seduce the super stallion working on the wall. Once he'd braided his tail and put on his horse makeup, Loki ran out of the forest in front of Svaðilfari, and he was just so sexy that the horse broke his tackle, left his master, and ran after Loki-horse into the night, making it impossible to keep working on the wall.

As far as schemes go it was pretty successful, as the wall wasn't finished on time, but to make sure the stallion stayed distracted Loki had to let the other horse, uh, take their relationship to the next level, for the entire night. How do we know for sure that Loki got mounted that night? Well, a few months later Loki gave birth to an eight-legged foal named Sleipnir, which he then gave to Odin. Why does the horse have eight legs? Who the hell knows—maybe Loki also turned into a spider that night for some side action. He's the god of mischief, he does what he wants, and what he wanted was to have sex with a horse and then give birth to a baby horse.

But Sleipnir doesn't just exist in Norse mythology; he also makes a blink-and-you'll-miss-it appearance in the first *Thor* movie, where he is being ridden by Odin into Jotunheim, and he is also listed as Loki's child in the official *Marvel Pets Handbook*. Which means that no matter what dimension you're in, you can be fairly certain that Loki gave birth to a horse at some point just to get out of a bet. To be fair, though, he gave birth to one hell of a horse. Sleipnir is generally considered "the best horse among gods and men." He's such a good horse that, despite him literally being his grandson, Odin rode that thing everywhere, into every battle and even Hel itself. Thus proving that Sleipnir was a pretty sweet ride, just like his mother.

THE REAL REASON HOWARD
THE DUCK WEARS PANTS

"You think I might find happiness in the animal kingdom, Duckie?"
—Beverly Switzler, *Howard the Duck* (1986)

Howard the Duck first appeared in Marvel Comics in 1973 as an anthropomorphic, pants-less, cigar-smoking duck who provided a satirical take on the state of the world that struck a chord with many readers. There were some that were less enamored with Howard, however, including the Walt Disney Company, who threatened to sue Marvel due to Howard's physical similarity to their character Donald Duck. Having an aversion to being sued by one of the biggest companies in the world, Marvel reached an agreement with Disney in 1977 to redesign the character to be less Donald-like, specifically by giving Howard pants.

It was around this time that Howard's popularity started to wane, not because of the pants, but because fans became divided on the adult content and political satire in his comic. Fans were less divided on his 1986 self-titled movie, though, which was an undisputed flop despite being produced as a passion project by George "Star Wars" Lucas himself, proving that cinematic lightning is not guaranteed to strike twice. One of the film's most famous failures of a scene involves Lea Thompson's human character, Beverly Switzler, getting into bed and trying to seduce Howard, who is very much a three-foot-tall talking duck. Beverly only manages to kiss Howard on the bill before other characters burst in, but if the scene had continued uninterrupted, and this human woman fully attempted to have sex with this outer space duck, the movie would have quickly changed from a comedy into a horror movie. Why? Because those court-appointed pants that Howard wears are hiding his terrible duck penis, nature's most horrifying and constantly evolving mistake. And what's even worse than this nightmare sexual organ is exactly what Howard uses it for.

Dating in Duckworld

Before we talk about the natural endowment of ducks, let's venture into a safer venue: duck mating habits. Like a lot of species, male ducks often try to woo females into mating with them, employing several different methods. The males can draw a lady's attention by being incredibly handsome, by being a great duck singer, or by enticing her with a mating dance—or by being a fowl triple threat and doing all three. This is referred to as the Hugh Jackman of mating habits.

If the male duck doesn't dance, sing, or have a rocking bod, it can be pretty much guaranteed a female won't show any interest in him, which might be why Howard is so surprised when Beverly tries to seduce him. In his society, sex doesn't happen without a song and dance number first, which sounds whimsical and fun but that's only because we haven't gotten into the nitty-gritty details of duck sex yet. And we can confirm that Howard has had sex back on Duckworld (which is the actual name of Howard's home planet and not one of my grasping attempts at humor). In one scene, Howard falls asleep on the couch and Beverly goes through his wallet, finding a tiny, open but unused condom inside. Upon seeing it she smiles to herself, presumably because now she knows that Howard fucks and she might be able to get a piece of that giant fowl for herself, proven by the fact that she just kind of jumps into bed with him shortly thereafter. If she had bothered to unfurl that tiny condom, though, she probably would have ended up throwing it away in horror as she gazed upon what would be the prophylactic equivalent of a Slinky.

The Long and Sharp of Duck Penises

You see, ducks have penises. And if you're thinking about how you've never seen a bird with a penis, that's because 97 percent of birds don't have them.[182] Basically just ducks do. And they don't just have penises; they have *terrifying* penises. Beverly Switzler needs to get down on her knees and pray in gratitude every night that her se-duck-tion attempts got interrupted before a duck penis ever got anywhere close to her. Or perhaps I should say "closer to her," because those things are long! Ducks are considered one of the most well-endowed vertebrates on the planet, with a penis to body size ratio that is staggering. For example, the Argentinian lake duck has a penis that's four inches longer than the length of its body.[183] It is truly more penis than duck. If we scale up those proportions for Howard, who is 3 feet tall, that means his front-facing duck-tail would be 4 feet long when extended. Dear God, that condom would have been unfurling for hours. And that might just be Howard's off-season penis. During mating season a duck's penis can grow up to 10 percent bigger than they are during the rest of the year, so plan accordingly, Beverly.[184]

The only good news if you're a human female encountering a duck penis is that they're pretty flexible when erect, all things considered. The bad news is everything else, like the fact that these reproductive ropes they're packing are covered with tiny teeth to hook onto the interior of a female's reproductive tract during penetration. This means that once the penis is in, it stays in until the male decides he's done. Geez. Okay, so duck schlongs are superlong and ribbed not-for-her pleasure, but that's not even the worst of it.

Duck penises are also corkscrew shaped, spiraling counter-clockwise with six to ten full twists in them, which is more than most actual corkscrews.[185] When the penis is completely unfurled, the male duck looks more like he's about to start drilling into the ground for oil than attempt any kind of sexual feat. That must be one hell of a song and dance that male ducks perform to convince the ladies to let them use those things on them. A sensible female duck would fly for the hills the second she sees one of these spikey drill bits coming toward her most sensitive areas, but unfortunately that's not much of an option because these horrible sexual organs move too fast to be avoided. Unlike most penises out there, duck dicks don't need a few minutes to come to attention, as they don't actually become engorged with blood to become erect. Instead, male ducks will do their mating rituals then strategically line themselves up behind a female and eject their penis into her vagina like a shotgun blast.[186] That metaphor might be inaccurate only because a duck's penis shoots out in one third of a second, and a shotgun blast might actually take longer than that.

To recap, sex with Howard could potentially involve a four-foot-long duck penis suddenly appearing inside you in a corkscrew motion that then latches onto the inside of your body with a bunch of little spikes. This sounds less like having sex and more like one of the deathtraps Jigsaw would set up in the *Saw* movies to kill you. No thank you.

Reproductive Defense

As awful as all of this sounds, if Beverly does decide to go through with this horrific sexual encounter, she can at least be assured that Howard is a nice guy who will treat her right, as he's seen protecting her from thugs at several points in the movie. This is sweet and fairly standard for ducks, as males and females will generally bond for a whole mating season and stay loyal to each other. Unfortunately, that's not true for all male ducks.

Out in the wild some males have been known to use their Quack-Fu for "forced copulation" when a female refuses to have sex with them (probably because she saw a duck penis once and is staying as far away from them as possible). This involves an unpaired male duck physically bullying a female into sex instead of wooing her with a song and dance routine. It's hard to play defense against a jerk with a penis that shoots out faster than a speeding bullet, but nature found a way by giving female ducks a vagina with more twists and turns than a labyrinth. This means that if a male has penetrated her against her will the female can send his penis down the wrong reproductive path and make sure he doesn't actually impregnate her, which is a great way of ensuring jerk ducks don't get to continue their lineage.[187] Now, a human woman like Beverly doesn't have a reproductive tract filled with fake passageways like an Indiana Jones movie but also wouldn't have to worry about getting pregnant as a four-foot-long, barbed penis uncoiling inside a human would overshoot the vagina by several feet and end up in the abdomen where insemination doesn't tend to happen. In fact, there's an almost certain chance it would kill her. So, when the Marvel Cinematic Universe reboots the Howard the Duck franchise into a terrifying body-horror escapade, you'll know what scene to look out for.

When we last see Howard in his 1986 self-titled movie, he is performing onstage with Beverly's band, singing and dancing with her in what could conceivably be considered a duck mating ritual. The two seem to be having a genuinely good time, but Howard should probably enjoy the attention he's getting from Beverly while he can. Because when she finds out about his giant, corkscrew-shaped, shotgun-blast penis, she might think he has a power worthy of being a superhero, as that sounds dangerous as hell, but she will absolutely never have sex with him.

PLEASE DON'T DO WHATEVER
A SPIDER CAN

"Does it just come out of your wrists or does it come out of anywhere else?"
—Peter Parker to Peter Parker, *Spider-Man: No Way Home* (2021)

We all know the song: "Spider-Man, Spider-Man, does whatever a spider can." It's ingrained in the subconscious of not just super-hero fans but the public at large. Spider-Man can do whatever a spider can, whether that be sticking to walls, creating webs, or display-ing incredible physical strength. But what if getting bitten by a radioactive spider passed on more than physical abilities? What if spider-people also inherited a spider's sexual habits? And beyond that, what would it look like if two of those spider-people dated each other? Well, we kind of have an answer to that.

Let's not forget, Peter Parker isn't the only spider-person out in the world. In another dimension of the spider-verse is Miles Morales and his love interest Gwen Stacy, both of whom were bitten by radioactive spi-ders and granted a wide range of spider-like abilities. If these two also took on the sexual habits of the spiders that bit them, they are going to have a very interesting and, shall we say, unbalanced relationship ahead of them. Because if Spider-Gwen does have a sex life that's in any way similar to a female spider, she's in for a treat, quite literally. And if Miles inherited the sexual traits of male spiders, well, let's just say that if he wants to know "what's up, danger," it's his penis(es).

A Tale of Two Penises

We've talked about penises a lot in this book (some would say too much, but that's for God to decide). To truly understand the sex lives of super-heroes, we must dive into the gritty details of things like Reed Richards's stretched-out seven-foot member, or Wolverine's engorged testicles, or the penis sword play of the ninja turtles. But it's time to shift the penile conversation away from the shockingly huge and talk about our friendly neighborhood wallcrawlers who have not only a relatively small penis but technically no penis at all. What spiders *do* have is a tiny appendage called a pedipalp that they use to store sperm in (okay), and they also have two of them (okaaaay), and one of them usually gets broken off when they have sex (not okay!). The exact fate of a spider's quasi-penis varies from species to species, but most male spiders lose the appendage at some point in the sex process, usually willingly, and, in case you're wondering, no, they don't grow back.

Break Me Off a Piece of That Pedipalp

Interestingly, many male spiders lose their penis by their own hand (so to speak) for a variety of reasons. Sometimes the male will approach a female, entice her into having sex, and then break off their own penis mid-action to purposely leave it inside the female spider as a way of blocking other males from having sex with her. If this seems like a raw deal for both the male and female, well, you should know that it really sucks for the guy and doesn't seem to bother females all that much. For example, female black widow spiders have commonly been found with up to five spider palps gumming up their genital area, but not in a way that's particularly bothersome.[188] If there's more than one broken-off penis in the works it means that several other males have successfully penetrated the female spider despite the appendages in the way, so clearly the female spider isn't letting men dictate her sex life, which honestly fits what we know about Spider-Gwen's no-nonsense attitude when it comes to dealing with Miles. This also means the males didn't have to cut their own dicks off to create some kind of penis chastity belt in their spider-lady loves because it didn't actually do anything to stop the females from finding other mates. The only solace to be found in this penile tragedy is that spider penises don't have nerve endings so when they crack off a piece of themselves in the name of procreation, it isn't some form of sadomasochism, but a willing sacrifice for the next generation. Which actually sounds a lot like Miles Morales, a man who will give you the shirt off his back and the penis off his body (apparently).

But there are many other reasons spiders break off their dicks and become Peter-Less Parkers (or Miles Mora-less, whichever pun you prefer). For some it's a survival mechanism. Out in the wild there are way more males than females so sometimes a bunch of guys will all show up on a female spider's web at the same time to woo her. If other males show up when one is already having sex with the female spider, the first male breaks his penis off, leaves it in his partner, and starts duking it out with the other guys while his unattached penis continues to expel semen.[189] This is simultaneously the grossest and raddest form of multi-tasking known to (spider)man.

It's also worth noting that breaking off his ninth leg will actually give that spider a huge advantage in the fight. When a spider loses his penis, he becomes a more agile and superior fighter, like an extreme version of shaving all the hair off your body so you can swim faster. Some spiders will even break off one of their penises before they ever have sex just to gain an advantage in a fight with other males.[190] So theoretically, someday Miles's spider-sense could warn him of danger, and he'd just tear off his manhood to get the upper hand in the upcoming fight. Eep. With great power comes great responsibility indeed (or doesn't cum, as the case may be).

A Girl's Gotta Eat

We mentioned that when a spider cuts his penis off, it doesn't grow back. Since they usually leave a penis behind when they bone, this means that male spiders can have sex a maximum of two times in their entire life, and that's only if they survive the first time. You see, there's a really good chance that if a male spider has sex, he's going to get eaten by his partner and not in the fun way—at least, it's not fun for him. I can't emphasize enough how much female spiders love eating dudes. It's their version of having a cigarette after sex to wind down, except they also do it before sex and during sex. They will basically eat a guy at any moment. Knowing this, the reason some male spiders break off their penises mid-coitus is to leave it behind to supply semen to the female while they run away to avoid being eaten. The reverse dine and dash, if you will. But a lot of male spiders aren't so lucky, like the Tidarren spider who breaks off one penis to make himself more mobile in battle, uses his remaining penis to penetrate his mate, gets twisted around by the female until his second penis breaks off inside her, and then gets eaten by her as a post-intercourse snack.[191]

Perhaps more tragically, there is also the fishing spider, who can only have sex a single time because he dies immediately after he ejaculates for the first time, like the world's worst magic trick. And if he ejaculates before he ever meets a woman, he just dies alone as a virgin.[192] But losing his virginity is no easy task. To successfully mate with a female, the fishing spider has to perform about ninety minutes of spider-foreplay, which includes abdomen jiggling and light caresses. This seems like a long time and a lot of work, but remember, he literally only gets one shot at this, and if he doesn't do a good enough job the female will eat him before they ever have sex. If he does do a good job then she allows him to have sex with her, he dies upon ejaculation, and then, you guessed it, she eats him. Thankfully, the fishing spider is mostly found in Asia and not common in North America, so let's start a prayer circle that this isn't the type of spider that bit Miles, or his love life is going to be shorter than Spider-Gwen's buzzcut.

And then there's the curious case of the redback spider, who also dies after sex but not of natural causes like the fishing spider.[193] Instead he initiates sex with the female and then *insists* that she eat him by flipping his body into her mouth. Scientists theorize this sacrifice is to make sure the female is well fed and healthy enough to have the male's babies, which makes the redback both an excellent father and a perpetually absent one. Redbacks can also have sex for a whopping four and a half hours, because if you're only going to have sex once in your life, you want to make it count. Or that's how long the male needs to work up the courage to yeet himself into the female's mouth and get cannibalized. In any case, things really work out for the female, all things considered. Unless she was hoping for a second date.

Who Runs the Spider-World? Girls!

All things considered, in the spider kingdom it's pretty much always good to be a woman. Females basically rule the spider ecosphere, with more sexual agency than most human women will ever experience. Generally speaking, female spiders are much larger than their male counterparts, usually between three to ten times bigger. The biggest size difference in the spider kingdom are the orb weavers, where the females are ten times as long as males and up to 125 times heavier.[194]

This size difference usually makes the females the dominant partner when it comes to anything involving sex. They get to choose which males have sex with them and which males fertilize their eggs, and if they don't like you, they eat you. Honestly, I'm a little jealous and hope Spider-Gwen knows just how good she has it as a female spider dating in a spider-verse. For example, some males perform mating dances to attract a mate, and Gwen loves dancing (but also if the female doesn't like the dancing, she might eat the potential suitor). Other male spiders play a game of peekaboo with the females, their version of a spider pickup line. Or sometimes male spiders will spread silk on a female's back, which is the spider version of giving her a massage. This reportedly works very well for getting the female in a good mood to have sex and rarely ends in being eaten, so take note, spider and human males alike.

And then there's the king among spider bachelors, the man who puts all others to shame, the Darwin bark spider, who actually performs oral sex on his potential mate and goes all out while doing it.[195] This guy hooks his fangs onto a female's genitals and salivates over them, before, during, and after copulation. It's also normal for the Darwin bark spider to repeat this action up to a hundred times in one mating session. Spider-ladies, a piece of advice: get yourself a man who's not a man, he's actually a Darwin bark spider. Oh, and if a male doesn't perform oral sex on the female Darwin bark spider, well, you're not going to believe this, but she eats him. Yeah, it's kind of her answer to everything.

Spider-Jerks

But much like in the human dating world, there are jerks out there that female spiders have to look out for. For example, the males in several different spider species have been known to wrap a woman's legs up in silk before attempting to copulate with her. These are called "bridal veils" and sometimes release pheromones to make the female feel happier, but mostly they're just used for restraint, and sure, some ladies like that, but consent is always key.[196] To be fair, if she's not restrained by the male, it's very likely she'll chomp down on a guy who tries to have sex with her, but that's a woman's prerogative. A girl's gotta eat, after all.

Then there are some male spiders who actually get the whole dating thing right and avoid the fangs of a potential lover by bringing her a tasty treat for her to snack on instead of him. These guys will catch an insect, wrap it in silk, and present it to the female as a gift, like a human showing up for a date with a box of chocolates. As the female chows down on the present, the male mounts her for sex, and since she's no longer hangry, she usually lets him live afterward. But there are, of course, the jerks.

Some males will just pretend to bring a female a snack as a distraction. Instead of bringing her an insect they wrap a rock or leaf in silk, present it to the female, then penetrate her before she's finished unwrapping the present and take off before she discovers the ruse.[197] These spiders are who J. Jonah Jameson is actually referring to when he says Spider-Man is a menace.

But there's one more really cool thing about being a female spider, which is that she gets to choose when she gets pregnant, and by whom. You see, even if a male spider forces or tricks her into having sex with him, a female spider can still make sure he doesn't fertilize her eggs and become her baby-daddy longlegs. When female spiders have sex, the male spider's semen doesn't go directly to her eggs. Instead the ladies have sacs called spermathecae that hold the semen until she's ready to fertilize her eggs.[198] The female gets to decide which sac of semen she wants to use to father her children and throws the rest away, thus ensuring a jerk spider's genes don't propagate any further, which is especially true if she also ate the guy after sex (I may have mentioned that she is often inclined to do this).

So, after all this, what dating advice can we give to dear Miles to avoid figuratively, or literally, getting his head bitten off by his spider-girlfriend? Well, scientists have found that male spiders have a 97 percent survival rate when they try to mate with females who have just molted their skin and only a 20 percent survival rate with females with a fully hardened exo-skeleton.[199] So if her skin looks hard, or her hackles are up, it may be best to stay away.

On a more basic level, we can say that female spiders are most recep-tive to men who bring them a snack, offer them a massage, perform a good mating dance, and are willing to break off their own penises to fight for them. Gwen probably doesn't need Miles to take things to such an extreme degree, as she can fight for herself, but taking your girl out for dinner and dancing and giving her a massage are excellent pieces of advice for both spiders and humans alike. It also wouldn't hurt if Miles was ready to run away if she starts looking hangry on their date. She might get mad that he suddenly bailed, but at least he'll be alive.

CONCLUSION

Agnd that's it.

Thank you for joining me on this journey from radioactive spider-semen to steel vaginal walls, to corkscrew penises and beyond. I appreciate you being strong enough to power through so many pages of sexual innuendo to get to the tiny morsels of science and canon that I had to offer. Not a lot of people would do that. And if you don't like dick jokes or puns about penises, God, I'm so sorry. This book must have been really hard-on you. (Okay, I'm not actually sorry.)

As we reach the end of our journey into the sex lives of superheroes, let's consider what we now know. We've learned that some superpowers are a huge benefit in the bedroom, some powers will shut you down for business permanently, and some are just weird, so if a stranded alien, mysterious wizard, or brilliant scientist ever offers you superpowers, hopefully you now find yourself equipped to make an informed decision about whether or not those powers come with a sexual sacrifice you're not willing to make.

And I hope you learned something else from this book, dear reader, not just about the sex lives of your favorite superheroes, but about sex and relationships in general, the different forms they can take, and how, much like a super stretchy penis, they can expand wider and further than you'd ever imagine. Maybe this book even awakened something in you that you never expected. If that happened, please, never tell me about it. Do not reach out. I am not a valuable resource. I will not reply. But I'm happy for you. Really.

But if you have any questions about the sex lives of superheroes, please do let me know, because in this book we answered all of mine (since I wrote it) and, even more importantly, all of Brodie's from *Mallrats*. And I could use some material for a sequel.

Take care, and remember: always use a condom, just in case.

ACKNOWLEDGMENTS

The deepest, biggest thank-you to my life and business partner, Andrew Ivimey, for his unwavering support while I wrote this book, whether it be in the form of cooking meals, bouncing ideas around with me, or just being generally chill all of the time. I couldn't do any of this without you, and I wouldn't want to.

To all my friends and family who enthusiastically asked how the book was going and would get me hyped up to finish it. I love you all.

To my mom, for supporting every artistic pursuit I've ever taken, even the ones she doesn't understand. (You'll figure out what podcasts are someday, Mom; I know it.)

To my dad, who raised me to love words, comedy, and movies, a recipe that made this book happen.

To Incognito Mode for allowing me to conduct research on this book without creating a search history that will haunt me until the end of time.

To Glenn and everyone else at BenBella Books, for immediately believing in this book.

To Marc Sumerak, Daniel Wallace, and Jonah Lobe for their book *Marvel Anatomy*, which made my life so much easier.

To Larry Niven for his essay "Man of Steel, Woman of Kleenex," which showed this idea could work.

To all the scientists and researchers whose work I referenced, thank you for being smarter than me.

To Dr. Jesse Ory and Dr. Josh White, who graciously and enthusiastically offered their valuable time to discuss some very silly topics with me.

To the Toronto Public Library for having so many books about sex and not asking any questions about why I needed them all.

To you, the wonderful reader who embarked on this journey with me. I hope you learned a few things and had fun doing it (and yes, I mean too much fun).

ENDNOTES

1   Jeff Christiansen, Sean McQuaid, Stephen Faulkner, et al (w). *WORLD WAR HULK: GAMMA FILES* (Marvel Comics, 2007).

2   J. Wortsman, S. Frank, and P. E. Cryer (1984). "Adrenomedullary Response to Maximal Stress in Humans," *American Journal of Medicine* 77(5): 779–784. doi. org/10.1016/0002-9343(84)90512-6.

3   T. Kruger (2003). "Specificity of the Neuroendocrine Response to Orgasm During Sexual Arousal in Men," *Journal of Endocrinology* 177(1): 57–64. doi.org/10.1677/joe.0.1770057.

4   A. D. Struthers, J. L. Reid, R. Whitesmith, et al. (1983). "Effect of Intravenous Adrenaline on Electrocardiogram, Blood Pressure, and Serum Potassium," *Heart* 49(1): 90–93. doi.org/10.1136/hrt.49.1.90.

5   Kaare Andrews (w) (p). *Spider-Man: Reign* No. 3 (Marvel Comics): February 2007.

6   "Risk Factors: Radiation," National Cancer Institute, last updated March 7, 2019, https://www.cancer.gov/about-cancer/causes-prevention/risk/radiation.

7   "What Causes Cancer?," Stanford Medicine, accessed March 9, 2024, https://stanfordhealthcare.org/medical-conditions/cancer/cancer/cancer-causes.html.

8   "Radioactive Contamination and Radiation Exposure | CDC," Centers for Disease Control and Prevention, accessed March 25, 2022, https://www.cdc.gov/nceh/radiation/emergencies/contamination.htm.

9   Daniel Engber, "Is Radiation Contagious?," *Slate*, November 27, 2006, https://slate.com/news-and-politics/2006/11/is-radiation-sickness-contagious.html.

10 "Radionuclide Basics: Uranium," United States Environmental Protection Agency, last updated February 16, 2023, https://www.epa.gov/radiation/radionuclide-basics-uranium.

11 The Occupational Cancer Research Centre (2015). "Ontario Uranium Miners Cohort Study Report," https://www.occupationalcancer.ca/wp-content/uploads/2023/01/RSP-0308.pdf.

12 M. A. McDiarmid, P. Gucer, J. A. Centeno, et al. (2018). "Semen Uranium Concentrations in Depleted Uranium Exposed Gulf War Veterans: Correlations with Other Body Fluid Matrices," *Biological Trace Element Research* 190(1): 45–51. doi. org/10.1007/s12011-018-1527-3.

13   S. J. Genuis, D. Birkholz, I. Rodushkin, et al. (2010). "Blood, Urine, and Sweat (BUS) Study: Monitoring and Elimination of Bioaccumulated Toxic Elements," *Archives of Environmental Contamination and Toxicology* 61(2): 344–357. doi.org/10.1007/s00244-010-9611-5.

14   "FAQs: Uranium | CDC," Centers for Disease Control and Prevention, accessed January 1, 2024, https://www.cdc.gov/nceh/clusters/fallon/uraniumfaq.htm.

15   Elizabeth Gamillo, "Chernobyl Survivors Do Not Pass Excess Mutations on to Their Children After All," *Smithsonian Magazine*, April 28, 2021, https://www.smithsonianmag.com/smart-news/children-chernobyl-survivors-do-not-have-excess-mutations-study-shows-180977596/.

16   "CDC Radiation Emergencies | Treatment for Radiation Exposure," Centers for Disease Control and Prevention, accessed June 2, 2022, https://www.cdc.gov/nceh/radiation/emergencies/countermeasures.htm.

17   "Blade (Eric Brooks) in Comics," Marvel.com, accessed May 20, 2023, https://www.marvel.com/characters/blade-eric-brooks/in-comics.

18   Sana Suri, "Spiders Disguise Themselves as Ants to Hide and Hunt Their Prey," *The Conversation*, November 13, 2014, https://theconversation.com/spiders-disguise-themselves-as-ants-to-hide-and-hunt-their-prey-33953.

19   Anne Rice, *The Queen of the Damned* (New York: Ballantine Books, 1989).

20   "Lexicon—Vampire the Requiem," Word Anvil, accessed March 9, 2024, https://www.worldanvil.com/w/creation/a/lexicon---vampire-the-requiem-article.

21   *Buffy the Vampire Slayer*, season 5, episode 22, "The Gift," directed and written by Joss Whedon, featuring Sarah Michelle Gellar, aired May 22, 2001, on the CW.

22   Stephanie Meyer, "Frequently Asked Questions: Breaking Dawn," *Stephanie Meyer* (blog), accessed March 21, 2023, https://stepheniemeyer.com/the-books/breaking-dawn/frequently-asked-questions-breaking-dawn/#pregnancy.

23   Chris Clarement (w), Jon Bogdanove (p), and Terry Austin (i). *Fantastic Four Versus the X-Men* No. 3 (Marvel Comics, 1987).

24   Marc Sumerak (w), Daniel Wallace (w), and Jonah Lobe (i). *Marvel Anatomy: A Scientific Study of the Superhuman* (San Rafael, CA: Insight Editions, 2022).

25   Warren Ellis (w) and Stuart Immonen (p). *Ultimate Fantastic Four* No. 8 (Marvel Comics, 2003).

26   Alexa Tsoulis-Reay, "What It's Like to Have a Micropenis," *New York Magazine*, November 6, 2014, https://www.thecut.com/2014/11/what-its-like-to-have-a-micropenis.html.

27   Sara C. Nelson, "Rafe Biggs, Quadriplegic Learns to Orgasm Through His Thumb," *Huffington Post*, June 22, 2013, https://www.huffingtonpost.co.uk/2013/04/22/rafe-biggs-quadriplegic-orgasm-thumb-pictures_n_3130545.html?utm_hp_ref=uk.

28   Cheryl Alkon, "Male Orgasm: Understanding the Male Climax," *Everyday Health*, last modified August 1, 2022, https://www.everydayhealth.com/sexual-health/the-male-orgasm.aspx.

29   Dilshan Pieris (2018). "'The Fastest Man Alive'—but How?," *Journal of Interdisciplinary Science Topics*, 7, https://www.researchgate.net/publication/325157782_The_Fastest_Man_Alive-but_how.

30   Scott Beatty, Robert Greenberger, Phil Jiminez, and Dan Wallace, *The DC Comics Encyclopedia: The Definitive Guide to the Characters of the DC Universe, Updated and Expanded* (New York: DK Publishing, 2008).

31   Roger Dobson, "New Study Reveals Average Time for a Woman to Orgasm," *New Zealand Herald*, June 2, 2019, https://www.nzherald.co.nz/lifestyle/new-study-reveals-average-time-for-a-woman-to-orgasm/CA2ZNMHEWGX4QYMFLOL3LAD2PM/.

32   Roger Dobson, "New Study Reveals Average Time for a Woman to Orgasm," *New Zealand Herald*, June 2, 2019, https://www.nzherald.co.nz/lifestyle/new-study-reveals-average-time-for-a-woman-to-orgasm/CA2ZNMHEWGX4QYMFLOL3LAD2PM/.

33   Noleen Arendse, "Average Running Speed by Age and Ability—Adults and Kids," *Calories Burned HQ*, accessed April 25, 2024, https://caloriesburnedhq.com/average-running-speed/

34   InformedHealth.org, "Premature Ejaculation: Overview," September 12, 2019. Originally published in Cologne, Germany, by the Institute for Quality and Efficiency in Health Care (IQWiG), 2006. Available from: https://www.ncbi.nlm.nih.gov/books/NBK547548/.

35   Noleen Arendse, "Average Running Speed by Age and Ability – Adults and Kids," *Calories Burned HQ*, accessed April 25, 2024, https://caloriesburnedhq.com/average-running-speed.

36   C. S. Easthope, C. Hausswirth, J. Louis, et al. (2010). "Effects of a Trail Running Competition on Muscular Performance and Efficiency in Well-Trained Young and Master Athletes," *European Journal of Applied Physiology* 110: 1107–1116. doi.org/10.1007/s00421-010-1597-1.

37   Geoff Johns, "Too Young to Die," in *Teen Titans* No. 3 (DC Comics, 2003).

38   B. Whipple, B. R. Myers, and B. R. Komisaruk (1998). "Male Multiple Ejaculatory Orgasms: A Case Study," *Journal of Sex Education and Therapy* 23(2): 157–162. doi.org/10.1080/01614576.1998.11074222.

39   M. E. Dunn and J. E. Trost (1989). "Male Multiple Orgasms: A Descriptive Study," *Archives of Sexual Behavior* 18(5): 377–387. doi:10.1007/bf01541970.

40   P. Haake, M. Exton, J. Haverkamp, et al. (2002). "Absence of Orgasm-Induced Prolactin Secretion in a Healthy Multi-Orgasmic Male Subject," *International Journal of Impotence Research* 14: 133–135. doi.org/10.1038/sj.ijir.3900823.

41   Brenton Stewart, "Justice League Anatomy: The 5 Weirdest Things About the Flash's Body," *Comic Book Resources*, last modified September 30, 2021, https://www.cbr.com/justice-league-anatomy-flash-facts/.

42   Tim Jewell, "How Long Does It Take for Sperm to Regenerate? What to Expect," *Healthline*, last modified September 19, 2018, https://www.healthline.com/health/mens-health/how-long-does-it-take-for-sperm-to-regenerate.

43   N. Prause, V. Roberts, M. Legarretta, et al. (2012). "Clinical and Research Concerns with Vibratory Stimulation: A Review and Pilot Study of Common Stimulation

Devices," *Sexual and Relationship Therapy* 27(1): 17–34. doi.org/10.1080/14681994.2012. 660141.

44 J. E. Rullo, T. Lorenz, M. Ziegelmann, et al. (2018). "Genital Vibration for Sexual Function and Enhancement: Best Practice Recommendations for Choosing and Safely Using a Vibrator," *Sexual and Relationship Therapy*: 1–11. doi. org/10.1080/14681994.2017.1419558.

45 J. E. Rullo, T. Lorenz, M. Ziegelmann, et al. (2018). "Genital Vibration for Sexual Function and Enhancement: Best Practice Recommendations for Choosing and Safely Using a Vibrator," *Sexual and Relationship Therapy*, 1–11. doi.org/10.1080/146819 94.2017.1419558.

46 "Orgasms 101: Male vs. Female," *Dr. Shannon Chavez*, accessed March 21, 2023, https:// drshannonchavez.com/orgasms-101-male-vs-female/.

47 B. Whipple, B. R. Myers, and B. R. Komisaruk (1998). "Male Multiple Ejaculatory Orgasms: A Case Study," *Journal of Sex Education and Therapy* 23(2): 157–162. doi.org /10.1080/01614576.1998.11074222.

48 Marc Sumerak (w), Daniel Wallace (w), and Jonah Lobe (i), *Marvel Anatomy: A Scientific Study of the Superhuman* (San Rafael, CA: Insight Editions, 2022).

49 Justin R. Garcia, Elisabeth A. Lloyd, Kim Wallen, et al. (2014). "Variation in Orgasm Occurrence by Sexual Orientation in a Sample of U.S. Singles," *Journal of Sexual Medicine* 11(11): 2645–2652. doi.org/10.1111/jsm.12669.

50 Mary Roach, *Bonk: The Curious Coupling of Science and Sex* (New York: W. W. Norton, 2008), 70.

51 Janet Brito, "Can the Size of Your Clitoris Affect Your Ability to Orgasm?," *Healthline*, November 2, 2020, https://www.healthline.com/health/healthy-sex/clitoris-size-orgasm#1.

52 "Women's Orgasms May Be Influenced by Genes," *NBC News*, June 7, 2005, https:// www.nbcnews.com/health/health-news/women-s-orgasms-may-be-influenced-genes-flna1c9442418.

53 "Vaginal Changes After Childbirth," Cherokee Women's Health, accessed March 12, 2023, https://cherokeewomenshealth.com/2019/10/vaginal-changes-after-childbirth/.

54 Alison Maloney, "Your Best Orgasm Will Happen at This Age," *New York Post*, May 29, 2017, https://nypost.com/2017/05/29/womens-orgasms-only-get-better-with-age/.

55 G. De Cuypere, G. TSjoen, R. Beerten, et al. (2005). "Sexual and Physical Health After Sex Reassignment Surgery," *Archives of Sexual Behavior* 34: 679–690. doi.org/10.1007/ s10508-005-7926-5.

56 Marc Sumerak (w), Daniel Wallace (w), and Jonah Lobe (i), *Marvel Anatomy: A Scientific Study of the Superhuman* (San Rafael, CA: Insight Editions, 2022).

57 H. Wessells, T. F. Lue, and J. W. McAninch (1996). "Penile Length in the Flaccid and Erect States: Guidelines for Penile Augmentation," *Journal of Urology* 156(3): 995–997. doi.org/10.1016/s0022-5347(01)65682-9.

58 James Roland, "How Much Blood Does It Take to Get Hard?," *Healthline*, last modified June 29, 2021, https://www.healthline.com/health/mens-health/how-much-blood-does-it-take-to-get-hard.

59   Kimberly Holland, "How Much Blood Can You Lose Without Severe Side Effects?," *Healthline*, February 26, 2022, https://www.healthline.com/health/how-much-blood-can-you-lose.

60   Gigi Engle, "Soft Penetration Can Be Used as an Aid for Erectile Dysfunction," *The Body*, April 28, 2022, https://www.thebody.com/article/soft-penetration-erectile-dysfunction-aid.

61   Jennifer Mitri Williamson, "All About Viagra," *Healthline*, last modified January 26, 2024, https://www.healthline.com/health/drugs/viagra#q-a.

62   Tim Jewell, "Everything You Need to Know About Jelqing," *Healthline*, last modified on February 26, 2023, https://www.healthline.com/health/jelqing#research.

63   M. F. Usta and T. Ipekci (2016). "Penile Traction Therapy for Peyronie's Disease—What's the Evidence?" *Translational Andrology and Urology* 5(3): 303–309. doi.org/10.21037/tau.2016.03.25. PMID: 27298777; PMCID: PMC4893512.

64   E. Chung and G. Brock (2013). "Penile Traction Therapy and Peyronie's Disease: A State of Art Review of the Current Literature," *Therapeutic Advances in Urology* 5(1): 59–65. doi.org/10.1177/1756287212454932. PMID: 23372611; PMCID: PMC3547530.

65   Giancarlo Marra, Andrew Drury, Lisa Tran, et al. (2020). "Systematic Review of Surgical and Nonsurgical Interventions in Normal Men Complaining of Small Penis Size," *Sexual Medicine Reviews* 8(1): 158–180. doi.org/10.1016/j.sxmr.2019.01.004.

66   Tim Jewell, "Penis Enlargement Surgery: How Much Does It Cost and Is It Worth the Risk?," *Healthline*, last modified on February 28, 2019, https://www.healthline.com/health/mens-health/penis-enlargement-surgery-cost.

67   Jon Johnson, "Penis Enlargement Surgery: Does It Work and Is It worth It?," *Medical News Today*, February 16, 2023, https://www.medicalnewstoday.com/articles/penis-enlargement-surgery.

68   J. Lever, D. A. Frederick, and L. A. Peplau (2006). "Does Size Matter? Men's and Women's Views on Penis Size Across the Lifespan," *Psychology of Men & Masculinities* 7(3): 129–143. doi.org/10.1037/1524-9220.7.3.129.

69   Lizette Borelli, "Size Matters: Teen Undergoes 'World's First' Penis Reduction Surgery to Have Sex," *Medical Daily*, February 12, 2015, https://www.medicaldaily.com/size-matters-teen-undergoes-worlds-first-penis-reduction-surgery-have-sex-321952.

70   S. Zhong, J. M. Pinto, K. E. Wroblewski, et al. (2018). "Sensory Dysfunction and Sexuality in the U.S. Population of Older Adults," *The Journal of Sexual Medicine* 15(4): 502–509. doi.org/10.1016/j.jsxm.2018.01.021. Epub 2018 Mar 2. PMID: 29501426; PMCID: PMC5882521.

71   "Sensory Science: Testing Taste Thresholds," *Scientific American*, December 5, 2013, https://www.scientificamerican.com/article/bring-science-home-taste-thresholds/.

72   J. P. Melnyk and M. F. Marcone (2011). "Aphrodisiacs from Plant and Animal Sources—A Review of Current Scientific Literature," *Food Research International* 44(4): 840–850. doi.org/10.1016/j.foodres.2011.02.043.

73   Sofie Boterberg and Petra Warreyn (2016). "Making Sense of It All: The Impact of Sensory Processing Sensitivity on Daily Functioning of Children," *Personality and Individual Differences* 92: 80–86. doi.org/10.1016/j.paid.2015.12.022.

74 Sarah Lempa, "Sex Is Different When You're a Highly Sensitive Person—Here's How," *Healthline*, May 12, 2021, https://www.healthline.com/health/healthy-sex/sex-highly-sensitive-person-hsp.

75 R. S. Herz and E. D. Cahill (1997). "Differential Use of Sensory Information in Sexual Behavior as a Function of Gender," *Human Nature* 8(3): 275–286. doi.org/10.1007/bf02912495.

76 L. F. Jacobs, J. Arter, A. Cook, et al. (2015). "Olfactory Orientation and Navigation in Humans," *PLoS One* 10(6): e0129387. doi.org/10.1371/journal.pone.0129387. PMID: 26083337; PMCID: PMC4470656.

77 I. Savic, H. Berglund, B. Gulyas, et al. (2001). "Smelling of Odorous Sex Hormone-like Compounds Causes Sex-Differentiated Hypothalamic Activations in Humans," *Neuron* 31(4): 661–668. doi.org/10.1016/s0896-6273(01)00390-7.

78 Tia Ghose, "Odd Reason Some Guys Have Fewer Sex Partners," *NBC News*, November 30, 2012, https://www.nbcnews.com/id/wbna50024588.

79 J. Bendas, T. Hummel, and I. Croy (2018). "Olfactory Function Relates to Sexual Experience in Adults," *Archives of Sexual Behavior* 47(5): 1333–1339. doi.org/10.1007/s10508-018-1203-x. Epub 2018 May 2. PMID: 29721723.

80 Cemal Cingi, Nuray Bayar Muluk, Glenis K. Scadding, and Ranko Mladina, *Challenges in Rhinology* (Springer Nature, 2020), 51–55.

81 S. Hicks, "Relationship and Sexual Problems of the Visually Handicapped," *Sexuality and Disability* 3(3): 165–176. doi.org/10.1007/bf01100751.

82 "The Higher the Altitude, the Hotter the Sex, Survey Says," *Toronto Sun*, June 14, 2017, https://torontosun.com/2017/06/14/the-higher-the-altitude-the-hotter-the-sex-survey-says.

83 Dan Brennan, "What Is Sexual Asphyxiation?," *WebMD*, accessed on June 29, 2021, https://www.webmd.com/sex/what-is-sexual-asphyxiation.

84 Natasha Umer, "9 Reasons Why Having Sex in Space Would Be Gross," *BuzzFeed*, February 6, 2015, https://www.buzzfeed.com/natashaumer/sex-in-space.

85 Mary Roach, *Packing for Mars: The Curious Science of Life in the Void* (New York: W. W. Norton & Company, 2011).

86 Ian Lecklitner, "Space Boners: It's Harder to Get Hard in Space," *Mel Magazine*, March 9, 2018, https://medium.com/mel-magazine/space-boners-its-harder-to-get-hard-in-space-8e766b0e645a.

87 Mark Hodge, "Sex in Space Would be a Nightmare, Scientist Says," *New York Post*, December 7, 2018, https://nypost.com/2018/12/07/sex-in-space-would-be-a-nightmare-scientist-says/.

88 Annalise Mabe, "Sex in Space Will Look Like Nothing We've Ever Seen Before," *The Daily Beast*, September 22, 2022, https://www.thedailybeast.com/sex-in-space-will-look-like-nothing-weve-ever-seen-before.

89 Mark Hodge, "Sex in Space Would be a Nightmare, Scientist Says," *New York Post*, December 7, 2018, https://nypost.com/2018/12/07/sex-in-space-would-be-a-nightmare-scientist-says/.

90 Seth T. Barbrow, "Policy Memo: Radiation Effects on Astronautic Fertility in Space: Deep Space Policy," *Journal of Science Policy & Governance*, April 13, 2020, https://www.sciencepolicyjournal.org/article_1038126_jspg_16_01_01.html.

91 Max Fisher, "International Space Station Bans Astronaut Sex," *Atlantic*, June 29, 2010, https://www.theatlantic.com/technology/archive/2010/06/international-space-station-bans-astronaut-sex/340614/.

92 Marc Beaulieu, "Scientists Are Worried About How We're Going to Have Sex in Space," CBC, June 23, 2017, https://www.cbc.ca/life/wellness/scientists-are-worried-about-how-we-re-going-to-have-sex-in-space-1.4175735.

93 "NASA Studying How Herpes Mutates in Space," *Australia Broadcasting Corporation*, January 29, 2016, https://www.abc.net.au/news/2016-01-30/nasa-funds-study-on-the-effects-of-herpes-in-space/7126382.

94 Steve Englehart (s), Joe Staton (p), Mark Farmer (i), Andy Helfer (e), in *The Green Lantern Corps*. Nos. 201–206 (DC Comics, 1986).

95 National Research Council, *The Polygraph and Lie Detection* (Washington, DC: National Academies Press, 2003), 292. doi.org/10.17226/10420.

96 William Moulton Marston, *Emotions of Normal People* (Los Angeles: Read & Co. Science [Reprint], 2019).

97 Christie Marston, "What 'Professor Marston' Misses About Wonder Woman's Origins (Guest Column)," *The Hollywood Reporter*, October 20, 2017, https://www.hollywoodreporter.com/movies/movie-news/what-professor-marston-misses-wonder-womans-origins-guest-column-1049868/.

98 Tim Hanley, *Wonder Woman Unbound: The Curious History of the World's Most Famous Heroine* (Chicago: Chicago Review Press Incorporated, 2014).

99 Diana McCallum, "The 5 Weirdest Changes Demanded by Comic Book Editors," *From Superheroes*, June 12, 2022, https://www.fromsuperheroes.com/post/the-5-weirdest-changes-demanded-by-comic-book-editors.

100 Tim Hanley, *Wonder Woman Unbound: The Curious History of the World's Most Famous Heroine* (Chicago: Chicago Review Press Incorporated, 2014).

101 A. Hébert and A. Weaver (2015). "Perks, Problems, and the People Who Play: A Qualitative Exploration of Dominant and Submissive BDSM Roles," *Canadian Journal of Human Sexuality* 24(1): 49–62. doi.org/10.3138/cjhs.2467.

102 A. Hébert and A. Weaver (2015). "Perks, Problems, and the People Who Play: A Qualitative Exploration of Dominant and Submissive BDSM Roles," *Canadian Journal of Human Sexuality* 24(1): 49–62. doi.org/10.3138/cjhs.2467.

103 Jason Badower (w) (i), *Sensation Comics Featuring Wonder Woman*, Chapter 48 (DC Comics, 2015).

104 Tim Hanley, *Wonder Woman Unbound: The Curious History of the World's Most Famous Heroine* (Chicago: Chicago Review Press Incorporated, 2014).

105 P. J. Kleinplatz, A. D. Ménard, M.-P. Paquet, N. Paradis, M. Campbell, D. Zuccarini, and L. Mehak (2009). "The Components of Optimal Sexuality: A Portrait of 'Great Sex,'" *Canadian Journal of Human Sexuality* 18(1–2): 1–13.

106 Robert Hart, "Kids Raised by Same-Sex Parents Fare Same As—or Better Than—Kids of Straight Couples, Research Finds," *Forbes*, March 6, 2023, https://www.forbes.com/sites/roberthart/2023/03/06/kids-raised-by-same-sex-parents-fare-same-as-or-better-than-kids-of-straight-couples-research-finds/?sh=19b633c7738e.

107 Meilan Solly, "The National Zoo's Female Asian Water Dragon Successfully Reproduced Without a Male," *Smithsonian Magazine*, June 6, 2019, https://www.smithsonianmag.com/smart-news/zoos-female-asian-water-dragon-successfully-reproduced-without-male-180972363/.

108 "Misattribution of Arousal (Definition + Examples)" *Practical Pie*, October 2, 2023, https://practicalpie.com/misattribution-of-arousal-definition-examples/.

109 D. G. Dutton and A. P. Aron (1974). "Some Evidence for Heightened Sexual Attraction Under Conditions of High Anxiety," *Journal of Personality and Social Psychology* 30(4): 510–517. doi.org/10.1037/h0037031.

110 Travis Langley, *Batman and Psychology: A Dark and Stormy Knight* (New Jersey: John Wiley & Sons, Inc., 2012).

111 Bill Finger (w), Bob Kane (p), and Sheldon Moldoff (i), "The Cat," in *Batman* No. 1 (DC Comics, 1940).

112 Bob Kane, *Batman & Me* (Rolla, MO: Eclipse Books, 1989).

113 Senate Committee on the Judiciary, Comic Books and Juvenile Delinquency, Interim Report, 1955 (Washington, DC: United States Government Printing Office, 1955).

114 Robin S. Rosenberg and Jennifer Canzoneri, *The Psychology of Superheroes: An Unauthorized Exploration* (Dallas: BenBella Books, 2008).

115 Grant Morrison (w) and Ethan Van Sciver (p), "Germ Free Generation" in *New X-Men* No. 118 (Marvel Comics, 2001).

116 William J. Broad, "I'll Have What She's Thinking," *New York Times*, September 28, 2013, https://www.nytimes.com/2013/09/29/sunday-review/ill-have-what-shes-thinking.html.

117 William J. Broad, "I'll Have What She's Thinking," *New York Times*, September 28, 2013, https://www.nytimes.com/2013/09/29/sunday-review/ill-have-what-shes-thinking.html.

118 James G. Pfaus and Karolin Tsarski (2022). "A Case of Female Orgasm Without Genital Stimulation," *Sexual Medicine* 10(2): 100496, ISSN 2050-1161. doi.org/10.1016/j.esxm.2022.100496.

119 Sarah Hunter Murray, "Why Women Fake (and No Longer Fake) Having Orgasms," *Psychology Today*, September 25, 2019, https://www.psychologytoday.com/ca/blog/myths-desire/201909/why-women-fake-and-no-longer-fake-having-orgasms.

120 B. Whipple, G. Ogden, and B. R. Komisaruk (1992). "Physiological Correlates of Imagery-Induced Orgasm in Women," *Archives of Sexual Behavior* 21(2): 121–133. doi.org/10.1007/BF01542589. PMID: 1580785.

121 Barbara L. Wells (1986). "Predictors of Female Nocturnal Orgasms: A Multivariate Analysis," *Journal of Sex Research* 22(4): 421–437. http://www.jstor.org/stable/3812289.

122 Debby Herbenick and J. Dennis Fortenberry (2011). "Exercise-Induced Orgasm and Pleasure Among Women," *Sexual and Relationship Therapy* 26(4): 373–388. doi.org /10.1080/14681994.2011.647902.

123 D. Herbenick, T. Fu, C. Patterson, et al. (2021). "Exercise-Induced Orgasm and Its Association with Sleep Orgasms and Orgasms During Partnered Sex: Findings from a U.S. Probability Survey," *Archives of Sexual Behavior* 50(6): 2631–2640. doi.org/10.1007/ s10508-021-01996-9.

124 W. Surbeck, A. Bouthillier, and D. K. Nguyen (2013). "Bilateral Cortical Representation of Orgasmic Ecstasy Localized by Depth Electrodes," *Epilepsy & Behavior Case Reports* 1: 62–65. doi.org/10.1016/j.ebcr.2013.03.002.

125 *Captain America: The First Avenger* (movie), directed by Joe Johnston (2011, United States: Marvel Studios).

126 Johannah Cornblatt, "A Brief History of Sex Ed in America," *Newsweek*, October 27, 2009, https://www.newsweek.com/brief-history-sex-ed-america-81001.

127 Jack Dougherty, "Curriculum Changes of Sex Education Through the Years," Trinity College, accessed June 6, 2023, https://commons.trincoll.edu/edreform/2016/05/ curriculum-changes-of-sex-education-through-the-years/.

128 Johannah Cornblatt, "A Brief History of Sex Ed in America," *Newsweek*, October 27, 2009, https://www.newsweek.com/brief-history-sex-ed-america-8100.

129 Seth Millstein, "Sex Education in the United States, 1835 Through Today," *Digg*, July 27, 2015, https://digg.com/2015/sex-education-history.

130 Thomas H. Sternberg, Ernest B. Howard, Leonard A. Dewey, and Paul Padget, "Venereal Diseases: Preventive Medicine in World War II," accessed June 6, 2023, https://achh.army.mil/history/book-wwii-communicablediseasesv5-chapter10.

131 Hallie Lieberman, "A Short History of the Condom," *JSTOR Daily*, June 8, 2017, https://daily.jstor.org/short-history-of-the-condom/.

132 Ally Hickson, "8 of the Craziest Myths About Women's Bodies You Never Heard," *Refinery29*, May 13, 2016, https://www.refinery29.com/en-us/old-wives-tales-womens- health-bodies#slide-7.

133 Ivan Cenzi, "The Strange History of Men Going Nuts for Monkey Testicle Transplants," *Vice*, January 11, 2021, https://www.vice.com/en/article/gy747y/monkey- testicle-transplant-serge-voronoff.

134 Emory University, "Penicillin, Not the Pill, May Have Launched the Sexual Revolution," *ScienceDaily*, January 28, 2013, https://www.sciencedaily.com/ releases/2013/01/130128082906.htm.

135 Beth L. Bailey, *From Front Porch to Back Seat: Courtship in Twentieth-Century America* (Baltimore: Johns Hopkins University Press, 1989).

136 Steve Englehart (w), Gene Colan (p), and Tom Palmer (i), "This Dream No More," in *Dr. Strange Master of the Mystic Arts*, No. 18, (Marvel Comics, 1976).

137 Dr. Jesse Ory and Dr. Josh White, interview by Diana McCallum, March 3, 2023.

138 Tim Jewell, "How Long Does It Take for Sperm to Regenerate? What to Expect," *Healthline*, last modified September 19, 2018, https://www.healthline.com/health/ mens-health/how-long-does-it-take-for-sperm-to-regenerate.

139 Dr. Jesse Ory and Dr. Josh White, interview by Diana McCallum, March 3, 2023.

140 Julia Belluz, "Sperm Counts Are Falling. This Isn't the Reproductive Apocalypse—Yet," *Vox*, May 30, 2019, https://www.vox.com/science-and-health/2018/9/17/17841518/low-sperm-count-semen-male-fertility.

141 Sarah Biddlecombe and Dr. Amanda Kallen, "Here's How Long It Takes Sperm to Reach the Egg After Sex," *Flo Health*, last updated March 17, 2022, https://flo.health/getting-pregnant/trying-to-conceive/fertility/how-long-does-it-take-sperm-to-reach-egg.

142 Tim Jewell, "12 Widely Believed Sperm Facts That Are Actually False," *Healthline*, September 18, 2018, https://www.healthline.com/health/mens-health/sperm-myth-and-facts.

143 Robert D. Martin, "Why Too Many Sperms Spoil the Egg," *Psychology Today*, August 11, 2017, https://www.psychologytoday.com/ca/blog/how-we-do-it/201708/why-too-many-sperms-spoil-the-egg.

144 "Conception: How It Works," University of California San Francisco, accessed April 5, 2023, https://www.ucsfhealth.org/education/conception-how-it-works.

145 Tim Jewell, "12 Widely Believed Sperm Facts That Are Actually False," *Healthline*, September 18, 2018, https://www.healthline.com/health/mens-health/sperm-myth-and-facts.

146 H. Jónsson, P. Sulem, B. Kehr, et al. (2017). "Parental Influence on Human Germline de Novo Mutations in 1,548 Trios from Iceland," *Nature* 549(7673): 519–522. doi.org/10.1038/nature24018.

147 Tim Jewell, "12 Widely Believed Sperm Facts That Are Actually False," *Healthline*, September 18, 2018, https://www.healthline.com/health/mens-health/sperm-myth-and-facts.

148 S. R. Killick, C. Leary, J. Trussell, et al. (2011). "Sperm Content of Pre-ejaculatory Fluid," *Human Fertility* (Camb), 14(1): 48–52. doi.org/10.3109/14647273.2010.520798. Epub 2010 Dec 15. PMID: 21155689; PMCID: PMC3564677.

149 Larry Niven, "Man of Steel, Woman of Kleenex," *Knight* 7, no. 8 (December 1969).

150 N. Prause, V. Roberts, M. Legarretta, et al. (2012). "Clinical and Research Concerns with Vibratory Stimulation: A Review and Pilot Study of Common Stimulation Devices," *Sexual and Relationship Therapy* 27(1): 17–34. doi.org/10.1080/14681994.2012.660141.

151 Kurt T. Barnhart et al. (2006). "Baseline Dimensions of the Human Vagina," *Human Reproduction* 21(6): 1618–1622. doi.org/10.1093/humrep/del022.

152 D. Herbenick, M. Reece, V. Schick, et al. (2014). "Erect Penile Length and Circumference Dimensions of 1,661 Sexually Active Men in the United States," *Journal of Sexual Medicine* 11(1): 93–101. doi.org/10.1111/jsm.12244.

153 William Kremer, "Can Couples Really Get Stuck Together During Sex?," BBC, February 2, 2014, https://www.bbc.com/news/magazine-25827175.

154 Kristin Grenero, "4 Insane Things That Happen to Your Lady Bits During Sex," *New York Post*, July 1, 2016, https://nypost.com/2016/07/01/4-insane-things-that-happen-to-your-lady-bits-during-sex/.

155   Kelly Classic, "Answer to Question #11747 Submitted to 'Ask the Experts' Category: Pregnancy and Radiation" *Healthy Physics Society*, September 21, 2016, http://hps.org/publicinformation/ate/q11747.html.

156   Dr. Jesse Ory and Dr. Josh White, interview by Diana McCallum, March 3, 2023.

157   S. D. Perry, Matthew K. Manning, and Ming Doyle, *DC Comics: Anatomy of a Metahuman* (San Rafael, CA: Insight Editions, 2018).

158   Al Plastino (p) (i), "Supergirl: Superman's Super-Courtship!" in *Action Comics* No. 289 (DC Comics: June, 1962).

159   P. Jóźków and M. Rossato (2017). "The Impact of Intense Exercise on Semen Quality," *American Journal of Men's Health* 11(3): 654–662. doi.org/10.1177/1557988316669045.

160   "Combat-Related Injuries and Male Fertility," Stork OTC, accessed May 23, 2023, https://storkotc.com/blog/combat-related-injuries-male-fertility/.

161   L. Mínguez-Alarcón, A. J. Gaskins, Y. H. Chiu, et al. (2018). "Type of Underwear Worn and Markers of Testicular Function Among Men Attending a Fertility Center," *Human Reproduction* 33(9): 1749–1756. doi.org/10.1093/humrep/dey259.

162   S. C. Krzastek, J. Farhi, M. Gray, et al. (2020). "Impact of Environmental Toxin Exposure on Male Fertility Potential," *Translational Andrology and Urology* 9(6): 2797–2813. doi.org/10.21037/tau-20-685.

163   D. Norman Buckley and J. B. Brodsky (1987). "Nitrous Oxide and Male Fertility," *Reproductive Toxicology* 1(2): 93–97. doi.org/10.1016/0890-6238(87)90002-5.

164   Jerry Ordway (w) (p). "Green Death in Crime Alley," in *Superman* Vol. 2, No. 44 (DC Comics, 1990).

165   Kenneth L. Miller, "Radiation Effects—Effects on Tissues and Organs," Health Physics Society, October 15, 2004, http://hps.org/publicinformation/ate/q3996.html.

166   S. D. Perry, Matthew K. Manning, and Ming Doyle, *DC Comics: Anatomy of a Metahuman* (San Rafael, CA: Insight Editions, 2018).

167   Darren Nash, "The Terrifying Sex Organs of Male Turtles," *Gizmodo*, June 20, 2012, https://gizmodo.com/the-terrifying-sex-organs-of-male-turtles-5919870.

168   Magdalene Taylor, "The Terrifying Orchid Penises of Turtles and Tortoises," *Mel Magazine*, accessed June 1, 2023, https://melmagazine.com/en-us/story/turtle-penis.

169   Wallace J. Nichols, "Sea Turtles Get It On, and On, and On . . .," *Deep Sea News*, May 19, 2009, https://deepseanews.com/2009/05/sea-turtles-get-it-on-and-on-and-on/.

170   Darren Nash, "The Terrifying Sex Organs of Male Turtles," *Gizmodo*, June 20, 2012, https://gizmodo.com/the-terrifying-sex-organs-of-male-turtles-5919870.

171   Darren Nash, "The Terrifying Sex Organs of Male Turtles," *Gizmodo*, June 20, 2012, https://gizmodo.com/the-terrifying-sex-organs-of-male-turtles-5919870.

172   Kellen Perry, "11 Weird Dolphin Mating Facts," *Ranker*, accessed June 3, 2023, https://www.ranker.com/list/weird-dolphin-mating-facts/kellen-perry?ref=collections_top&l=2424647&collectionId=1666.

173   Corryn Wetzel, "Nine of the Weirdest Penises in the Animal Kingdom," *Smithsonian Magazine*, November 17, 2020, https://www.smithsonianmag.com/science-nature/nine-weirdest-penises-animal-kingdom-180976274/.

174 "Amorous Dolphin Targeting Swimmers," *CNN*, June 4, 2002, https://www.cnn.com/2002/WORLD/europe/06/04/uk.dolphin/index.html.

175 Jennifer Abbasi, "Can Animals Really Be Gay?" *Popular Science*, October 5, 2011, https://www.popsci.com/science/article/2011-10/can-animals-really-be-gay/.

176 Corryn Wetzel, "Nine of the Weirdest Penises in the Animal Kingdom," *Smithsonian Magazine*, November 17, 2020, https://www.smithsonianmag.com/science-nature/nine-weirdest-penises-animal-kingdom-180976274/.

177 Chetana Babburjung Purushotham, "Mate and Die: Mysteries of Octopus Sex," *Roundglass*, March 13, 2023, https://roundglasssustain.com/photostories/octopus-sex.

178 Julie Kalupa, "Creating Pacific Octopuses," *BioWeb*, Spring 2012, http://bioweb.uwlax.edu/bio203/s2012/kalupa_juli/reproduction.htm.

179 Kellianne Matthews, "Are Octopuses Poisonous?," *A–Z Animals*, December 31, 2022, https://a-z-animals.com/blog/are-octopuses-poisonous/.

180 Julie Kalupa, "Creating Pacific Octopuses," *BioWeb*, Spring 2012, http://bioweb.uwlax.edu/bio203/s2012/kalupa_juli/reproduction.htm.

181 Michael Hoskin (w), *Marvel Pets Handbook* (Marvel Comics, 2018).

182 Susannah Cahalan, "The Horrible Thing You Never Knew About Ducks," *New York Post*, May 6, 2017, https://nypost.com/2017/05/06/dont-be-fooled-ducks-are-sadistic-raping-monsters/.

183 Susannah Cahalan, "The Horrible Thing You Never Knew About Ducks," *New York Post*, May 6, 2017, https://nypost.com/2017/05/06/dont-be-fooled-ducks-are-sadistic-raping-monsters/.

184 Susannah Cahalan, "The Horrible Thing You Never Knew About Ducks," *New York Post*, May 6, 2017, https://nypost.com/2017/05/06/dont-be-fooled-ducks-are-sadistic-raping-monsters/

185 Ed Yong, "Ballistic Penises and Corkscrew Vaginas: The Sexual Battles of Ducks," *Discover Magazine*, December 22, 2009, https://www.discovermagazine.com/planet-earth/ballistic-penises-and-corkscrew-vaginas-the-sexual-battles-of-ducks.

186 Kathryn Vera, "How Do Ducks Mate?," *Sciencing*, March 13, 2018, https://sciencing.com/ducks-mate-4569594.html.

187 Susannah Cahalan, "The Horrible Thing You Never Knew About Ducks," *New York Post*, May 6, 2017, https://nypost.com/2017/05/06/dont-be-fooled-ducks-are-sadistic-raping-monsters/.

188 Menno Schilthuizen, "The Nihilistic Sex Lives of Spiders," *Slate*, June 10, 2014, https://slate.com/technology/2014/06/spider-sex-why-male-spiders-intentionally-castrate-themselves-during-copulation.html.

189 Matt Soniak, "The Bizarre Sex Lives of Spiders," *The Week*, January 8, 2015, https://theweek.com/articles/451434/bizarre-sex-lives-spiders.

190 Stephanie Pain, "The Ungentle Joy of Spider Sex," *Knowable Magazine*, October 28, 2020, https://knowablemagazine.org/article/living-world/2020/the-ungentle-joy-spider-sex.

191   Menno Schilthuizen, "The Nihilistic Sex Lives of Spiders," *Slate*, June 10, 2014, https://slate.com/technology/2014/06/spider-sex-why-male-spiders-intentionally-castrate-themselves-during-copulation.html.

192   Michael Greshko, "Bondage, Cannibalism, and Castration—Spiders' Wild Sex Lives," *National Geographic*, February 14, 2017, https://www.nationalgeographic.com/animals/article/spiders-sex-valentines-day-cannibalism.

193   Stephanie Pain, "The Ungentle Joy of Spider Sex," *Knowable Magazine*, October 28, 2020, https://knowablemagazine.org/article/living-world/2020/the-ungentle-joy-spider-sex.

194   Stephanie Pain, "The Ungentle Joy of Spider Sex," *Knowable Magazine*, October 28, 2020, https://knowablemagazine.org/article/living-world/2020/the-ungentle-joy-spider-sex.

195   Karl Gruber, "These Male Spiders Perform Oral Sex—and Lots of It," *The Washington Post*, May 6, 2016, https://www.washingtonpost.com/news/speaking-of-science/wp/2016/05/06/its-better-to-give-these-male-spiders-perform-oral-sex-up-to-100-times-a-night/.

196   Michael Greshko, "Bondage, Cannibalism, and Castration—Spiders' Wild Sex Lives," *National Geographic*, February 14, 2017, https://www.nationalgeographic.com/animals/article/spiders-sex-valentines-day-cannibalism.

197   Matt Soniak, "The Bizarre Sex Lives of Spiders," *The Week*, January 8, 2015, https://theweek.com/articles/451434/bizarre-sex-lives-spiders.

198   Matt Soniak, "The Bizarre Sex Lives of Spiders," *The Week*, January 8, 2015, https://theweek.com/articles/451434/bizarre-sex-lives-spiders.

199   Stephanie Pain, "The Ungentle Joy of Spider Sex," *Knowable Magazine*, October 28, 2020, https://knowablemagazine.org/article/living-world/2020/the-ungentle-joy-spider-sex.

ABOUT THE AUTHOR

Diana McCallum is a writer, podcaster, internet comedian, and co-creator of the From Superheroes Network. She co-writes the webcomic *Texts From Superheroes* and co-hosts the *Talk From Superheroes* podcast. In 2019 she was nominated for Best Podcast Host in Canada and lost to a child. (It's fine.) Her superhero musings have appeared on sites such as Cracked, TopTenz, and Dork Shelf, as well as in the Dark Horse anthology *The Secret Loves of Geek Girls* and its sequel, *The Secret Loves of Geeks*. She lives in Toronto, Canada, with her partner, Andrew, and their dog, Scar.